AF316674

History of the Talmud

The Babylonian Talmud, Book 10

Michael L. Rodkinson

FV Editions

Contents

History of the Talmud

Preface   3

Introduction   7

1. Origin of the Talmud   11
2. Development of the Talmud in the First Century   14
3. Persecution of the Talmud from the destruction of the Temple to the Third Century   17
4. Development of the Talmud in the Third Century   21
5. The Two Talmuds   26
6. The Sixth Century: Persian and Byzantine Persecution of the Talmud   33
7. The Eight Century: the Persecution of the Talmud by the Karaites   36
8. Islam and Its Influence on the Talmud   45
9. The Period of Greatest Diffusion of Talmudic Study   49
10. The Spanish Writers on the Talmud   56
11. Talmudic Scholars of Germany and Northern France   65
12. The Doctors of France; Authors of the Tosphoth   72
13. Religious Disputes of All Periods   77
14. The Talmud in the Sixteenth and Seventeenth Centuries   93
15. Polemics with Muslims and Frankists   117
16. Persecution during the Seventeenth Century   122
17. Attacks on the Talmud in the Nineteenth Century   125
18. The Affair of Rohling-Bloch   130
19. Exilarchs, Talmud at the Stake and Its Development at the Present Time   136

Appendix A   141

Appendix B   163

Historical and Literary Introduction to the New Edition of the Talmud

1. The Combination of the Gemara, The Sophrim and the Eshcalath   193
2. The Generations of the Tanaim   199
3. The Amoraim or Expounders of the Mishna   216
4. The Classification of Halakha and Hagada in the Contents of the Gemara   233
5. Apocryphal Appendices to the Talmud and Commentaries   240
6. Epitomes, Codifications, Manuscripts and Printed Editions of the Talmud   245
7. Translations of the Talmud   253
8. Bibliography of Modern Works and Monographs on Talmudic Subjects   256
9. Why Should Christians Feel Interested in the Talmud?   269
10. Opinions on the Value of the Talmud by Gentiles and Modern Jewish Scholars   276
11. Talmudical Ethics   281
12. Ethical Teachings of the Talmud   286
13. Method of Translation   296
14. Criticism   303
15. The Arrangement of the Six Sections in Their Sixty Tracts   307

History of the Talmud

Preface

THE ancient authors used to begin the prefaces to their works with the proverb *"Sepher be Lo Hakdamha kegnph be Lo nechamaha,"* which means "A book without a preface is similar to a body without a soul"; and, indeed, this proverb remains forever true. At the time we began our translation of the Talmud, we were aware that to the study of it a clear preface which should explain its nature and the character of the sages mentioned in it was necessary, as without it there would be great difficulty for students in catching the real meaning, and in some places the reader would be confused, not being aware of its history and of the names mentioned--who these were and when they existed.

With this in mind, we had already prepared the present work in 1897, when only a few volumes of our translation had been issued. Although we gave a brief general introduction to the first volume of the translation, and also some prefaces and introductions in the succeeding volumes, they do not suffice for the student who desires to have a clear idea of all that he is studying.

However, the translation has taken up so much of our time that it has hitherto been impossible for us to look up everything pertinent to our purpose that has been written and to submit it in presentable form. Now, after the completion, with the Divine help of the two large sections, containing twenty-seven tracts, and in response to many inquiries from the reading public for some explanations, we find that now is the time to put forth this work; and, instead of adding two more volumes to the translation of the Talmud in the current year, we have decided to furnish the two volumes which form our "History of the Talmud."

It may be inferred that what was written several years ago has had to be thoroughly revised and corrected, according to the literature which has appeared since that time. There is an old witticism, *"Koshe Atika Me Chadtha"*; *i.e.*, "It is more difficult to correct an old thing than to write a new one"; and, as a matter of fact, it has taken a great deal of time to make the necessary changes and corrections in what we had written. As a natural consequence, the work is enlarged, and many chapters have been added since the issue of our prospectus. All this concerns the first volume of this work, as it relates to the history of the Talmud only, as to which there has been little new information. True there have been some new dissertations on the Talmud in Germany, but they do not add much to our knowledge concerning it, and may therefore be ignored.

The second volume, however, we have had to recast and rewrite. In this labor the wonderful work of that western light which was recently extinguished--we mean the Rev. Dr. Mielziner--"Introduction to the Talmud," which has reached a second edition and has been so favorably received by all students of both continents, was of great service to us. As Dr. Mielziner's work contains essentially all that concerns the Talmud itself, we resolved to take it as a text for our historical introduction, adding and abating as we deemed necessary. We have done so, also, with the second part, "The Ethics of the Talmud," which he arranged so admirably. Here, also, we have added whatever, according to our knowledge, there was left for us to bring to the attention of the reader.

Now, the work being finished, we regard it as a suitable preface to our translation and one which will enlighten the understanding of the reader in many places. At the same time, it seems to us to be interesting to the general reader who has neither time nor inclination for the study of the Talmud.

This is all we need say in the preface, referring the reader for more details to our introduction, which follows.

THE AUTHOR.

NEW YORK, *September*, 1903.

Introduction

The persecutors of the Talmud during the period ranging from the first century B.C., when it began to take form, to the present day, have varied in their character, objects and actions. In one respect, however, they all agreed, namely, in their general wish to destroy its existence. Careful consideration of its many vicissitudes certainly justifies the assertion that the Talmud is one of the wonders of the world. During the twenty centuries of its existence not one of them has passed without great and powerful enemies vying with each other and exhausting every effort to destroy it; still it survived in its entirety, and not only has the power of its foes failed to destroy even a single line, but it has not even been able materially to weaken its influence for any length of time. It still dominates the minds of a whole people, who venerate its contents as divine truth, and countless numbers have sacrificed their lives and their possessions to save it from perishing.

A review of its persecutors, before going into their history would not be amiss. They are the Seleucidae, in the time of Antiochus Epiphanes, the Roman Emperor Nero, Domitian, Hadrian, etc., the Samaritans, the Sadducees, Boethuseans, the followers of Jesus, and all the sects opposed to the Pharisees.

Before the development of the Talmud had been completed,

when hardly a single section had been arranged systematically and written down, it having been known merely as oral teaching in the mouths of the sages, and reconsidered and analyzed constantly by their disciples in the colleges, it was violently attacked. But no sooner had the Talmud been completed in Babylonia, and the Saburites had put their seal upon it, so to speak, deciding that nothing was to be added to or subtracted from, when Justinian decreed practically its death; that is to say, what amounted to the same thing, capital punishment to all those who were occupied in its study (550). Then followed the Karaites, in the days of the Gaonim, who seriously threatened its existence. Time and time again they triumphed over Talmudic Rabbis and were near making an end of the Talmud and of them. The Rabbis next encountered the Popes. From the time of Pope Innocent III., the Talmud was burned at the stake in nearly every century from the 11th to the 18th, in Italy, France, Germany, Spain, and many other countries, and in the 18th, also in Poland by the Frankists, by Bishop Dembovski, where copies were dragged through the streets of the city, tied to horses' tails and then delivered to the executioner to be burned at the stake in Kamenetz, Lemberg, Brody and elsewhere. In most places, before it was resolved what was to be done with Talmud, the Israelites were forced to dispute with its enemies, and had to pay heavy fines for arriving late to the dispute, as well as for being vanquished in argument, the judges, being their enemies. Still what has been the result? The Talmud exists to-day, and not one letter in it is missing. It is true, the persecutions against it are not yet at an end; accusations and calumnies by its enemies, under the new name of anti-Semites, are still directed against it, while the government of Russia legislates against and restricts the rights of the nation which adheres to the Talmud. No modern persecutions, however, can seriously endanger its existence, and it would appear that the Talmud will also survive them and continue as long as the sky spans the earth.

A desire to know all that has befallen the Talmud and all its vicissitudes since its inception would require the reading of all the scattered passages in countless volumes which have been compiled in various ages, languages, and countries. Its history, however, has never yet been written by a single author. Treaties on the Talmud itself, or on certain subjects contained therein, have briefly related part of its history, each according to the subject and the aim of its theme. Such are the works of Zunz and Grätz, the one dealing with rabbinical literature, and the other writing concerning the history of the Jews. Similarly the historians of the world, relating in detail the occurrences of every century, have briefly made mention of what happened to the Talmud in each century. Even in the year there appeared a pamphlet entitled "Anklager und Vertheidiger des Talmud" (accusers and defenders), by Dr. B. Kurrein, of Frankfort-on-the-Main, apparently giving the entire history of the Talmud from its origin to the present time, but it contains only dates (and not even these in full) and not occurrences. No mention is made of Karaites, who persecuted it in the times of the Gaonim, or of the Frankists of the 18th century, of its fate during the 15th century; the Pfefferkorn and Reuchlin episode is mentioned only in part, and by no means satisfactory to the reader curious about the details, not to speak of the Rohling-Bloch, at the end of the 19th century. It is, indeed, a matter of astonishment that hundreds of books have been written about the Talmud by exponents of all sects and in all ages, to say nothing of the extensive modern literature dealing with the Talmud in whole or in part, amounting to thousands of volumes--in particular a work, "Dik-duke Sophrim," published in the last century, containing only the dates and publishers' names of the various editions of the Talmud, in seventeen large volumes, with a comparison of all words and letters of the different editions and manuscripts, and this only of two-thirds of the Talmud--the fate of the Talmud, the charges brought against it, the repeated persecutions, the burning at the stake, have not been recorded in a separate work, as though unworthy of notice. It has been thus left for us to supply the deficiency. For we, who have taken upon ourselves the difficult task of editing the old Talmud, to punctuate it in conformity with works in other languages, to systematize and arrange it for a new edition, and to translate it into a modern language, deem it our duty to collect into one book all the records of the vicissitudes of the Talmud in a systematic manner, at the same time stating the causes of many occurrences.

It is quite true, that in many places we have been constrained to be brief where a more ample account would not have been out of place, but it must be borne in mind that to expatiate on every incident would lead to the writing of a volume equal in bulk to the Talmud itself, perhaps even larger, and time would not permit such an undertaking. In one respect, however, we will do our duty; we will arrange all the events chronologically, and we have taken pains to denote the time and place of different events and likewise to name the persecutors of the Talmud. We trust this volume will meet with a favorable reception from the readers, for our work was done conscientiously, and to the utmost of our talents. To save space, we have not on every occasion mentioned the authorities from whom we derived our facts, but only when we had to refer the reader for details to other books we gave the name and page of the book. We may state, however, that the sources on which we have drawn are all the books which speak of this subject, viz.: the Talmud itself, the books of the Gaonim, and those written on this topic in the Middle Ages, as well as the extensive literature relating to it of the last century, from Zunz, Jost, Herzfeld, Graetz, etc., to the pamphlet we have mentioned. At the conclusion of the book the reader will find an explanation of the method employed in the new edition and translation of the Talmud, and at the same time a full introduction. We made it as lucid as possible, and also endeavored to reply to some criticisms that have appeared in various periodicals since the new publication had first appeared.

MICHAEL L. RODKINSON.
NEW YORK, *AUGUST*, 1903.

Chapter 1
Origin of the Talmud

The Origin Of The Name "Talmud"--The Samaritans--Antiochus Epiphanes--The Sadducees.

The name "written law" was given to the Pentateuch, Prophets and Hagiographa, and that of "oral law" to all the teachings of the "sages" consisting of comments on the text of the Bible. The word Torah alone was applied to the entire Bible, the term "Talmud" was reserved for the oral law, though the meaning of these two words is identical; namely, "teaching" or "study." Still, because it is written *Velimdo* (Deut. xxxi, 19), and *teach it* the children of Israel (put it in their mouths; that is to say that the teacher's duty was to explain and comment on the laws and ordinances until the children understood them thoroughly and were conversant with them by heart)--the name "Talmud" was applied to what was styled by a long phrase "Oral Law" (Torah-she b'al-Peh). This word designated all the commentaries of the sages on the Scriptures which the Pharisees had begun to interpret figuratively.

Figurative interpretation was inaugurated in the days of the Great Assembly when its members resolved to keep themselves distinct from the Samaritans, their inveterate enemies, who adhered to the literal interpretation of the text, which, in the opinion of the

Pharisees, was falsified by them. This study, however, commenced to make progress at the time of the Sanhedrin, or from that of the Macedonian conquest of Judea, when the term "Great Assembly" was changed to the Greek "Sanhedrin." It spread into every college where were assembled sages entrusted with the guidance of congregations, with instruction of the Law, of ordinances relating to clean and unclean, to property, to crimes. All sages who interpreted the biblical passages figuratively, unlike the Samaritans, were called "Pharisees." The Samaritans of course persecuted those Pharisees (see App. No. 1), objected to their interpretation, and did them great injury whenever they had the power. At last, Janai, Hyrcanus the First, overcame them, burned their temple, devastated their city, and compelled them by force of arms to conduct themselves according to the doctrines of the Pharisees, though he himself in his latter years became a Sadducee.

Until the time of Antiochus Epiphanes, before which period all the high priests since the erection of the second temple had been of the family of Zadok, King David's high priest (see App. 2), and the priests had been also among the sages of the Pharisees and no disputes arose between them as to the interpretation of the law. From the time of Antiochus, however, when the high priesthood passed from the descendants of Zadok to other families, finally coming into the possession of the Maccabees, who were not descendants of the house of Zadok, began to differ from the Pharisees in the interpretation of the Torah, and to explain the texts on the basis of oral tradition. They founded a distinct sect, styled "Sadducees" (after Zadok), and the dispute with the Pharisees and their teaching, *i.e.* with the Talmud, was begun. They persecuted the Pharisees to the utmost; being mostly men of wealth and rank, and in their hearts leaning toward the Hellenes, who then held sway in Palestine, they joined the Samaritans, the foes of the Jews, whose aim was to eradicate the study of Judaism. Thus united, they gave their aid to Antiochus Epiphanes, who was anyhow the enemy of the Jews, and who decreed on the pain of capital punishment that the Pharisees should discontinue their studies, that circumcision should be performed in a manner other than that prescribed by the Pharisees (see App. No. 3);

that the Sabbath should not be observed according to the interpretation of the Sabbath law by the Pharisees, etc. The obvious intention
was to destroy the Talmud together with Pharisees who adhered to it.
These persecutions against the Talmud ended usually in favor of the
Sadducees until the time of Simon ben Shetah, and the above
mentioned Janai, Hyrcanus I. (Johanan the High Priest). Then the
Pharisees triumphed over their foes, and the oral law was the
absorbing subject of the Sanhedrin, under the leadership of Joshuah
b. Prachia, Simon b. Shetah and Jehudah b. Tabai. The Talmud was
then studied in all colleges of Palestine, Egypt and wherever Jews
lived. Owing to the enmity of the Samaritans and the opposition of
the Sadducees, many laws and regulations were added to the Talmud
of the Pharisees. From that time the Pharisees began to restrict their
interpretations so as to make them agree with the deep though literal
meaning of the texts, employing therein much sophistry. They
counted all the letters of the Torah, and if they found a word or letter
not absolutely necessary to the understanding of the text, they said it
was placed there only to add to or subtract from the meaning. But at
that period the Mishna was not a separate and distinct thing from the
Talmud, though many ancient Mishnas already existed in writing,
but without a separate title. The Pharisees studied the ancient Mishnayoth, added (see App. No. 4) to them, and explained the biblical
texts. All this was entitled Oral Law, or, shortly, "Talmud."

Chapter 2
Development of the Talmud in the First Century

The Development Of The Talmud During The Last Century Of The Second Temple's Existence (I.E. The First A.C.) Shemaia--Abtalian-- Hillel--Shammai--The Princes (Nasis) Of Israel--R. Johanan B. Zakkai--Sanhedrin Of Jamnia--The Jewish Christians.

After the triumph of Simon b. Shetah over the Sadducees, when he had finally cleared the Sanhedrin of them, and only the Pharisees remained there, the development of the Talmud progressed rapidly, for the number of the sages, the adherents, reverers, sanctifiers of the Talmud, increased greatly in the colleges of the Ashkaloth (Duumviri) who succeeded to ben Shetah: Shemaia and Abtalian, and, after them, Hillel and Shammai. And although at that time new enemies arose, in the Boethuseans, Essenes, and many other sects who were opposed to its particular doctrines, yet those had not the power to check its progress or to weaken its influence--not only on all Israelites, wherever they dwelt, but also on many Gentiles: for at that time we see that prominent persons of other nations (App. No. 5) come to the chief men of Israel and express their wish to adopt Judaism. Hillel the Elder received them with open arms. Helen the Queen, and her son, Isotis, also accepted the creed of the Talmud. All this was due to the fact that its morality came at this time to be before the world. The Polytheists began to perceive the great difference between the teaching of their priests in the names of the gods, and the Torah as explained by its sages. From all places of the world came persons to learn the doctrines and the morality of the Talmud. This period of good fortune, however, was only of short duration, as the time of the destruction of the Temple was nigh, and with it the victims of the sword and of hunger were many. Among these were the great sages who bore the banner of the Talmud, and their wisdom died with them. The Sanhedrin had been forced, while the Temple was still in existence, to transfer their meeting places from the "marble hall" to the "shops." Rabban Gamaliel the Elder, the son of Hillel the Prince (Nasi) was persecuted by them, and his son Simeon was slain, together with many sages. Thus, if R. Johanan b. Zakkai had not, risking his life, petitioned Vespasian to spare the Sanhedrin, who had been compelled during the tumults at Jerusalem to move with their college to Jamnia, there would have remained no vestige of the Talmud, since most of those who cherished it had passed away by the sword, by hunger and by the plague. Besides, the disciples of Jesus (see App. No. 6), who then believed in his Messiahship, but not in his divinity, began secretly to undermine the Talmud, which laid more stress on external ceremonies than they deemed necessary, and endeavored with all their might to weaken its influence among the populace, but R. Jehanan b. Zakkai and the Sanhedrin in Jamnia, with Rabban Gamaliel, the son of the slain Simeon, at their head, restored the Talmud to its prestige, and took pains to raise up others in the places of the murdered sages.

Thus the study of the Talmud flourished after the destruction of the Temple, although beset with great difficulties and desperate struggles. All his days, R. Johanan b. Zakkai was obliged to dispute with Sadducees and Bathueians and, no doubt, with the Messiahists also; for although these last were Pharisees, they differed in many points from the teaching of the Talmud after their master, Jesus, had broken with the Pharisees and their doctrines in public. So R. Johanan b. Zakkai was obliged to introduce many reforms; and Rabban Gamaliel of Jamnia, notwithstanding his office of Nasi, and his lofty bearing towards his colleagues and adversaries, was compelled to go many times to Rome to ask for mercy for his college and the Pharisaic sages. And this first Nasi, after the Temple's destruction, also had to witness the evil consequences of quarrels in the midst of his own nation, added to the calamities from without.

As the interpretations of every letter and vowel point of the written law had multiplied, and liberty had been given to every learned man to construe biblical texts at his pleasure, the differences of opinion multiplied, and the disciples of Shammai and Hillel, whose master's characters differed to the utmost, split into two factions and studied in separate colleges. Thus the teaching of the Talmud was differently interpreted by two parties, and what the one permitted, the other forbade. This circumstance was of more danger to the Talmud than any external foe, for when there is no internal union, the whole fabric will go to pieces, and its influence will, of course, diminish. Therefore the sages of Jamnia, with R. Gamaliel at their head, strove not only to decide the law according to the school of Hillel, but also to decree that the words of Shammai's school in the place of Hillel's had no value at all. And what a world of difficulty the sages had to surmount before they succeeded! .R. Simeon ben Gamaliel rightly says "If we proceeded to record all the troubles and calamities we had endured, time would not suffice."

But in the long run they did succeed in widening and increasing the sphere of influence of the Talmud, for both the internal dissensions and external opposition only tended to sink more deeply into the hearts of the people its doctrines (Halakhas), legends (Hagadas) and morals. At the end of the first century it was to them a substitute for their destroyed Temple; it was their stronghold, their entertainment by day and by night. It was only when they were occupied with it that they forgot all the calamities past and present; it was the sole bond which kept together the scattered colonies of Israelites, which strengthened them to bear the yoke of the Romans, to hope for brighter days, to be patient unto the end.

Chapter 3
Persecution of the Talmud from the destruction of the Temple to the Third Century

The Destruction Of The Temple--The Fall Of Bethel--The Massacre Of The Sages Of The Talmud, Till The Writing Of The Mishna In The Beginning Of The Third Century.

The Temple had been destroyed; Rabban Gamaliel and many of his colleagues were dead; the family of the Nasi extirpated, excepting only his son R. Simeon, who succeeded to his father as Nasi and established a college at Usha; and new persecutions, awful in their extent, were directed against those who were engaged in the compilation of the Talmud. The sages, the chief men of Israel, were slaughtered without pity by Trajan and his successors through the entire period of fifty-two years from the destruction of the Temple to the fall of Bethel. Some of these founders of the Talmud who forfeited their lives for its sake are known to us only by their names: R. Ishmael, Simeon b. Azai, Papus b. Jehudah, Yishbab the Scribe, Huzpeth the Dragoman (interpreter), Jehudah the Baker, Hananiah b. Tradion and Aqiba; the last, the main pillar of the Talmud, and who contributed much to its diffusion and completion, died with joy at being enabled to sacrifice his life for it.

One of the causes of the great revolt against the Romans at this time was the prohibition by the Roman government of the study of the Torah, wherein alone the Jews found comfort, since only in their houses of learning could they enjoy complete peace and freedom. But as the death penalty had been decreed against all who occupied themselves with religious study and observed its precepts, and as this prohibition deprived them of their only source of consolation, they rebelled, led by Bar Kochba. R. Aqiba was the first to become his adherent, who journeyed from town to town, inciting the Israelites to rebel, and bringing them the message that a saviour of Israel had arisen in Bar Kochba, the Messiah. It is not surprising, therefore, that Hadrian, when he had ascended to the throne, was not content barely with the massacre of the sages of the Talmud, but was intent also on the destruction of the Talmud itself. Unable to find a pretext for killing all the sages who kept it tip, he decreed that if any of the old rabbis Should qualify a young rabbi for Israel, both should be put to death, and the place in which such took place should be destroyed, believing that with the death of the elder generation the Talmud would be forgotten and Israel would blend with the nations and its memory be obliterated; because he very well knew that as long as the Talmud existed there was little hope for the assimilation of the Jews with other nations. This decree, however, was not executed, and his murderous plan was further frustrated by R. Jehudah b. Baba, who, forewarned of the decree and comprehending its consequences, betook himself to a place between two great mountains between Usha and Shprehem and licensed six of the older men of R. Aqiba's disciples to be rabbis (*i.e.*, teachers of the Talmud): R. Meir, R. Jehudah b. Elai, R. Jose b. Halaphta, R. Simeon b. Jochai, R. Eleazar b. Shemua, and R. Nehemiah. Having done this, and feeling sure that as long as these men lived the Talmud would be kept alive, he thus addressed them: "Fly, my sons, and hide from the wrath of the enemy. I alone will remain, and will offer my body to satiate their vengeance." And in fact the Romans pierced his body with three hundred iron lances, so that it resembled a sieve; but the newly consecrated rabbis were saved, and with them the Talmud.

Thus the efforts of Hadrian met with no success, so that at last he said to himself: "Great is the sheep that stands among seventy wolves." He saw the Talmud still existing, bringing to naught his plan for converting the Jews, uniting Israel into one people, and establishing it still more firmly as a national and a religious whole. For the six rabbis named above very soon became the soul of Talmudic study; some of them were with R. Simeon, the Nasi, in Shprehem, and others founded colleges of their own. Through them the Talmud regained its former power and influence, and one of them, R. Ilai, became the chief teacher of R. Jehudah the Nasi, the compiler of the Mishna.

The translation of the Bible (written law) into Greek also contributed very much to the popularization of the Talmud. As long as the Torah was in the sacred language only (for the Aramaic version of the time of Ezra had been concealed or destroyed as early as the time of Rabban Gamaliel the Elder, the son of Simeon who had been slain, or probably even during the life of the latter),[1] all Jewish sects and foreign scholars interpreted it in their own way. But a wise Greek, a convert of Judaism, Aquila the Proselyte, who received the doctrines of the Talmud from the disciples of R. Johanan b. Zakkai and also from R. Aqiba, translated the Bible into Greek. This version was not acceptable to the Jewish believers in Jesus (Messianists)--who must already at that period have constituted a large sect--because their construction of many passages in the Messianic spirit was flatly disregarded by the new translation; nor to the Romans, because all expressions seeming to imply the materiality of the Deity were translated in a figurative sense--as for example, "the hand of the Lord"; "the glory of the Lord," which the statue-worshipping Romans could not endure with equanimity, and further because by this translation the nature and doctrines of the Talmud became known to many nations, who found no evil in it. In our opinion the version of Aquila was the sole cause of the despatch of censors from Rome to revise the Talmud, and these censors avowed that its teaching was true. Be it as it may, in studying the history of the Talmud during the first three centuries the reader is easily convinced of the great courage and patience of the sages of the Talmud, For no year of that period passed without trouble from its external as well as from its internal foes, as R. Simeon b. Gamaliel, the Nasi of Jamnia, himself testifies. For even after the death of Hadrian it enjoyed but a short respite, for Antoninus Pius renewed the decree of Hadrian, and only with much trouble and at great risk of his life did the Nasi succeed in inducing R. Simeon b. Jochai and R. Josi to go with him to Rome to petition the Cæsar to repeal the decree, which, according to the tradition of the Talmud, they effected only through the intervention of "Ben Temalion" (a demon, according to some; a man, according to others). And yet, in spite of this, during this very period, the Talmud became so popular that every town wherein Jews had their habitation possessed also a house of learning for the study of the Talmud; so that everywhere it bloomed and flourished, and bore the fruit of the Mishna, as we shall see in the next chapter.

----

1. See our "Pentateuch, its Languages and Characters," pp. 16-17.

Chapter 4
Development of the Talmud in the Third Century

The Third Century--The Arrangement Of The Mishnas--The Talmudic Colleges Of Palestine And Babylonia.

The sages, the commentators of the Talmud, differed in opinion as to the epoch when the Talmud began to be written down. The scholars of Spain, and their colleagues and disciples, said that it had been recorded from notes possessed since schools had begun in Israel, a long time before R. Jehudah the Nasi. The scholars of France, among them "Rashi," however, declared that not a line was written till the completion of the Talmud, before which its study had been oral. Each school adduced proofs in behalf of its assertion. Modem scholars have made a compromise between these various versions, by asserting that during the first centuries the commentators of the Talmud in the beginning had taken notes of their studies, and later had written them out in a permanent form. It would seem that as the persecutions had at their commencement been very severe, and the sages (see App. No. 7) felt that their lives were in peril, they decided to write its teaching in secret and to conceal it from its foes. No sooner had the Pharisees granted permission for this (for till then it was absolutely forbidden to put in writing oral law) than the number of manuscripts became very great; and when R. Jehudah the

Nasi came to occupy the seat of his father and had been confirmed in authority (since he enjoyed the friendship of one Antonius, who was in power at Rome), he discovered that from the multitude of the trees the forest could not be seen; that is, from the multitude of the Mishnas the people had lost sight of the Talmud. He therefore resolved to compile, selecting out of all the written and the unwritten law, clear Mishnayoth, and to systematize them.

Indeed, the period was very favorable to this undertaking, for the Talmud enjoyed a respite from persecutors external and internal. The Jewish followers of the Messiah, Jesus, began at this time to gradually blend with the foreigners who adopted the new creed; hence their influence on their brethren who persisted in the old faith was weakened. Still he met with many obstacles. The chief one was the division of opinion among the students of the Talmud themselves. For although his grandfather, Rabban Gamaliel the Elder, had succeeded in fixing the law in accordance with Hillel's school, and declared, with the consent of many of the sages of the Talmud, the school of Shammai of no validity when at variance with Hillel's, still the decree was weakened, when later he was deposed for a short time from his office of Nasi, and in his college were assembled four hundred students more, of diverse opinions. In view of this, and it was decided again that individual opinions, even those of the minority, should be considered, the differences between the students and the sages of his college were renewed with greater vigor. This state of things continued till the time of 'Rabbi, and in order that his Mishnayoth might be accepted he was compelled to give due weight to all the varying opinions, slighting none, even of those who were in direct contravention of the decision.

The second difficulty was in selecting, from among the mass of incongruous doctrines and laws--many of which had become obsolete, and others found to be unnecessary or impracticable--those which were both practicable and of direct application (for a tradition relates that Rabbi found six hundred sections of Mishnayoth; and even if we admit that this number is greatly exaggerated, still if even one hundred existed, it was no light task to reduce them to six).

The third difficulty was that as the subject had been studied in divers places, differing in dialect or language, all the Mishnayoth had to be made uniform in their dialect. Added to all this, he was forced to clear the Mishnayoth from the insertions incorporated into it by the Messianists; for being many and considerable persons, and in close alliance with their colleagues the Pharisees during two centuries, they could not have failed to introduce into the Mishnayoth their own peculiar opinion and beliefs, many such passages, indeed, being found in the Gemara.

Reason compels us to admit, at least, that there were passages in the Mishnayoth concerning Jesus and his teachings; for how is it possible that an occurrence which holds so important a place in the history of Israel, and which has spread its influence among the nations for centuries, should not be even hinted at in the Mishnayoth? We must, therefore, conclude that Rabbi thought it well to clear the Mishnayoth of any reference to the occurrence itself, as well as to the adherents of the new faith. In this he acted wisely, for he knew beforehand that the Mishnayoth would be the foundation upon which Judaism and the Talmud should be built, and that the interpretations of it would be many, each interpreter following the bias of his mind. Therefore it was deemed best by him to avoid all mention of the new event, to treat it as though it had no existence. Nothing can withstand a strong will. When once he had resolved to carry out his project at any cost, all difficulties vanished. He went from college to college, in cities far and near, in places where the great masters taught and learned; and though they "surrounded him as cocks of Beth Bukia," he was not shaken in his resolution, and with the help of his many friends and sympathizers he was finally enabled to arrange in order six sections of Mishnayoth, condensed from hundreds. Each section is given up to a general subject, and is subdivided into tracts dealing with matters which come naturally within the scope of the section, The tracts are further divided into chapters.

The subjects of the sections and the tracts are as follows:

1. *The Section of Seeds.*--The general subject of this section is the law relating to vegetables, heave offerings, tithes, the sabbatical year, Kilaim, etc.; and at the head of this section he placed the tract on benedictions which man owes to his Maker every morning, beginning

with those of the evening, which commences the day according to the Jewish custom.

2. *The Section of Festivals.*--This treats of the Sabbath holidays (to each holiday being devoted a separate tract), and incidentally also of the duty of taxes before the holidays, and of mourning during the festivals. (See App. No. 8.)

3. *The Section of Women.*--This deals with laws having reference to women, marriage, divorce, in separate tracts, and thereto are added laws concerning vows and Nazarites, as women's vows are dependent on the decision of their fathers and husbands, and Nazarites depend on women, who may legally consecrate the child previous to its birth, as for example, Hannah and the mother of Samson.

4. *The Section of Damages.*--This section treats of laws of Property, of the judges, of the penalties which the court may Prescribe, and is divided into the tracts "Sanhedrin," "Penalties" (Makkoth), etc.; but as the first part treats only of damages and their prevention, it is divided simply into three parts without distinct titles: but as first, second and third Geths, and as it treats of damages for which men are responsible, a tract on morals has been added--"Abboth." (Sections "Festivals and Jurisprudence" have been already translated into English by us in eighteen volumes; the synopsis of which will be here appendixed.)

5. *The Section of Sacred Things* (sacrifices), divided into tracts on sacrifices (Zebachim) firstlings (Bekhoroth), and by the way also Chulin; it treats of slaughtering, and examination of the slaughtered animal used for profane purposes.

6. *The Section of Purifications* (Tohoroth).--This deals with the subject of defilements and purifications in general, and has for special topics the defilement of vessels (Kelim), of plagues (Nega'im), of tents (Aholoth), etc., and a tract relating to a Nidah (menstruated woman).

Thus he arranged all the laws relating to the Hebrew religion and to civil matters, and called his entire work Mishnayoth (Mishna), *i.e.* meaning "teaching" to distinguish it from "Torah" and "Talmud," and probably because it is written (Deut. vi. 7) V'shinantam--"and thou shalt teach them diligently to thy children"--in the original version (Mishna Tohroh), which signifies really to explain

24

and comment upon it. Thus the Mishna is an explanation of and a comment upon the Pentateuch (see footnote for a different explanation, in the introduction to "Sabbath"), and teaches men how to conduct themselves in relation to their fellow-men, and incites them to all good and praiseworthy (actions).

In the short introduction to "Sabbath" (vi.-vii.) we have already described briefly the character of the Mishnayoth which Rabbi arranged, and how he succeeded in imparting to it the sanctity of the Pentateuch itself, so that nothing is to be added to them, and what was done later after Rabbi's death, is not the place to expatiate on this subject; we may, however, state briefly that as soon as the Mishnayoth was completed, colleges were founded in Palestine and Babylonia to explain the meaning of the Mishnayoth and develop their laws to their ultimate consequences. After Rabbi's death, when Boraithoth and Toseptheth were discovered which did not form part of his compilation and which in many places contradicted the Mishnayoth, these colleges busied themselves in reconciling them with the Mishnayoth and with each other. They accounted for contradictions in Baraithoth by saying that one spoke of a case under same circumstances, while another meant a like case under different circumstances. So they explained the differences in the Mishnayoth themselves, often dividing a Mishna, whose parts seemed to contradict each other, and giving as explanation of the contradictions that the first part was according to one tana, but the latter part according to another. These discussions and comments on the Mishna they called "Gemara," which also signifies "teaching" in Aramaic, which was the spoken language of the sages of the Gemara (see in the above-mentioned introduction for a different reason), and to the combined Mishnayoth and Gemara they gave the old name, "Talmud".

Chapter 5
The Two Talmuds

The Talmud Of Jerusalem, The Talmud Of Babylonia, The Character Of Their Halakha And Hagada, The Dates Of Their Completion And Their Systematization.

The sages of the Gemara, called Amaraim, and the commentators of Mishnayoth were of different characters. Some were intent only on diligently collecting Mishnayoth and Baraithoth, wherever found, to compare them with each other, to correct their reading in conformity with Rabbi's Mishnayoth, and to separate the wheat from the chaff, *i.e.* to decide which Boraithoth was valid and which was not worthy of consideration (Boraithoth which were not studied in the colleges of R. Hyya and R. Ushia were not considered). On the other hand, there were others who devoted themselves to ingenious construction of the Mishnayoth and the Boraithoth itself, without adducing proofs from elsewhere. (See App. No. 9.) This consisted in scrupulously examining the letters in the Mishna, to eliminate or to amplify it where they judged necessary, to trace laws to their origin and to discover what tana agreed with this Mishna and what differed from it, whether the same tana contradicted himself at different places, and whether it was incompatible to explain them in various ways, and the like. In the language of the Gemara they are distinguished by different titles. Those who studied the Mishnayoth were styled "Sinai, the master of the wheat," and the dialecticians "the uprooters of mountains" or "acute men"; and although the preference was given to the former, as it was said, "all must resort to the master of the wheat," yet the study of the Babylonian Talmudists being based on scholasticism, their acuteness is evinced in their so harmonizing the contradictions and disagreements, that they appear to point to the same meaning.

Not only did they interpret the Boraithas at variance with the Mishnayoth, but when even one of the great Amoraim appeared to differ from the Mishna they so distorted the latter that it should seem to agree with the Amora. A similar difference existed among the authors of the Hagada; some gave to biblical texts a new reading remote from the plain meaning, interpreting them in strange and marvellous ways, and basing on them legends of natural impossibilities, while some adhered closely to the literal meaning of texts, without adorning them with exaggerations. Though in the Palestinian and the Syrian, as well as in the Babylonian colleges, there were many scholars who assisted each other in their studies and comments on the Mishnayoth, the Palestinian differed from those of Babylon in this respect, that in the former the chief labor consisted in the collection of Halakhas, without profound researches into the deeper meanings and implications, even in the study of the mere Mishnayoth, all of which was totally unlike the manner of study in the Babylonian schools. Indeed, the Palestinians were inferior to the Babylonians in scholastic profundity and ingenuity, and but few of them distinguished themselves therein, except R. Johanan, R. Simeon b. Lakish, and several others of that period. Therefore, in the schools of Palestine, scholasticism was esteemed of little value, and in them the study of Halakhas fell into decay, so that finally the Hagada came to occupy the principal place, the Halakhas holding a subordinate position. In addition to this, they found themselves compelled to give their attention to the biblical texts, as the Messianists, who had grown in numbers, construed these texts favorably to Christianity, and challenged the Jews to dispute with them. Therefore, the sages found themselves obliged to give the preference to the study of the Scriptures and Hagada. As at that time the impression was general that the most important element in the study of the Torah is ingenious reasoning on Halakha, it is not surprising that the Babylonian Talmud came to be received as the important and essential part of the Oral Law, while that of Palestine held a subordinate position.

It is difficult to describe accurately and clearly the mode of thinking and ways of reasoning of the Talmud, which in truth is known only to one who has made it the study of his life. It is easier, however, to give a picture of the Talmudists' views and notions. as gathered from the Hagada. In this respect the Hagada of the Palestinian Talmud is superior to that of Babylon, as it had its birth in Palestine, and was borrowed thence by the Babylonians.

Many books of Hagada had existed in Palestine, whose contents were incorporated later in various Midrashim, and some also in the Talmud, and even at that period there was a difference of opinion as to their value. Some valued them, and some despised them. The Hagadas consist of two elements: first, the external garment of the thought, the tradition, and secondly, the internal idea, allegorically shadowed forth, which constitutes literary value. The latter can be divided into three kinds: "P'shat," the interpretation of the meaning of biblical words; "Drash," a free untrammelled interpretation of the scriptural texts; "Sod," the deep mystic, religious meanings construed from the texts. By these three kinds of construction of Scripture, all subjects, topics and times are embraced and discussed. The Hagada, with its mystic and veiled religious wisdom, has exercised a great influence in the Oriental and heathen world, which has borrowed from it many precious gems of profound religious thought having Palestine for their birthplace. And indeed we find that the multitude of legends based on the Bible which have been current in, and reverenced by, the Mohammedan world for twelve hundred years, delighting both sages and the unlearned, are to be found in the Talmudic Hagada. Whether entire or only in the leading idea, their identity is recognizable. Many also of the legends of the Middle Ages to be found in the works of Dante, or those of Boccaccio, Cervantes, and Milton, are taken, consciously or unconsciously, from their original source, the Talmudic Hagada. The Fathers of the Christian church have likewise drawn on it, as Basilius of Cappadocia, Hieronymus, Chrysostomus, and many others who construed passages in the Bible in accordance with the Hagada. The moral code contained in the Hagada, teaches man how to conduct himself toward all men and in all situations of life. We shall deal with this moral law in a future chapter on the Ethics of the Talmud.

The two Talmuds contain, then, Halakhas, Hagadas, references to all branches of science known in those days, but without any system or order. Many times a Hagada is interpolated in the middle of a Halakha, and again in like manner a digression on a scientific subject extraneous to the Halakha is inserted in it. The compiler of the Talmud, whether from careless method or from the great labor involved, could introduce no order. In this respect there is little difference between the two Talmuds; nor is there much difference in the sources whence each drew its material. Sayings from the Talmud of Palestine are quoted in that of Babylonia, sometimes under the name of their author or their citer in Babylonia; other passages are stated to emanate from the "West." "In the West (Palestine) it was said." In the Talmud Palestinian, similarly (*vide* I. H Weiss, Vol. III., 127, etc.), the Babylonian authority is often given; *e.g.*, "*There* they learn" or "say." It is clear however that when the Babylonian Talmud was compiled that of Palestine was unknown to its compilers, although, according to the opinion of many, the Talmud of Palestine was arranged by R. Johanan and concluded by R. Jose bar Bun about one hundred years before the Babylonian; others, however, affirm that the Talmud of Palestine was concluded only in the eighth century or even as late as the ninth (in the time of Anan, the founder of the Karaite sect), and adduce evidence in substantiation. We may assume, as a compromise, both assertions to be true; the greater part had indeed been arranged and systematized in the time of Hillel, the last of the Nasis in the West, but it was not employed to any extent in the colleges remaining in Palestine and Syria, because the Babylonian Talmud had spread until it reached the West. But in the time of the Karaites many things were added to the Talmud of Palestine (to oppose the doctrines of the Karaites, as the small tract on Tephilin and the like, which that sect repudiated) by those who wished their words to be held as of equal sacredness with the Talmud, as was then customary. (We shall speak of this further on.) The bulk of the Palestine Talmud, after all the additions, is much less than that of the Babylonian, albeit it contains Gemara on two additional tracts (thirty-nine instead of thirty-seven, as will be explained) and fragmentary chapters of other tracts. This is owing to the fact that the discussion of the Mishnayoth is not so elaborate, and there is less of scholastics. We have already stated that its quality, as regards the Halakhas, is also inferior. It was not as popular as that of Babylonia, therefore fewer copies were made of it than of the latter. For this reason, since its conclusion its opponents have been less numerous, though it was very much persecuted at the time when it was studied in the colleges. The government rulers persecuted Israel and its Torah, since the death of Rabhi, and the persecutions did not stop until the death of Hillel, the last of his descendants, with whom the office of Nasi ceased to exist (360). This was alone one of the causes why the Talmud of Palestine spread less widely than its younger brother of Babylonia. The lot of the Talmud in Babylonia was better, since from the time of the death of Rabbi (223) till Mar b. R. Rah Ashi, one of the last of the Amoraim (500), it was not persecuted by the Persian rulers. For about a hundred years, the heads of the Exile were diligent in their studies, uniting thereunto its political power. If it sometimes happened that some kings were ill-disposed to the Jews, still they did not interfere with their studies.[1] For this reason the study of the Talmud flourished in the colleges of Sura, Nahardea and Pumbeditha, and the number of its students was counted by thousands. (The Talmud counts the auditors of Abba Arikha's [Rabb's] lectures as 12,000.) And so the Talmud became a vast sea, and its waves rose with might. R. Ashi (355-427) saw, therefore, that the time had come for revising, systematizing and concluding it, when he came to restore the college of Sura (Matha Mekhasia), which had fallen into decay on the death of Rabh.

About this R. Ashi it was said (Sanhedrin, p. 108) that from the time of Rabbi to his time there is not to be found a man who was

unique in the possession of wisdom, riches and glory. He was in favor
with King Izgadar II., rich and long-lived. Therefore, he undertook in
the course of one year to systematize two tracts. Whether he arranged
them in the order in which they are found in the Mishnayoth, or
differently, or whether he revised and improved them, is not known
to us; but this, at least, is clear, that some tracts he revised twice, and
the second time in a manner opposite to the first.[2] Be this as it may, it
is also certain that the Talmud which we possess is not that which
came from R. Ashi's hands, since additions by seven heads of the
colleges who succeeded him in Sura, and by their colleagues, Meremar, Idi bar Abin, Nabman bar Huna, Tabyomi (Mar b. R. Ashi) his
son, Rabba Tosphoah, Rabina bar Huna, Rabbana Jose, who presided
together 125 years, are mentioned in the Talmud, none of which are
found in R. Ashi's edition. Perhaps they also made eliminations in his
edition though they did not attain the learning and religious wisdom
of R. Ashi, except his son, Tabyomi. The latter filled the place of his
father in learning and wisdom, though not in his breadth of view, for
in his time reigned King Peros, the son of Izgadar III., who persecuted
the Jews, the Talmud, and those who cherished it. Therefore, even if
we suppose that his son Mar was diligent in arranging and revising
the Talmud, as traces of his insertions and corrections are found in it,
yet he did not succeed in completing it, owing to the persecutions of
the government, especially as he did not occupy his office long, and
thus the Talmud has remained uncorrected. But as the sages became
aware that the times were changing, the number of learned men
diminishing, they began to fear lest in the course of time, passages
would multiply in the Talmud which would rather detract from than
add to its value; therefore they concluded it, and decreed that thence-
forth nothing should be added to it. They also ordered that the sages
should no more be called "Amoraim." (signifying commentators of the
Mishna), but Saburaim (*i.e.*, explainers of the Talmud to the people).
Thus the Talmud was concluded in the age of Rabbana Jose (about
525), without further revision or rearranging. In reality, however,
these sages achieved almost nothing; for, despite their decree, the
Soburites (as also many of its enemies) as well as the Gaonim, and the
rabbis succeeding them, added to and eliminated from it and altered

in many places its version, as 1. H. Weiss has proved beyond dispute and also we ourselves in our book "L'baker Mishpat" and in the journal "Hakol" many times, as will be mentioned further on. (See App. No. 10.)

---

1. See Getzow, "Al Naharoth Babel."
2. Vide "Last Gate," 356b.

Chapter 6
The Sixth Century: Persian and Byzantine Persecution of the Talmud

The Persecutions Of The Talmud In The Persian And Byzantine Empires In The Sixth Century After The Close Of The Talmud.

In the reign of Kobad (Cabades) in Persia, a fanatic reformer named Mazdak desired to introduce the doctrine of the community of property and wives, thus modifying the Zoroastrian creed. (501). The king became an adherent of the new doctrine and decreed its acceptance by the people. The lower classes eagerly availed themselves of the license thus granted. To this communism, the Jews, led by Mar Zutra II., son of R. Huna, the young exilarch, offered an armed resistance. The occasion of the revolt was the murder of Mar Isaac, president of one of the colleges. It is related that they established an independent Jewish state, having for king the Prince of Captivity, with Machuza as the capital. At last, after seven years, Mar Zutra and his grandfather, Mar Chanina, were taken prisoners, executed, and their bodies nailed to the cross on the bridge of Machuza (about 520). On account of the ensuing persecutions the office of Exilarch remained for some time in abeyance. The colleges were closed, as the teachers were compelled to conceal themselves, and Abuna and Giza, two of the most, eminent, fled. When peace was restored after Kobad's death, the college at Sura, received Giza as president, and that at Pumbeditha, Semuna. A third name of eminence survives, that of Rabbi or Rab (near Nahardea), of whom little is known. Men of religious mind of the period devoted themselves to the study of the Talmud, the love for which persecution had but increased, which satisfied religious zeal and promoted tranquillity of mind, and the knowledge of which raised its possessor to positions of honor and trust.

The original development of the Talmud had at that period ceased. Giza and Semuna conceived the desire to fix the laws for practical use, casting aside theoretical speculation, for it was necessary that there be no doubts or wavering. Their activity in this work was but a continuation of that which had begun at the close of the Talmud. The labors of the presidents of the colleges were confined to this task and to assembling, as of old, the disciples in Adar (March) and Ellul (September) and instructing them by lectures, and to assigning themes for private study. To fix the laws, the arguments *pro* and *con* needed to be weighed; therefore they were called Sabureans (Saburai). Many points of practice in the ritual, the civil law, and the marriage code were settled at this period.

Giza and Semuna gave chief attention to committing the Talmud to writing, making use of oral traditions and of notes made to aid the memory by various individuals. All legends were incorporated, and the obscure passages elucidated by their additions, for everything emanating from the Amoraim was thought important. In this form it has reached us. The vowel points to the Bible were also invented at this time, according to Graetz.

"The names of the immediate successors of Giza and Semuna have not been preserved either by chronicles or tradition"--forgotten in the persecution visited on the colleges during this century by both Christian and Zoroastrian churches.

Hormisdas IV., Chosroes Nushirvan's son, was unlike his father. Led by the Magi, who strove to check the approaching dissolution of their religion by persecution of the adherents of other faiths, he vented his wrath upon the Jews and Christians of his empire. The Talmudical colleges at Sura and Pumbeditha were closed, and again many teachers fled (about 581) this time to Firuzshabar, where, under an Arabian governor, they were less exposed to espionage. New colleges arose there, among which that of Mari was eminent, and there they continued their Talmudic labors. A general, Babram Tshubin, who had experienced the ingratitude of the king, usurped the Persian throne. In this he was assisted by the Jews with money and men, and in return granted them many favors and concessions. As a result, the colleges of Sura and Pumbeditha were reopened; Chanan of Iskia returned from Firuzshabar to Pumbeditha, and restored the college there; it is also probable that the president of Sura, which was of far greater repute, was elected at that time, though his name is not mentioned in the chronicles.

With Babram's fall the vengeance of the lawful heir to the throne, prince Chosru, was visited on the Jews. With the aid of the Byzantine emperor, Mauritius, and the loyal portion of the Persian people, he defeated the usurper, putting to the sword also the greater part of the Jewish population of Machuza, and probably of other cities as well.

Chapter 7
The Eight Century: the Persecution of the Talmud by the Karaites

The Eighth Century. The Dominion Of The Gaonim. The Opposition Of The Karaites. The Establishment Of A Sect Of That Name.

The Pharisees had been victorious over the Sadducees and the other sects opposed to the Oral Law, but had not annihilated them entirely; since only because these latter could not withstand them, they kept silence and were discontented in their hearts, As the Talmud gained strength and became more severe in its decrees against the Sadducees and Samaritans, so that in the end the Kuthim were declared as idolaters in all respects, then their indignation burned and they awaited a favorable time for revenge. In the time of the dominance of the Gaonim, who carried out the Talmud in practice, the measure became full, and Anan, the nephew of the Gaon at Sura, when he was not elected as Gaon, for the reason of his liberal ideas and his opposition to the Talmud, established the Karaite sect.

Those who hold that the Karaites were a new sect founded by Anan (760 C.E.), are mistaken, for a small sect under the name of Karaites, or adherents of the Text, had existed already in the days of the Talmud, where they are mentioned in many places, as "adherents of the Text," or once "the Karaites add" (Pesachim, 117a in text; in our edition, Vol. V., p. 145). Doubtless the remainder of the Sadducees assumed this name, having lost political influence since they had been vanquished, and the word "Sadducees" being hated by the people. Therefore the remains of the sect called themselves "Karaites," *i.e.* those who occupy themselves with the text of Scripture, and endeavor to understand its real meaning. Owing to their. small numbers, or to the lack of a great man to head them, this, sect kept secret its hatred of the Talmud, though it existed so long as to outlive even the close of the latter, and the Talmudic sages paid no attention to them. Finally, however, chance gave them a man fit to be their leader, who publicly opposed the Talmud so that all its enemies made one league against it, and they were at first a great power; and in the course of 700 years they did not cease to persecute the Talmud and almost destroyed it; finally, however, they lost their influence which they never regained, and to-day are decayed so that small numbers only live in Austria, Crimea, and many other places in Russia, numbering in all to-day no more than 4,000 or 5,000 souls altogether.

This man was Anan ben David, nephew of the exilarch Solomon, in Bagdad, who had died childless. Anan expected to be elected as his successor, but his younger brother was chosen instead, and he was rejected because of his liberal ideas and want of sympathy with the Talmud. Then he publicly began to make war on the Talmud and Talmudists, and became the head of all its opponents and ill-wishers. He made his headquarters at Jerusalem, after having been, it seems, obliged to leave Babylonia. There he assumed the title of exilarch, and around him were assembled a great multitude who made, war on the Oral Law, its scholars, and in particular on the two colleges of Sura and Pumbeditha.

By his general precept, "Search well in the Scriptures," he declared as naught the whole Oral Law. And wishing to find favor in the eyes of the Caliphs, who fixed the dates of their festivals by observation of the new moon, he also renewed this custom, once in force among the Jews while the Temple had existed, repealing thus the calculation of R. Adda received among all Talmudists. He openly said to the Caliph Almanzur that the Jews had been guilty of persecuting Jesus and opposing Mahomet, though (said he) both these men did much to drive idolatry out of existence, and cannot be attacked without guilt. Of the first he said that he had been a holy man who did not want to appear as a prophet, or a god, but only desired to reform the faith which the Pharisees had perverted. Of the second he said that be really was a prophet for the Arabs, only he does not believe that the Law (of Moses) is repealed by Mahommedanism.

His first work was to separate himself from the Jews by fixing the date of Pentecost to be fifty days after the first Sabbath after Passover, as the Sadducees fixed it formerly. The dates of New Year and the Day of Atonement, Passover and the Feast of Booths were determined by watching for the new moon, which did not agree with the Jewish dates. As in the leap year one month is added to the year, he allowed, in case of need, to begin Passover when barley is ripe in the fields. The Phylacteries (not a grave ceremony among the Jews, at any rate), the four species of the Lulab and the semi-holiday Hanuka (Dedication), he abolished. On the other hand he made the observation of Sabbath more burdensome, so that the lighting of candles was prohibited on the eve of Sabbath, even by a non-Jew, also the leaving of one's house during Sabbath when most neighbors are not Jews, *i.e.* Karaites; the dietary laws he also made stricter, so as to prohibit his adherents eating in company with Jews for the latter are not careful enough and oftentimes eat with Gentiles.

Soon Anan saw that if every one were left to interpret the Biblical text according to his own mind, etc., his sect would be split, and not endure (as actually was the case in the course of time, as will be explained further on), and that a fixed commentary is needed at least for those passages which can by no means be interpreted literally. *Therefore he claimed many great authorities, long deceased, as Karaites, and declared that R. Jehuda b. Tabai,* the colleague of Simeon b. Shetah, etc. Shamai the elder, the colleague of Hillel the Elder, and other such, were some of the founders of their sect, and he ascribed to them some interpretations of passages which he claimed to have received by tradition from them. "Abandon the Talmud and Mishna," he said to his followers, "and I will make you a Talmud of my own, according to the traditions I have." Though in reality he took the rules of the Mishna as basis, yet he said that as far as details are concerned he is as wise as the sages of the Mishna, or more so, and can construe the Biblical texts by his own intellect.

His hatred of the Talmud became so great that he said that if he could have swallowed the Talmud, he would cast himself into a lime-kiln, that it might be burned with him and leave no vestige of its existence. Thus the people of Israel separated itself then into two hostile hosts. The Talmudists declared the Karaites not to be Jews, and forbade to give them any holy ceremony to perform, while the Karaites said of the followers of the rabbis that they are Jewish sinners, and it is sinful to intermarry with them. The city of Jerusalem witnessed for the third time a splitting of Israel into parties.

Of Anan's writing we know nothing, although according to the Karaites he wrote some comments on the Bible and prayers. From the compositions imputed by them to him, we can see that only the love of resistance and victory absorbed him; how great his learning was we can not judge, as in general his biography is unknown to us, but it is known that he was not given, to philosophy, nor ingenious in interpreting Scripture. One good effect we can ascribe to him, that, owing to his opposition, the Talmudic rabbis were also forced to pay more attention to the Scriptures, and make researches and learn the niceties of the Hebrew language, so that Anan and his sect were the prime cause of all the compositions on grammar, Massorah and vowel points, and even poetic compositions that the Talmudists gave birth to in the course of time.

After Anan's death Saul, his son, succeeded him as exilarch of the Karaites, but Anan's disciples separated from him, as they did not agree with him about some ceremonies, according to Saul's interpretation of biblical passages. They became a distinct sect calling themselves Ananites; so it also happened after the death of Saul, who was succeeded by Josiah, his son. And so almost every age sprang a new Karaite sect with a name of its own, each interpreting Scripture in its own way. Some of them will be mentioned presently, It is self-evident that an attempt to get at the profound meaning of the Scriptures was the business of every such sect; through their activity the knowledge of Hebrew grammar, of Massorah, the vowel-points and punctuation

marks, was diffused; theological philosophizing was also not strange
to some Karaites, as they had to explain such words as God's "hand,"
"eye," "finger," which they were unwilling to take literally and materi-
alize God, just as the other Jews. Thus gradually a large literature
sprang among the Karaites, not inferior, taken as a whole, to the
Talmud itself in bulk.

At all events, the Talmud was menaced by a much greater danger
from these internal enemies than from its external foes. For the latter
did not attack the Talmud itself, except so far as it was an obstacle in
their way, but their main and avowed object was to convert
the *Jews* to another religion, or even merely to fill their own pockets
with Jewish gold, given to avert the persecution instigated for that
very purpose. The Talmud was then attacked only incidentally, not
for its sake, while the main object was something else.

But the Karaites made it their great aim to drive the Talmud itself
out of existence, to direct their arrows against it for its own sake, and
endeavored to bring about, that the Jews should become Christians,
or Mussulmans, or join any sect whatever, the Karaites did not care
which, provided that the Jews should forsake the hateful Talmud,
and its Halakhas and Hagadas should get lost. Therefore the struggle
with them was very great, especially as they pretended that their
traditions were based on the great authorities of the remnants of the
nation.

As their doctrines, however, were not fixed, and as almost every
age the Karaites were split into diverse sects, therefore they could not
resist or make headway against the Talmud, whose strength is, to
those who rightly understand it, that it has never purposed to make
fixed rules, to last for all ages; deliberation and reasoning concerning
the Halakhas according to the circumstances, is the principle of the
Talmud; and the saying of the Talmud, "even when they say to you
of *right* that it is *left*, and of *left* that it is *right*, thou shalt not swerve
from the commandment," shows the opinion of the Talmud, that the
practice of the ceremonies and precepts is dependent on the time,
place and other circumstances. With this power the Talmud
combatted all its enemies, and was victorious.

The controversies between the Jews and the Karaites are

recorded in many books, Karaite and Talmudistic, from the age of R. Saadia the Gaon, and his opponent Sahal ben Matzliah to the present time. In them can also be found the history of their alternate triumphs. But this is not our task here: we will remark only that from the days of R. Saadiah the Gaon, when the Rabbis had begun to have polemics with them, can be seen the deep mark the Karaite literature left on the Rabbinical one. Philosophy was from that time used in conjunction with the Torah; many Gaonim followed R. Saadiah's method of harmonizing the Torah and the philosophy of that time, that they should seem as mutual enemies. So the Karaites charged such men with infidelity, but others were themselves compelled to imitate them, and called in the aid of philosophy, of the divinity, to interpret the texts of the Holy Scriptures.

The effect of the Karaites on the Talmudist Rabbis is made evident also in this: that since their time the rabbis also began to write down fixed Halakhas taken from the Talmud, that the readers should not otherwise by error adopt the Karaite rules, made by the Karaite leaders, which they might mistake for the rules of the Talmud itself, since they could not know the whole Talmud by heart. They composed, therefore, the "Halakhoth G'doloth" (Great Halakhas), "Sh'iltoth'derab A'bai" (Queries of R. Ahai), for the sake of the students, who could not themselves wade through the whole Talmud. But thereby they opposed the spirit and object of the Talmud itself, that the Halakhas should be matter for discussion, and modified in accordance with the requirements of the time and place. As soon as the Gaonim had permitted to propound decisions of the Halakhas, and to fix them, those Gaonim, who succeeded them, were compelled to teach that these decisions of the former Gaonim, even though given without proofs, are holy for the people, as if giver, from Mount Sinai. This circumstance added fuel to the quarrel of the Karaites, and gave them new points of attack. The hope of some great men of the nation to reconcile the Jews with the Karaites became naught, for although the Karaites quarrelled among themselves, and split into rival sects, yet they all equally hated the Talmud, reviled it, and insulted it, styling the two colleges, at Sura and Pumbeditha, "the two harlots" spoken of in

Ezekiel, who (claimed they) referred to these colleges in his prophecy.

According to Makrizi there were among the Karaites ten sects, differing from each other in their opinions, practice and festivals; they had no permanence, some rose, some fell, and in the tenth century only five large sects were found, named:

1. Jod'anim or Jodganim.
2. Makrites or Magrites.
3. Akhbarites.
4. Abn Amronites or Tiflisites.
5. Balbekites.

The reader will find in the books of Jost, Grätz, Fürst, Geiger, and in Hebrew, in "Bequoreth L'toldoth Hakaraim" an account of the particulars about which the various sects of the Karaites differed, and also the names of their leaders. We do not think it necessary to give these details in this place. We will mention for illustration the latest sect, which wished to fix the day of Atonement only on a Saturday every year, because it is said "Sabbath Sabbathan," which means a Sabbath of rest (Lev. xxiii. 32), and they translate "a Sabbath of Sabbaths," and the first day of Passover on Thursday. Thus each Karaite sect celebrated the Biblical festivals on different days, for each sect construed the texts in the Pentateuch by preference without being able to come to an agreement. Thus also in respect of the observation of Sabbath: for some Karaites, their houses were during the Sabbath their prisons, where they did sit in darkness, and which they could not leave when their neighbors happened not to be Karaites like themselves. In this we see the power of the Talmud, that even those who were inimical to it or hostile to a large portion of it, Halakhas never had different opinions concerning the festivals and other such things, important to one particular nation; for they could not deny its general tradition.

The effects of Karaism are also traceable in some religious practices, which had not been usual among the people of ancient times. Thus Phylacteries, which it had not been customary to use, in spite of the literal interpretation of the Talmud of the passage "and thou shalt bind them for a sign upon thy hand, and they shall be as frontlets between thine eyes," (Deut. vi. 8); perhaps for the reason that Hillel had said: "Leave Israel alone; if they are not prophets, they are children of prophets," (Pesachim); for after all, the arguments of the Talmud in favor of the literalness of that passage, the people felt that it was only a figurative expression; and the Talmud itself prohibited the use of phylacteries to the people, permitting it only to confirmed scholars. But when the Karaites interpreted the passage figuratively, the Gaonim permitted the use of Tephilin to the people also, to show their difference from the Karaites.

The opposition of the Karaites effected also that the Gaonim should declare that the Hagada of the Talmud is not obligatory to believe for any man; and that it is not to be taken literally, but as allegorical. "Leave to every one the right to hold what opinions he chooseth about the Hagada of the Talmud" says R. Samuel b. Hopni, father-in-law to Hai Gaon, to ward off the attacks of the Karaites and opponents of the Talmud generally, who made it responsible for many Hagadic things cautioned in it. And indeed we see that the collections of Halakhas from the Talmud, as Rab Alphasi and his colleagues inserted but little of the Hagada, as if to show that the Hagadas are not minded. Though in truth the Hagadas of the Talmud relating to morality are the main element of the Talmud, mostly require no change, addition, or subtraction, even in our age. While on the other hand, the absence of the ethics of the Talmudic Hagada is painfully felt in Karaite literature to the present day. In points of morality their opinions are as various as concerning the Halakhas, in the course of time issued from the Karaite ascetics who abstained from meat and wine, left their homes, dwelt in deserts, and mourned over the destruction of Jerusalem. The Karaites styled them "the sixty heroes who are around Solomon's bed," for there were sixty in number, and called them the great teachers, for they had been taught by them that it is not legal to eat meat in exile, since a text says one should not slaughter outside the camp. In contrast with these, from among the Karaites came also Hiri Hakalhi or Habalki who, owing to his opposition to the Talmud, denied also Moses' Torah, providence, creation, etc., so that the Karaites repulsed him also. There were among them also some who believed in a material God, eating something of the sacrifices, and enjoying the agreeable flavor of them. Such was the destiny of those who rejected tradition, and relied on their own intellect.

The issue was that, though among the Karaites were also great men and great sects--and many times they triumphed over the Talmudists for centuries--the following peculiarities made them a sect secluded from the whole world (especially from the Rabbis, who were to them as if unclean); their scrupulousness about cleanliness and uncleanliness, their separation from anybody who was not a Karaite Jew, so as not to take from him bread and other articles of the bakery, and so as not to eat anything that had been touched by a non-Jew (some prohibited even meat fit for a sacrifice). Gradually their numbers diminished, so that now they number only about four thousand souls in the world, and even these few differ among themselves in their usages and festivals. To this day the Karaites in Egypt and the East remain in the dark during the eve of Sabbath; the dates of their festivals are not alike every year, and by their attacks on the Talmud they not only failed to weaken its influence or diminish the number of its adherents, but brought about its increased influence and accepted holiness. Though the Rabbis kept apart from them, and said to those who wished to make peace between them, "the Karaites (or *torn pieces, Kraim Kra'im*), never became joined," still they did not forbear to borrow from them what seemed to them good, adopting the Massorah and vowel points of Ben Asher, who was one of them.

About the Judaized Chazars, of their time, the Karaites say that they had the Karaite form of Judaism, but modern scholars contradict this. They say that the Chazars were Talmudic Jews and A. B. Gottlober has written admirably about this subject. His argument seems to savor of the truth. But there is no doubt, that among the Jewish tribes of Arabia, and those of the Judaized Arabian kingdom, there were Talmudic Jews who rendered many services to the Jews of the Byzantine empire; but as these matters do not pertain to our subject, we will not speak further of them, and conclude hereby the present chapter. (See App. at the end of this volume.)

Chapter 8
Islam and Its Influence on the Talmud

Islam And Its Influence On The Talmud.

In 622, the Hebrew religion gave birth to a second daughter, Mohammedanism--founded by Mahomet of Mecca among the tribes of Arabia, who had lived unprogressive for ages in the large peninsula between the Red Sea and the Persian Gulf, keeping by the usages received from their ancestors traditionally. Hundreds of years had passed without making any impression on the development of this people, until Mahommed arose, and in the space of twenty years subdued with the sword and by the tongue the whole great land of Arabia. And like a stream of mighty waters the Arabs burst from their bonds, animated by a spirit of war, and fired by religious zeal, tore away from the Byzantine empire the whole of Syria and Egypt, and conquered also Persia, extended their empire to India and Caucasus, on the one band, and to Western Africa, on the other, spreading, at last, over Spain and Southern Italy to the heart of Christendom, preaching Islam, and bearing the banner of their prophet wherever they stepped.

For the second time, after an interval of six hundred years, Judaism witnessed a new faith born, all whose choice portions, all whose good and beauty, were taken from the storehouse of the

Talmudic Hagada. When Mahomet arose to say that through Gabriel, the angel, the Lord had destined him to confirm the truth of the Divine revelation previously to Abraham, Isaac and Jacob, Moses and the rest of the saints who had been on earth, he borrowed only the foundation of his idea from the Hagada of the Talmud. Likewise he borrowed many sayings, traditions, and historic legends from the same source, and these materials served him as the foundation of the principles he prescribed for the guidance of his people. All the Hebrew plants succeeded speedily on the Arabian soil, as if they had been native.

Islam grew in power and soon made progress, political and ecclesiastical, for new forces joined it. It reared a new civilization on the ruins of the heathen culture of Syria. During the first century of its existence it likewise exercised an influence on the scholars of the Talmud. As the Greek spirit had formerly been wedded to the Jewish spirit, so now the Arabian was wedded to it. It might have supplanted Jewish thought altogether had not the many sages, adherents of the Talmud, written excellent books in Arabic, extolling the Talmud, its system and its spirit.

When the Jewish tribes of Arabia, some of these powerful and independent, had refused to believe in the inspiration of the new prophet, Islam arose on its parent Judaism, as Christianity had done before; persecutions, massacres, blood and fire and exile were visited on the adherents of the Talmud. As long as Mahomet had entertained the hope of gaining Jews for converts, his treatment of them was favorable and he enjoined in the Koran not to be inimical to adorers of one God. He even wanted to make the date of the fast of Rhamadan on the tenth of Tishri (the Day of Atonement), as well as to make Jerusalem the centre of the pilgrims instead of Mecca. Perceiving, however, that notwithstanding all this, Islam gained few Jewish converts, he turned the enemy of the Jews and became wroth against them ("The Vision of the Cow"; a chapter in the Koran) and persecuted them with fury and bloodthirstiness as infidels. But at his death his hatred and intolerance died with him, the Jews found peace and protection under the Caliphs, and the Gaonim could establish their colleges. When Spain was added in 711 by the General Torick

46

Aben Zara, bright days ensued for the Jews; they were able to devote themselves to spiritual activity undisturbed, also to take a large part in the culture of science which flourished in Spain. Great offices and high posts were given to Talmudic Jews; councillors, authors of law articles, court physicians and ministers were taken from among them. Together with their civic prosperity their spiritual activity made progress, and they made great contributions to Judaism, and benefited their co-religionists. Rarely were they visited by storms, as in Granada, in 1603, and at Cordova, in 1157, and then they suffered only as citizens.

In Egypt, Syria, Fez and Morocco, wherever Islam dominated, Jewish communities flourished. In contrast to this, the study of the Torah decayed in the East, and from Babylonia it changed its place to Spain.

The prosperity and the power of the Jews called forth envy and opposition, resulting in the desertion of some Jews to Islam; and this spirit of opposition was kindled yet more by false Messiahs arising frequently, as Shiraini in 720 and Abu Eiei in 1464, in the reign of the Caliph Merian, who opposed themselves to the Talmud with all their might (the last abolished also divorce). In spite of all that, the Talmud was honored as before. For the Gaonim and the two colleges at Sura and Pumbeditha were as beacons to all the exiled Jews till the second half of the tenth century. Only a singular accident, which happened about 960, put an end to this unlimited and undivided dominion of Babylonia over the Jewish minds. Four scholars had left Sura with the purpose of collecting money among their European brethern, for the benefit of encouraging a more assiduous study of the Talmud at the college of Sura; the vessel being captured by an Arab pirate, the four sages were sold as slaves. One, R. Shemariah b. El'hanan was then brought to Alexandria; there the Jewish community ransomed him, and appointed him as supervisor of religion and teacher of the Talmud in Cairo. The second, R. Hushiel, was sold into slavery at the African coast, and brought to Kairuban. The third, R. Moses b. Enoch was ransomed from his owners after many hardships, at Cordova, where the community chose him as Rabbi. The name of the fourth has not transpired. It is possible that he reached

France. The four men, not having attained their object of collecting money for Sura, and its college having been closed seven hundred years after its foundation, brought to an end the spiritual dominion of Babylonia over the Jewish mind and scattered the seeds of Talmudic study throughout all lands.

The college of Pumbeditha, though it continued to exist for some period after that of Sura, spreading the light of the Torah among all the exiled, sank from its preëminent rank, gradually, till its existence came to an end (about 1040). With it was extinguished the light of the Gaonim. From that time the centre of religious activity for the Jews was in Europe. The Talmud had its home in Spain, whence it spread to other countries, as will be seen in the coming chapters.

Chapter 9
The Period of Greatest Diffusion of Talmudic Study

The Victory Of Karaism Over The Spiritual Dominion Of The Talmud And The Mind Of The Jewish Nation--The Last Gaonim At Sura And Pumbeditha--The Centre Of Talmudic Study Transferred From Mesopotamia To Spain--The Scholars Of Kairuban--The Period Of The Greatest Diffusion Of Talmudic Study.

Though Rabbinism came out victorious from the struggle with Karaism, it can not be denied that in one respect the latter triumphed. The unlimited dominion which the Talmudic spirit of the colleges of Sura and Pumbeditha had at that time on the minds of the nation of Israel in general in all places of their abode--this spiritual dominion waned greatly. The glory of these colleges irresistibly declined, in spite of all efforts to the contrary, even of a supreme man like Saadiah the Gaon. The spirit of investigation and free thought at Bagdad induced the disciples, to whom the religious teachings of their master Saadiah gave the example, to engage in the study of philosophy, grammar and the interpretations of the text of the Scripture, and to abandon the hard and exhausting studies of Sura. A slight cause, the voyage of the four scholars mentioned above to Europe, sufficed to hasten the end of this college, which did not exist long after the death of R. Saadiah the Gaon, so that it was closed forever after centuries of its existence.

The college at Pumbeditha continued some time longer; it put forth its last efforts, before the lights of its Gaonim and Exilarchs were extinguished, before the glory and religious and spiritual pre-eminence of Babylon departed from there to honor Spain; and as the light of a candle blazes up before it is extinguished, so there shone on the Babylonian horizon three Gaonim, Sherira b. Hanina, Hai his son, and Samuel b. Hophni the father-in-law of the latter (960-1038). The activity of these men in the field of Talmudic literature persists and exercise their influence yet.

R. Sherira placed the Talmudic studies too much above all other studies, whereas in the college at Sura, in accordance with the spirit of Saadiah the Gaon, the sciences also stood in the first rank of studies and a critical spirit reigned in studying Scripture and in commenting on the Talmud. At Pumbeditha the Talmud was the only dish offered to the students, the only subject of the curriculum. R. Sherira was the first who fearlessly taught and said: "The utterances of the Gaonim require no demonstration; whoso rebels against their decisions, rebels against God and betrays His Torah." His book "Megilath Stharim." (Scroll of Mysteries), which was undoubtedly written in this autocratic spirit, is lost. But, on the other band, he has bequeathed to us a fragment which enlightens us at present, being the chief basis of all Jewish literary and theological history. This is the letter he sent to the congregation of Kairuban, termed "R. Sherira's Epistle," which treats of the history of the Talmud and of the Gaonim and is the key to the otherwise mysterious history of that epoch. From this letter only can we take the essential information for arranging the history from the close of the Talmud to his time. Without this document many and important periods, from the time of the Maccabees to those of the Gaonim, over a thousand years, would remain to us obscure and unknown. The epistle is wonderfully accurate in respect to chronology, and is free from any bias. Only by means of it, and of other compositions of this class, as the Megilath Taanith (Scroll of Fasts), Seder Olam (Order of the World), the Sedar Tanaim and Amoraim, together with the remnants of information of R. Nathan bar Izhak the Babylonian (956) concerning the colleges at Sura and Pumbeditha, and the methods of study at their time, can the modem scholar compile the known histories, so very necessary to the understanding of the Talmud and its literature.

R. Hai, his son, was indeed more inclined towards the sciences than his father. He was proficient in Arabic learning. Nor was he averse to philosophic studies. He opposed himself with all his might against speculation about the hypothesis of religion. In theological and Talmudical knowledge, R. Hai surpassed all his colleagues and stood alone in his age. From Northern Africa and Spain, whither sparks of Talmudic literary activity had just penetrated and kindled, came to him questions in great number. He replied to them in Arabic or in Hebrew; the spirit of reconciliation between philosophy and theology is in all his answers. His list of Hebrew roots, commentaries on the Mishna, and compositions examining Scriptures exist mostly no longer, and only fragments of Talmudic jurisprudence, as laws of buying and selling, of oaths, etc., which he attempted to methodize in verse are preserved. So also is ascribed to him a didactic poem entitled "Musar Haschel" (Morality of Reason) very excellent in its thoughts, matter, and intention (purpose, aim, conception), albeit we can not extole the style or the poetic form. At all events this R. Hai, the last of the Gaonim is the first of all Talmudic scholars even at this day, and his words are oracular for all commentators and all those who decide Halakhas according to the Talmud.

His father-in-law, Samuel b. Hophni, held of the same opinions as he, but was more free in his criticism of the Scriptures than all his colleagues. Of his many works only fragments (which originally written in Arabic, we have in the Hebrew garb) of his commentaries to the Scriptures remain. But his compositions about Halakhas and essentials of religion are all lost, and only their names survive. The fundamental principle of this thinker was: "Things opposed to human common sense should not be admitted." He combated violently also the Karaites and was attacked desperately, as they mocked and scoffed at him and even wrote satiric Hebrew poems about him.

Those three were the last of those remaining at these colleges, and at their death the sources of wisdom in Babylonia were stopped

off. After the decease of ben Hophni (about 1034) the college at Sura
was abolished, and two years after the death of R. Hai (1640) the
college of Pumbeditha was closed. The wisdom of Israel removed to
North Africa (Kairuban) and Spain and bore fair fruit there.

The city Kairuban had a great reputation. In an antique commentary, imputed to a disciple of R. Saadiah the Gaon, this city is
mentioned as "the city of great sages." As is known, one of the four
above-mentioned rabbis, R. Hushiel, who with his colleagues had
been voyaging to collect money for the college of Sura, was cast
thither. All four introduced mental activity in all places they visited.
R. Hananel, the son of R. Hushiel, succeeded to his position (in
1050) and surpassed his father in wisdom and in energy. He
bequeathed to us fragments of commentaries on Scriptures and the
Talmud, which were of great help to the study in the conditions at
that time, when Talmudic activity was diffused among Jews. He and
his contemporary, Nisim b. Jacob, who also resided in Kairuban,
renewed the youth of the Palestinian Talmud, which had been
neglected. Especially did the latter contribute to bring about this. He
also issued the book "Maphteah" (Key) for several tracts of the Babylonian Talmud and in it he cast light on many difficult passages in the
Palestinian Talmud by comparing the two Talmuds.

R. Hananel also wrote a commentary on the Talmud, which was
published in separate parts. Therein he explains the subject and
meaning of the words in Hebrew, and draws a parallel between the
Babylonian and Palestinian Talmud. He wrote also a book containing
abstracts arranged in Talmudic order of the Halakhas, concerning
service and pecuniary matters.

A careful examination of the books of the two men will show that
they were in unison with their opinions with Saadiah the Gaon, and
diffused his teaching and ideas among the Jews. Friendship existed
between these two men and Hai and the learned men of Spain, as is
seen from their large correspondence. There is also a third one of the
sages of Kairuban, who contributed to the study of the Talmud, he is
Hephetz b. Jatzbiah, held in great esteem by his contemporaries, and
upon whom all titles of honor that great men receive were bestowed.
Of his works nothing is known except the name "Sepher Hephetz"

52

(the book of Hephetz or Desirable book) which he wrote as a commentary to the "books of duties."

The sages of Kairuban witnessed the end of the two colleges and the extinction of the Gaonim, but also the flourishing of Jewish literature in Spain, whither it had been spread from Northern Africa. After the decease of these learned men the glory of Kairuban became also extinct, and Jewish intellectual activity left the East and emigrated to the West.

An examination of the literary period after the death of the Gaonim shows that it surpassed by far the preceding period. Whereas, in the time of the Exilarchs and the Gaonim, only the Talmud had been the subject chiefly studied and only to it had contributions been made which helped to perpetuate the spirit of Judaism. Now, when Jewish learning removed to Spain and Southern France, it blossomed and became split into many branches, to each of which many good books were contributed. On the study of the Scriptures shone forth the light of free criticism; the studies of Masorah reached perfection; grammar and linguistic researches came to the front rank; the Talmud and Midrash, long ago concluded, were subjected to the analysis of commentaries and abridged into systematic abstracts. The basis of the philosophic conception of the Jewish faith was laid; and religious and ritual poems succeeded, when treated by the sublimely inspired Spanish poets. A broader and deeper comprehension of the Talmud was also the result of the intellectual awakening. It is true that the cause of this intellectual activity were the Arabs, while the polemics with the Karaites enhanced it, and made it penetrate through the wall of Judaism; but, taken up by the Jews, it made progress and continued to do so even when both Arabs and Karaites had abandoned knowledge altogether. This spiritual awakening caused even the remotest branch of Israelite stock, from which almost all life had fled, to bloom up and to awake to new life. Even the small community of Samaritans, whose existence had been quite forgotten, came to life and took part in the Jewish culture. The book of "Joshua" of the Samaritans, the "Reminiscences of Abul-Pathah" (a historical treatise of these events), the Samaritan version of the Pentateuch, and the Arabic version of the Scriptures by Abu-Laid appeared at this time. Also fragments of ritual composition there are a few left of many, but their value is small and they are not as ancient as had been at first thought. On the new Jewish literature the Samaritan sect never made any impression; but the intellectual movement of the Jews involved also the remnant of the Samaritans and aroused it from its slumber. But in the time of the Gaonim, when the bearers of the banner of the Talmud ranked themselves to battle with the Karaites, they did not condescend to notice the Samaritans.

When we say that this period surpassed the former, we are far from disparaging the great Gaonim, and from thinking them men inferior to their successors. In truth, these men were only dwarfs who stood on the shoulders of giants for had they not stood on the shoulders of those giants they could not have investigated deeply all those subjects to which in time of the Gaonim no attention had been paid. For, in spite of the precept of Sherira, above mentioned, "that the utterances of the Gaonim require no demonstration," they did not cease to give proofs, reasons, and to advance arguments in their replies to questioners. Only by means of thorough and deep research in the Talmud, by comparing and by reasoning, did the Gaonim bring the ideas of their time in accordance with the ancient Halakhas, thus increasing the practical importance of tradition and giving to the Torah a living interest. The Spanish and French scholars took up their work and carried it on, extending it to all branches of science. Then literature, therefore, attained its highest development, so that this period has been termed the "golden age of Jewish learning." The replies of the Gaonim only were the basis of their superstructure, reared when intellectual activity had removed from the banks of the Euphrates to the banks of the Tagus and the Rhine.

Their explanations of Halakha were of two kinds; either those induced by the bare love of knowledge, or answers which had to be given to question arising from practical exigencies, which occasioned the analysis of the Halakhas and the investigation whether the spirit of the Halakhas held good only at their time or applied to other times also.

Five compilations of this kind, termed "Replies of the Gaonim," exist in the Jewish literature, which have been compiled from the beginning of the seventh to the eleventh centuries. The first of the authors of those replies was the Gaon Hananai and the last Hai the Gaon. This literature of the Gaonim's replies is a large field for scientific researches in literary history in general, of historic events, and of intellectual progress. In all their replies and decisions we see that their aim is knowledge, not authoritativeness as is usual in the case of priests or even of Gaonim. For their decision they gave reasons and advanced arguments, and also forbade no learned or ingenious man to object to them.

This spirit of employing reason found in this literature of Replies still continues. By it the present is linked with the past and the future with the present. These replies touch almost all branches of thought as well as all practical questions, viz.: the value of the Agada in Talmudic literature; the value of the studies of the mysteries; opinions on philosophy, on the rights due to sciences, answers to questions about chronology and calculations of time. History, geography, and mathematics in some of their replies are also discussed. There are also answers with reasons to questions about Laws of Marriage, Gentiles, Proselytes, Testaments, Mourning, Sermons, Divorce. They also explain to those who question them different passages in Mishna and Talmud-questions even without any practical aim-only to increase and advance the Torah by the discussions made in the house of learning.

Chapter 10
The Spanish Writers on the Talmud

The Spanish Writers. A Brief Survey Of Their Writings Relating To The Talmud.

Although the aim of this, our work, is to give a history of the Talmud alone, not of the whole Jewish literature of that period (to which is devoted a work by Dr. Karpeles and others), we can not, however, skip over the writers of Spain and France of that time, who extended the literature according to the fundamental principles of the Talmud, and shine in history, the admiration of succeeding generations. We will not, however, speak at length of their work or examine it minutely, but merely mention the names; only those whose main work was elevated to Talmudic subjects we except from this rule of brevity, and shall speak about their work as far as is necessary for the purpose of this work.

The first of the distinguished men of Spain, whom the Babylonians honored with the title of "Resh Kalah" (synonymous with "Head of College"), was R. Hisdai b. Itzhak Ebn Spurt (915-970), who was counsellor and physician to the Caliph Abdul Rahman III., and he was the one who helped his co-religionists to rise from their degradation. Besides his diligence in other sciences, as the translation of the

56

botanical books of Disscroridus, the Greek, for his sovereign, the Caliph, he carried on a correspondence with the Gaonim. of the colleges of Sura and Pumbeditha, and through them succeeded in bringing scholars and books to his own country, and to found a college for Talmudical studies. He wrote the well known letter to the king of the Chosars, in which his love for his co-religionists and his Zeal for their welfare are manifested. Menahem b. S'ruk and Duns b. Labrat, the grammarians known through their polemics about the roots and the grammar of the Hebrew language, were invited by R. Hisdai to come to popularize the study of Hebrew. Jehud b. David Chilveg, Isaac b. Kapron and Isaac Giktalia were the disciples of Menahem, and Jehudah b. Shesheth was the disciple of Dun. These men by their controversies about the grammar carried it further and perfected the study. Jonah Ebn Ganah (1000-1050) surpassed even those, for he composed seven books about grammar in Arabic and Hebrew which are preserved to the present time.

Samuel Hanagid (and the Nasi Ebn Nagdilah, 993-1055) was a patron of Jewish learning in Spain, as Ebn Spurt had been before him. He was the author of twenty-two books, but not even one of them survives completely. Even from his great book "Introduction to the Talmud" only a small portion is preserved, but this testifies to the greatness of his knowledge and the acuteness of his intellect. With all his adherence to the traditions and to the cardinal principles of the Talmud, he did not exclude the use of common sense and human judgment. He says: "Every comment in the Talmud on passages of Scriptures other than commandments we have to admit only so far as seems to be rational, but as for the rest, it is not authoritative." From this we see that in his ideas about the Hagadah of the Talmud, he went a step in advance of the Gaonim, Saadiah, and Hai. His poems and prayers in his works "Ben Thilim" and "Ben Mishle" are based on the tradition of the Talmud. But of his "Ben Koheleth" nothing was preserved by us. He was held in great esteem by the contemporary learned men. Many wrote poems in his praise, among them is the "Orphan" (Jethoma), by R. Joseph b. Hisdai. The poets at that time used to say, "In the days of R. Hisdai, the Nasi, they began to twitter (in poetry) and in the days of Samuel the Nagid, they lifted their voice." (See App. No. 11.)

He was succeeded by the lofty poet Solomon b. Gabirol, 1012-1070. (We need not here dwell on his biography and work, as Messrs. Senor Sachs and Salomon Munk wrote whole books about him.) In his time, Jekuthiel Ebn Hassau, who was high in the court of King Jahia Ibu Mundhir at Saragossa, was also a patron of all Jewish learning, especially of ben Gabirol. The latter's poem, "Kether Malchuth" (Crown of Royalty), was very favorably received by all who bore the banners of the Talmudic and Kabbaldic studies, and also by Christian priests, so that it was translated into Latin by the priest Dominicus Gondizallo (1150) and also into Hebrew by him, with the assistance of Johannis Abudalu (an apostate Jew). The fact that his name "Ebn Gabirol" was altered to Abizatrol or Abizabran has been illuminated by Salomon Munk.

Bahayi b. Joseph Ebn Pekira, judge in Saragossa, his contemporary, is the author of the wonderful book "The Duty of Hearts" (Chobath Halbaboth) in Arabic, which has been translated by Samuel Ebn Tabun into Hebrew, and accepted as a guide in life by Israel everywhere they were found. (It has been translated also into German by Herr Baumgarten of Vienna.) This teacher Behayi absorbed himself wholly in the Talmud and gave it the preference to Arabic or Grecian philosophy. His object in this, his wonderful work, is the following: to conciliate morals with commandments and the duties of the heart with those of the other members of the body. The duty of the heart is purity of thought, that of the other members to carry out the commandments. (See App. No. 12.)

Five sages bearing the name Isaac lived at that time, viz.: 1. Isaac b. Reuben of Barcelona (1043), great in knowledge of the Talmud and an expert at translating. He translated the decisions of R. Hai Gaon, about buying and selling, from Arabic to Hebrew. 2. Isaac b. Jehudah Ebn Giath (1089), who composed prayers and ritual poems considered remarkable at that time. 3. Isaac b. Moses Sochni, who emigrated from Spain to the East, where he was qualified as Gaon and became the successor of R. Hai. Only his fame survives, his writings, however, are all lost. 4. Isaac b. Baruch Abudaly (1035-1094), who was a sage and astrologer to Caliph Al Mahmed. The latter made him Nasi over the Israelite communities in his domain, Seville. He wrote a commentary to difficult Halakhas in his book "Kupath Haruchim" (Book of Spices), which, however, he did not complete. 5. The greatest of all, Isaac b. Jacob Alphassi (1013-1103), who came from North Africa to Lucina (Alisa) and there founded a college for the study of the Talmud, in which he surpassed all his colleagues in Spain. Alphassi was the first to abridge the Talmud, compiling only the necessary Halakhas, transcribed textually. Sometimes he appended his opinions, and by this work is immortalized among all Israel in exile. In times of misfortune, when it was difficult to procure the Talmud, students occupied themselves with his work, called after him "Alphassi," to which they wrote many commentaries. His decisions, called "Questions and Replies of Hariph," have been accepted for all times. It is true that he wrote in Arabic and that it was translated into Hebrew. He also wrote three great Halakhas with an extensive commentary in Arabic, which was also translated into Hebrew, as well as 320 of his decisions above mentioned. (One was recently published with a new translation from the Arabic.)

The spirit of deep research, distinguishing this Spanish period, is also found in his works. The most difficult subjects in the Talmud and all intricate questions he explains easily. He strove in his books to smooth the contradictions between the Torah and Wisdom, reconciling them. His decisions extend over all provinces of the Torah in all questions concerning law and judgment; to all laws, both written and traditional laws, his reasons, based upon sound logic, were stated in a concise and ingenious manner. In the same way, he also explains the Hagada, to bring it in conformity with reason. He, Alphassi, did not devote himself to theological philosophy and criticism of the Scriptures, like his contemporaries, but to Talmudical studies, thus giving an example to those thinkers not to presume to give their religion a philosophic garb. At his death, all Jewish scholars, wheresoever found, lamented him. R. Jehudah Halevi, whose muse began then to shine, mourned for him thus:

Mountains on the day of Sinai for thee quaked,
For angels of the Lord met thee
And inscribed the Torah on the tablets of thy heart.
The glorious crown was placed around thee.
The wise had not power to stand
If they did not from thee wisdom beg.

Moses b. Samuel Ebn Giktali and Jehudah Ebn Bilan (1070) were free thinkers in his age and his opponents, but many of those scholars who explained the Talmud by simple logic were his disciples. Among these was also Isaac b. Baruch Albalia, mentioned above. The greatest of his disciples, however, was Joseph Ebn Migash b. Mair (1076-1141), who succeeded to his position in his college and inherited his greatness in Talmudic wisdom. His new contributions to Talmudic study, called by him "Megilath Setharim" (The Revelation of Hidden Scrolls) and the queries and answers collected into one book under the title of "Questions and Replies of Ebn Migash," bear testimony to his ingenuity, loftiness of spirit and gentleness. (These books were reprinted the second time by us in 1870, in Warsaw, with our preface and some remarks, but even this edition is already nearly out and scattered.) Most of his answers and questions were written in Arabic and translated later into Hebrew; only his explanations were written in Hebrew and in the Talmudic idiom. Particularly wondrous is his manner of examining all sides of a subject, so that not one possibility remains unconsidered.

As Ebn Migash was the greatest Rabbi after the death of his master, Alphassi, questions were addressed to him from all sides, and he, always following his disposition, answered them according to his inclinations, leniently. Let us cite one of his answers as an example:

A question was addressed to him by one who had vowed to abstain from meat and wine till he shall have reached the Holy Land, and found the project too difficult to carry out, but could find no ground for repenting. Ebn Migash found for him a ground for repentance, that, while he vowed he undoubtedly was ignorant of a saying in the Talmud: Whoever afflicts himself is guilty against a life.

Many were the disciples who trod in Ebn Migash's footsteps and carried on their activity in his spirit. Among these was his son who succeeded him also in his college. Of his contemporaries, who distinguished themselves as philosophers or poets, it is proper to mention Rabbi Joseph Ebn Zadok of Cordova (1070-1149), author of "Olam Katan" (Microcosm), a religious philosophy in which he is of the opinion (see App. No. 11) that man must know himself in order to attain to the knowledge of Divinity. The rabbi who was his predecessor at Cordova, Joseph b. Jacob Ebn Sahl (1103), was a poet and ritual author. (See App. No. 12.) In the north of Spain were also then found scholars and poets; Abraham b. Hyya, a minister in a Mahometan ruler's court, was a great astronomer and mathematician, who wrote four books on astronomy, three of which were printed, viz.: "The Form of the Earth" (T'urath Hoaretz), "The Book of Leap-Years" (Sepher Haibur), of the third, only the latter part, treating of mathematics, optics, and astronomy was printed. Next to him is Jehudah b. Barzilar, author of the book "Hoetim." (The Times).

We have reached to the three great poets, who enjoy a world-wide renown, Moses b. Ezra, Abraham b. Meir Ebn Ezra, and Jehudah Halevi, all of whom were bearers of the banner of the Talmud, and contributed to diffusing its ideas and morals among the nation. We think it, however, superfluous to expatiate on them, as they are well-known to every cultured person, and, as many books have been written about them at different epochs, we cannot refrain, however, from giving briefly their biographies, as far as they bear on no subject of this work.

The dates of the birth and death of the first of these, Moses b. Ezra, are unknown to us: it is known only to us that he lived later than ben Gabirol. His opinions in his poems and other works vacillate. He composed ritual poems and lamentations, which have a place in the prayer-books of the Spanish Jews; also the "Arugath Habossem" (Bed of Spices), on theological philosophy, and the "Sepher Hassichoth V'hazichronoth" (Book of Discourses and Reminiscences), about the poems of ben Gabirol and his character.

The second, Abraham Ebn Ezra, was one of the most wonderful phenomena of his age. His commentaries on the Bible, his poems and ritual poems, are known to everyone; but the contemporary scholars found it impossible to know his real opinions, nor can modern scholars fathom them.

The third, Jehudah Halevi, the father of poets, before whom none lived equal to him, and who knows whether after him any one like him will live. Besides inspiring with a very exalted national spirit every reader of his poems and lamentations, he powerfully defended the Talmud in his book the "Chosar," where the eloquent defender of the Talmud is represented by the disputant arguing with the King of the Chosars, and which to the present time is a shining example of compositions of this kind. (A lengthy account the reader can find in the works of Karpeles.)

After them is distinguished Abraham b. David Halevi (Ebn Daud) who died as a martyr (1180). He defended the Talmud in his book "Emuna Rama" (Exalted Faith) and in his great work "Hakabala" (The Tradition), in which he powerfully argues against all the deniers of tradition, and shows them in the wrong; supporting his logical arguments by historical facts, proving the continuance of tradition from the time of Moses to that time. In his polemics against the Karaites, he is so irritated that he styles them "dumb dogs."

With Moses b. Maiman, the Spaniard, called by all "Maimonides" or "Rambam" (1135-1204), the Spanish period concludes. With him died the mental activity in Spain, after having flourished there for three centuries. About this great man we have nothing to add to what the historians who have preceded us have written about his life, and disputed about his opinions. (The reader desiring minute information is referred to the *Life of the Rambam*, "Taldoth Horambam," by I. H. Weiss, and also Karpeles' work.) But we do not think it superfluous to remark on two points, viz.: 1. That the opinions of Maimonides are found too differ in the three different periods of his life: thus, in his commentary on the Mishnayoth, they are not the same as in his work "Yad Hachazaka," nor are they similar to that of his last work, "More Nebuchim," which he wrote in the evening of his life. For in all of them we see a development of his ideas according to the increase of his studies and knowledge; it is not true as some affirm that there is no change in his opinions. We have made it evident, long ago, in our book "Phylacterien-Ritus," that his decisions in his "Yad Hachazaka" or "Mishna Torah," do not accord with those in his commentary on the Mishnayoth; and, it is needless to say, that his statements in the "More" are at variance with things said in all his former works. And in truth, this is the case with all great thinkers, that they can not remain at a stand still from their youth to their old age, and to this we may apply [job, xxxii. 7]. "Multitude of years shall make wisdom known."

2. That Maimonides has omitted all references in the Talmud which treats of witchcraft, demons, interpretation of dreams, etc., not only because they were considered by him as vain superstitions and follies, for this reason alone he would not have ventured to omit them, in spite of the Talmud, for he left all that is found in the Talmud of Halakhas and moral Hagadas, even with which he himself could not agree; but his motive was, that, in his opinion, they had originally not been found in the Talmud, and that only the later men inserted them, according to their own ideas, for whatever purpose it might have been. (I. H. Weiss has insinuated this long ago, and it seems that the probability tends that way.)

So also, about the apology advanced by many for the words of Maimonides at the head of his work "Mishna Torah," that he had chosen this title, because if a man first read the Pentateuch, and then this work, he will know the entire Oral Law, and need read no inter-mediate book--that by these words he did not mean that his work should be a substitute for the Talmud, etc., etc.; we do not think this apology needful, even if he meant this. For as Maimonides had observed that much had been superadded to the Talmud, also things opposed to his general opinions--no wonder if he wished to prevent those who could not distinguish between the good and the evil, from. reading the spurious passages, to which they would attach as great importance as to the Talmud itself. After he had sifted it, and arranged all that is found in that sea, the Talmud, in fourteen volumes, of his "Mishna Torah," there is no pre-emption or oddity in these words, whereby he merely sought the real good of the students.

To enumerate in detail all his books, writings, epistles, polemics and apologies, we think superfluous here; as all biographical and crit-ical facts have already been given in detail in the above-mentioned works. We will only remark, that after all the great things which

Maimonides had done and accomplished, he did not attain his object. As the study of the. Talmud did not cease in any of the colleges, and, on the contrary, they who desired to criticize Maimonides, brought the rabbis to study yet more profoundly and attentively the Talmud, and to add new commentaries, decisions of Halakhas, etc., etc.

Chapter 11
Talmudic Scholars of Germany and Northern France

The Scholars Of Germany And Of Northern France, And What They Contributed To The Studies Of The Talmud.

At the time, when Talmudic study flourished in Spain, and made progress, and diffused itself in all corners of the earth, shone "the luminary of the exile" in Germany, who constructed a strong fortress around the Talmud, in his great wisdom--which was accepted in all places of the exiled as though canonical, and which not only contributed to strengthen the Talmud, but also to prevent all its adherents from *perishing*. Like Rabban Johanan b. Zakkai formerly, when he saw that the end of Jewish civic independence approached, founded by his wisdom a Jewish spiritual kingdom, which nothing could ruin, and by saving from the jaws of that lion, Vespasian, Yanmia and its sages, saved the existence of the Jewish people itself; so did Gershon b. Jehudah who came from Carraibe to Mayence, where his great teacher Jehudah b. Meir resided. This most important task he found to be his prohibition, which he made in the name of the Talmud, and at once all Israel (in Europe) hailed this luminary, and accepted without protests or hesitation, his prohibition, and made it a permanent law.

He saw and understood that the Jews scattered among Christian nations, among whom divorce is prohibited and polygamy regarded as a sin, will not exist long, if they persist to permit themselves these things, according to their laws, and, as he had not the power to forbid what was permitted in the Torah expressly, he strove to remove the causes leading to divorce; and thereby he made his co-religionists so far like the Christians that they should be able to live side by side.

He decreed, on pain of excommunication, and without revocation or qualification, that polygamy be prohibited to every Israelite (see App. No. 13), and only monogamy should be legal, and as long as the first wife lives, it is prohibited to add to her another, in the capacity of wife or concubine. Thereby, the main cause for divorce was also removed, but he did not content himself with this decree alone, but added thereto a decree opposed to the Pentateuch, that divorce cannot take place without the assent of the divorced wife, if the man and his wife should find it impossible to live together, then only if the woman is also willing, the husband can divorce her. Whereas, till then, the woman was dependent on the will of her husband, for good or for ill. It is superfluous for us to expatiate on the consequences of these two decrees, or rather reforms of how much utility they have been to social life and the feeble sex; as every thinking man can understand this.

Added to these prohibitions, he permitted Jewish apostates, who are penitent, to return to their faith, and also prohibited, on pain of excommunication, to open a strange man's letter and read it, without the assent of the person to whom it is addressed.

His energy, great wisdom, and deep observation of his nation's life, and strong wish to ensure its existence, we can see from these reforms, which we do not find made by any rabbis of his predecessors; and he was justly called, afterwards, "The Luminary of the Exile," as he illuminated in truth the eyes of all Israelites and gave to them a new life. He composed commentaries on several tracts of the Talmud, which became distinguished in his age, and the commentator on the Torah, Rashi (whom we are going to mention) borrowed from him much.

R. Machir, his brother (1030), was also a Talmudic scholar and the author of a Talmudic dictionary. Several ritual poets were also found in Germany and Northern France, as Meshulam bar Klein-mus, R. Simeon, b. Isaac, b. Abun of Mayence, who lamented the miseries of their paytonim in ritual poems and prayers for mercy (Sli'-choth), but their work in the study of the Torah was small; and only in Metz and Mayence in Germany, and Rheims, Loiret, in Northern France and Narbonne, Montpellier and Beziers in Southern France were many scholars, whose active occupation was mental activity in the field of the Talmud. (The college of Talmud in Narbonne was erected by R. Machir, who had arrived from Babylonia to France; and in the second half of the eleventh century came from this college R. Moses Hadarshon, known as the commentator on some tracts in the Talmud, and some books of Scripture; and later generations drew much on his wisdom, and made many quotations from him. All or most of his writings are collected in one work entitled "Breshith Rabthi." R. Joseph Tob Alm (Baufils, of Lemans), who has edited and systematized many subjects and speculations of the Talmud, a list of the Tanaim and Amoraim, and the answers of the Gaonim, and R. Elijah the Elder, both men of that age, were esteemed as poets, but did not approach those of Spain.

What is worthy of notice, considering the various countries at that age, is that whereas the scholars of Spain (see App. No. 14) exerted their great powers and displayed their knowledge in collecting Halakhas of the Talmud, the scholars of Germany devoted themselves wholly to collecting Hagadas and Midrashim, so that various compilers rose. Of the distinguished compilers of Midrash are: R. Moses of Narbonne, R. Jehudah of Toulouse, R. Simeon, author of "Yalkut Simoni," where he compiled words of wisdom, morals and Hogada, from fifty various ancient works and arranged them according to the portions of the Pentateuch. This Yalkut is a comprehensive reference book for Agadic lore, and drove out of the field the Agadic compilation "Lekach Tob," or "Psigtha Zutrha" by R. Tobiah b. Eliezer, his contemporary, who lived in Greece (Byzantium) at that time.

We will skip over a number of lecturers and Pashtanim for want of space, and we will come to our great teacher, through whom only we are enabled to comprehend the Talmud, and to read it and study it, namely: R. Soloman b. Isaac of Trayes, called (by using the initials) "Rashi" (1040-1105). He was the first who gave a complete piece of work in his commentary on the Talmud. He is one of the most wonderful phenomena given by Nature, perhaps once in thousand years; his advantage over Maimonides, his peer, is in the fact that he met with general acceptation in the whole world, and no one presumes to study the Talmud without him. The influence he has on Jewish students has met with no opposition or discontent. The generations subsequent to Rashi, styled him "Parshandatha" (a proper name in Scripture), that is, "Explainer of the Law." Justly was he called thus; in truth no man arose after him with such ability to shed light on the intricacies of the law or on obscure passages in Scripture.

His comprehensive intellect embraced that mighty and eternal structure, the whole vast province of the theological literature of Israel. By his commentaries he has introduced common sense into the study of the vastest and profoundest subjects. The study of the tracts lacking his commentary, although many different other men have attempted to supply the deficiency, gives us many pains and much trouble, till we come to understand the real meaning. As what Rashi elucidates in a few words, or sometimes even by one word added to the text before us, has to be commented upon by others in many laborious lines to make the student understand the simple meaning of the Talmud.

The life of Rashi has been written by many scholars, who have discussed at length his commentaries, legal decisions, and ritual poetry. The latest, A. H. Weiss, in the periodical "Beth Talmud" and in separate pamphlets. We think it therefore superfluous to repeat them, as this is not our task here. We have to remark, however, on several points relating to the Talmud here, on which those scholars have left something for us to add: An examination of Rashi's commentaries on the Talmud, on the Bible, and legal decisions in his "Hapardes," and so also his ritual poems, will show that they differ in their nature totally. In his commentary on the Talmud, which general criticism places above his other writings, we see that he is very cautious to decide any Halakha, and to draw from the statements of the Talmud definite conclusions as to a law or custom. We do not remember in his whole commentary on the Talmud, any place where he should decide "that such a Halakha prevails," or even, "so was the custom in his days," as we find on many occasions in the commentaries of his disciples "Tosphath," and we have long ago shown in our work about Phylacteries (p. 24), that he has interpreted an obscure passage in the Talmud in contradiction to the custom and Halakha accepted among the Gaonim, because, according to his method, it is the plain meaning of the passage. Everywhere he bewares of *dialectics*, and of contradictions between some passages of the Talmud and others, but he explained the subject of the passage according to its simple meaning in its own place. In case of Agadoth he also was careful to give only an explanation of the words, literally without any remark or opinion of his own, even hinted. This is his custom in his whole commentary on the Talmud. Where he found the text corrupted, he corrected it according to his opinion, and in accordance to his profound knowledge of the Talmud, of its style and language; and, if necessary, removed the old version, not fearing additions or eliminations, provided the real meaning of the Talmud he comprehended, without resorting to forced and far-fetched reasoning.

His commentary on the Bible, however, is different, as mostly he construes according to the Halakha; *i.e.*, as the sages had explained the biblical passages in the Talmud and Midrashim, without regard to the fact that the literal meaning of the biblical texts often does not bear out these constructions. Often he was not averse to interpret the text according to the Talmudic interpretation, even when its meaning is manifestly contrary thereto by all the rules of language. His object in this is unknown to us, and it can only be conjectured that he did not like that his commentary should be at variance with the Talmudic interpretations and conclusions, which correctness and justice he forces himself in his commentary on the Talmud to make manifest.

Not so in his decisions; he endeavors always to interpret the laws leniently (mildly), and is averse to rigor. There he also avoids dialectics, tries not to attain his object by strange and eccentric reasonings, but is only intent on finding the real deep meaning of the law, and to interpret it as mildly as it is in his power. It is true, that most of his decisions are written by his disciples, and we cannot find there that clearness of language and wonderful felicity of expression which he displays in his two above-mentioned commentaries. The Replies of the Gaonim and their works served to him also as a guide, but he did not tread in their footsteps blindfold, but he sifted their statements and construed them ingeniously into accordance with his own opinion; this we witness in his book Pardes,[1] which has been accepted as a great authority for all Poskim deciders of the law subsequent to him.

We do not possess his commentary on all the tracts of the Talmud, for of three tracts we know with certitude that the commentaries are not his; and in the case of other tracts, criticism is doubtful whether they are from his pen. And it may be that they got lost in the course of time, either because he did not compose his comments on the Talmud in the natural order, but in the order in which they were studied in the great college at the head of which he was, and whither pupils flocked from all places of the earth, after the decease of the celebrated scholars of Lorraine; or perhaps he left this world before he had completed his commentary on the whole Talmud, as he did not complete the commentary on the Bible, for those on the books of Chronicles, Ezra, and Nehemiah, and a part of the commentary on the books of Ezekiel and Job have not issued from his pen, though they bear no name, for they are easily distinguishable from his version in their style and by their nature.

What Rashi had done to the Talmud, his disciples have done to his commentary, which they have surrounded by comments and remarks on the margins, sometimes to make plainer his meaning, and sometimes they also made additions to amplify his statements by Agadas and Halakhas, and in the course of time they crept into his own commentary and were interpolated into the words of Rashi, but to separate them from his own words it is very difficult, even for the lancet of sharp criticism.

Modem criticism has rightly thought that Rashi (Isaacides) began his labor of the commentary on the Talmud, which was composed gradually, by the lectures which he delivered to the students. After this he turned to the Midrash, and from it passed to the books of Scripture. And as soon as his commentary was heard among the living, an echo sounded in the camp of Israel that if not Isaacides who laid his hand upon it to investigate and to commentate it, it would remain almost neglected as its brother, the Palestinian Talmud. No wonder, therefore, that after a short time, some fifty commentaries on the commentary of Rashi sprung up, which examine nicely every word and syllable that has proceeded from him; and the last, Kabbalist, R. Samson, of Astropol, was not incorrect when he said in his book, "Likute Shoshanim." ["Collections of Roses"], that every drop of ink that has come forth from Rashi's pen it is needful to sit seven days and to examine with one's whole attention.

Thus while Alphassi illuminated Spain by his elucidations of the Halakhas, another sun, Rashi, rose also in France to shed yet more light, to comment on the Talmud, its Halakhas and Agadas. And the latter had more success, in so far that his commentary was accepted in all the world (among Christian scholars also, as has avowed Nicholas de Lyra, some two hundred years after Rashi's decease, that to the right understanding of the words and simple meaning of the texts, Rashi's commentary has led him) by universal assent. And therein also is France superior to Spain, that though the latter has been studying diligently Torah, even from the ancient times, while the colleges at Sura and Pumbeditha existed yet, and after their fall, assumed pre-eminence in the usages and literature of Israel, their scholars could never agree, and were forever disputing. But in France, since Rashi's commentary began to shine, no voice dissented from the universal approval, and those who sometimes were at variance with him, did not withhold the great honors which were justly due to him, and endeavored to reconcile their own opinions with his. For two hundred years continuously, after Rashi's decease, his disciples were diligent at the holy work of spreading the study of the Talmud and a correct understanding of the great work of their master. They called their labors only "Additions" (Tosphoth), *i.e.*, their thoughts which suggested themselves to them to add to his commentary, and to explain it.

---

1. It was also reprinted by us at Warsau, 1870, with our preface and a few notes.

Chapter 12

The Doctors of France; Authors of the Tosphoth

The Doctors Of France. Authors Of The Tosphoth.

Through the Tosphoth which were begun by Rashi's own descendants as his two sons-in-law, Meir b. Samuel and Jehudah bar Nathan and the sons of the first Samuel and Jacob Tam, the activity of the scholars of France and Germany assumed great proportions and was exalted, so that all Israel in the Middle Ages accepted them unanimously, and in the course of time the numbers of their disciples and the pupils of their disciples increased. So that more than two hundred great Talmudists are known to the historian, but whom it is needless to enumerate here, except a few which we deem necessary for our work.

His grandson, R. Samuel b. Meir, or Rashbam (1085-1158), did not content himself with the commentary of his grandfather on the Bible, as well as on the Talmud, and tried his strength to explain them after his own method, that is, according to their deep literal meaning, and leaving ingenious but forced constructions to dialecticians, even when the literal interpretation will thus be in direct contradiction to the Halakha (see App. No. 15) however, without any opposition to the traditions expressed. He only added in his commentary "according to the deep literal meaning," but leaves one to think that even the traditional interpretation about the Halakha can find place. To the Hagada, however, which tries to interpret biblical texts according to its legends, he opposes with all the strength of his intellect, and makes manifest their contradiction, so as to demolish the Hagada to the foundation, In his commentary on the Talmud, however, he is given to lengthy reasonings and dialectics and also endeavors to arrive at decisions of Halakhas, which his grandfather took care to avoid. Whoever sees critically, Rashi's commentary on Tract Baba Bathra up to 29b, and from there onwards, Rashbam's commentary which is its substitute from that place onwards, will be astonished at the great difference between them, if but at the relative quantities of Rashi's comments and Rashbam's.

From his commentaries and compositions we see that he had much knowledge of diverse languages, and of the manners and customs of nations and their modes of life, and gave human reasons for many commandments of the Pentateuch. In Northern France his commentaries were accepted in the colleges and it became their main authority.

But his younger brother, Jacob, styled "Rabenu Tam," devoted his whole mind to studies of the Talmud chiefly, and he became the center of the authors of the Tosphoth, to him flocked men with questions from all ends of the earth, to whom he was as an oracle. justly we may entitle him the Pillar of the Talmud. He went to the depths of the sea of the Talmud, and made it his first task to reconcile apparent contradictions therein. He likewise mended many corrupted texts in the Talmud, though of him it has been said that he decreed on the pain of excommunication not to amend any text in the Talmud, and in many places he disagrees with his grandfather. Aside from this he did not at one's own conjecture, neglect commentaries on Scriptures and grammatical studies, and decided in favor of Menachem b. Sruk against Duns b. Labrat in his book "Hahakhraoth" (Reconciliations); he also tried his ability for poetry. As his biography has been written by the learned A. H. Weiss in a separate book, it is unnecessary to expatiate on it.

Here is the place to remark that in late generations the second pair of phylacteries which pietists put on after the prayer, have been styled after him on account of two or three words which he wrote in his commentary on an obscure passage in Tract Mena'hoth in opposition to Rashi's commentary, on account of a hair-splitting discussion in the language of the Gemara, though he had never the intention to decide so the Halakha, as his grandfather Rashi had also not intended in his commentary on the Halakha, still those phylacteries are called after him. In truth neither the one nor the other was used yet as phylacteries, as testifies the greatest among the authors of Tosphoth, R. Isaac the Elder (as this is explained in one book on Phylacteries).

Among the faithful disciples whom Pashi had in the college at Troy it is proper to mention R. Joseph b. Simeon Kara who was revealed to us recently by modem criticism; and R. Joseph Bchor Shor who was a disciple of Rabenu Tam, and composed a commentary on the Pentateuch in the spirit of that of Rashbam. The other commentators on Scripture among the authors of the Tosphath and their disciples, however, as the author of "Hagan" (The Garden) a commentary on the Pentateuch, which is to be found in two different versions, and some more commentaries by R. Hezekiah b. Manoah, R. Isaac Halevi, R. Jehuda b. R. Eliezer, R. Jacob d'Illesques, do not cling to the principle of literal interpretation, but of Drash and Mysticism. Rashi's commentary was, however, their model. The chiefs of the authors of Tosphoth in the period of from 1167 till 1300 were: R. Isaac b. Samuel, called R. Isaac the Elder, from Dampirere, the nephew of Jacob Tam, his son Elchanan, Eliezer b. Samuel ("Ram") of Metz, author of "Sepher Yereim" (Book of the God-Fearing), Isaac b. Abraham, Junior (Ritzba), his brother, Simsan of Chanz (Rashba), his great labors are called Tosphoth of Chanz, Jehudah b. Isaac from Paris, called Sirlian, Ephraim b. Isaac from Reugspurk, and Nathan Official, who will be mentioned by us further in a separate chapter. Among the latest of the authors of the Tosphoth, however, we may name the Rabbi Moses of Caucy, author of "Smag" who is also mentioned in Tosphoth thrice (Berakhoth, 14b, 43a, Aboda Zarah, 13a), and R. Jacob of Courbel to whom have been attributed the questions and answers *from Heaven*, and we doubt whether Isaac of Vienna author of the well-known book "Or Zarua" (Diffused Light), who also lived at that time, has also been mentioned in Tosphoth (see our work on *Phylacteries*), by the name of R. Isaac--simply, as not every time when the name R. Isaac--barely is mentioned in Tosphoth, R. Isaac the Elder is meant.

This last, R. Moses of Caucy, contributed much to restore the study of the Talmud to its former splendor in his days, when in Spain it was almost stopped, and along with it many ceremonies, as phylacteries, Mezuzoth and Tzitzith, which were not seen in his time in any part of Spain or other countries. Owing to the oppression of the other religions by the dominant religion, the Israelites began to blend with the nations, and thousands of them embraced ostensibly the dominant religion, and some even conscientiously, having despaired of the former hope of Israel, Moses of Coucy therefore devoted himself to his work and travelled from city to city, and from land to land, to encourage Israel in the study of the Talmudic literature, and restore the activity, and he is the first who required help for his aim from gentiles, his friends, though not co-religionists, and that his works should find acceptance he backed them by dreams and natural phenomena that took place at the time, which he warned the people that they were signs from heaven, and also by astrology, to arouse the people to return to the study of the Talmud and its commandments. As he testified himself in his book which he wrote in his later days (1288), "*Sepher Mitzvoth Gadol*" (Positive Commandments) whose title is abbreviated "Smag." After writing the sermons in exile, he concludes: "After the year 4995 after creation (1235), an event took place from heaven to chastize. And in the year 1236 I was in Spain *preaching* to and reproving them, God strengthened my arms by Jews *and Gentiles*' dreams, and visions of the stars and extended his mercy to me, and the earth trembled[1] and there was general terror, great repentances were made, and thousands as well as myriads accepted the sacred ceremonies of Tephilin, Mezuzoth, and Tzitzith. So I was afterwards in other countries, and they were accepted in all places, and I was asked for a commentary on these commandments in brief." Not only in France and Spain were such books written about the practical ceremonies in the spirit of the Talmud, but also in Germany, R. Baruch of Germisa composed "Sepher Hatrumah" and R. Isaac from Vienna, his book "Diffused

Light" (Or Zarua) which all treat of ceremonies and Halakhas after the rules of the Talmud, which those sages saw a great necessity to renew and arouse the nation to observe them, after the Halakahs of Alfasi and Maimonides had become already too ancient in their tone, and the violent persecutions then directed against the Talmud diminished the number of the students. It would seem that at that time was composed also the small book "Questions and Answers from Heaven" in the name of R. Jacob of Corbel who was known as a holy man, to show to the people that its hope was not yet at end, that in heaven all wards of the Talmud are venerated, and so are all sages who occupy themselves with it, as seen from the contents of the questions and answers given from heaven especially in case of R. Isaac Alfasi, about whom from heaven it was answered: "Not in an old man is wisdom, nor in schoolboys counsel, but my covenant I shall fulfil with Isaac," and this may be a kind of basis for the programme made by Shem Tobb, Joseph Falkira (1264), that diligent study of Alfasi may substitute the study of the Talmud.

---

1. See our "Phylacterien," page 85, concerning the trembling of the earth, mentioned here.

Chapter 13
Religious Disputes of All Periods

Religious Disputes Of All Periods.

From the earliest recorded times there have been disputes between men on faith and religion. When, in pagan countries, the idols had become great in number and each man considered his own the right one, he strove to convert his fellows to his own opinion, whether through benevolence or from wrath that the idol of his neighbor should be considered greater than his own. Traces of such disputes are found in the Prophets. To the Jewish people was probably due the increase in the violence and frequency of such disputes, since its mission was always the annihilation of idol-worship. Being monotheistic, it could not live at peace with any gods besides its own. No historical importance can be attached to such disputes among and with the heathen, because the number of idols was often as large as that of the worshippers. But when Christianity, whose great aim was to convert all humanity and to extinguish all theologies, began to spread over and to dominate the world, the matter of religious disputes assumed a new and baleful aspect, for persecutions and trials were mercilessly inflicted on all who opposed it, whether those who took an active part in the controversies or those who refused to enter into them.

In recording the history of the Talmud and of its persecutions we cannot pass over the disputes concerning it from the time of its birth, and continuing throughout its troubled history in succeeding ages. A minute history of all these controversies, however, their dates, the names of the disputants, the topics of the disputes, as well as the consequences to the Talmud, would require a volume twice the bulk of the Talmud itself. We will therefore content ourselves with devoting to it a separate chapter, mentioning only the greater historical controversies and giving a résumé of the subject matter of the disputes as we deem them of value to our readers.

Already in the first century we have seen that the disputes between the Jewish Christians and their brethren who did not believe in Jesus' Messiahship were many. In the Talmud are given the names of many sages and Amoraims who were compelled to enter upon disputations with their Christian brethern.[1] But in the second and third centuries, houses for disputations (see App. No. 10) had already been established, as well in Palestine as in Babylonia, and doubtless also in many other places where Jews dwelt. Those known to us by name are the house of Abidan, the house of Abiani, and that of Nitzraphi. The Talmud relates that the Jews were forced to come hither, or to furnish sufficient explanation for not so doing.

We have no record of the results of these disputes, but in the sixth century we see Priscus, a Jewish officer of King Eilprich, forced to a controversy. When ordered to embrace Christianity he naïvely replied "that he could not believe that, to save sinners, God was compelled to enter into marital relations with a woman, and finally, in order to redeem the world, underwent the death-agony, when at his command were hosts of angels not needed in heaven." For this he was imprisoned. Henceforward in almost every century of the Christian era there arose fanatics who forced the Jews into controversy. In the seventh century these disputes were used as weapons against the Jews of Spain in documents issued by Isidorie, Bishop of Seville. These and other writings against the Jews, added to the verbal disputes, finally resulted in the ninth century, during the reign of Charles the Bald, in invectives promulgated by the Bishop of Amulo, denouncing the Jewish creed as "superstition" and inciting all Christians to their duty in eradicating the error from the minds of the Jews, to force them to accept the Gospel in place of their belief in the two Messiahs, one a descendant of David and the other a descendant of Joseph. It is remarkable that in these documents the bishop complains that the Jews, by their eloquent sermons and lectures, made more impression on their hearers than did the preaching of the Christians, as he was convinced by personal experience. And, indeed, in this he was not mistaken; for where the Jews' lot was ameliorated, as in the reign of Louis the Saint--who, as well as his wife, Judith, honored the Jews, so much so as to change for their sake the fair-day from Saturday to Sunday--many Christians came to the synagogues to hear the Rabbis and the scholars among them read with pleasure the writings of Philo and Flavius instead of the Gospel, and likewise learned from Jewish scholars the interpretation of Scripture, as Rhabanus Maurus of Fulda avows in his commentary on the Bible.

The Jews in Arabia also were forced to dispute with the Mussulmans, who assured them that the teaching of the Talmud had its day and Islam was even then usurping its place. When Basilius, the Macedonian ascended the throne of Byzantium he summoned learned Jews to argue with Christian priests, who strove to convince them that Jesus had become the center of the law and prophets. But these disputes are insignificant compared with those of the last four centuries of the Middle Ages; during this period the number of Jewish apostates increased, who challenged their brethern of the old faith to arguments. Massacre and pillage were the results of these disputes, the invitation to which was, briefly, as follows: "If ye be willing and obey, the good of the land shall ye eat; but if ye refuse and rebel, by the sword shall ye be devoured." And, as if no loophole should exist through which the Jews, might evade persecution, if a Christian were converted to the Jewish faith and mocked his former religion the Jews were held responsible and punished. Thus in the ninth century the priest Boda accepted Judaism and ridiculed the Christians, going even so far as to beg the Mohammedan rulers in Spain to permit residence in that country only to Jews and Mussulmans, and not to Christians. Coystan Becelelonus in 1005, in the reign of Henry II., wrote a pamphlet in which he addressed his former co-religionists thus: "Fools read the prophet Malachai, who says in God's name, 'I am God, without change.' How then can you believe that the Divinity underwent any change?" The culmination of all this was a renewed outburst of wrath and persecution directed against the Jews.

The Christians did not consider the fact that he who exchanges his religion for another, from any motive whatever, by so doing is held in enmity by his former co-religionists and his affirmations esteemed of no value. They declared that the spirit of Satan had seduced the Jewish proselytes, while at the same time they gave credit to all the calumnies uttered by the Christianized Jews and granted them power to compel the Jews to enter into dispute with them. For this alleged guilt of Satan they punished the Jews with restriction of rights, confiscation of property, or total exile. An instance is recorded of the conversion in London in 1275, during the reign of Henry II., of the great Dominican preacher Robert de Redinge to Judaism, who adopted the name of Haggai. The Christianized Jews of France and Spain were also the cause of great trouble to the Jews in those countries during the Middle Ages, though Christianity had been the dominant religion but for a short period.

Of the more prominent controversies of that time may be mentioned that of Rabbi Nathan Haupniel, one of the writers of the commentaries called "Tosphoth" (Taanith IX., the Tosphoth beginning at "Aser T'aser"), known among Gentiles as Nathan Official, the colleague of Rabenu Tam and perfect under the Archbishop of Cens, with this same archbishop, and, near the close of the twelfth century, with Pope Alexander and the king himself. At this epoch the status of the Jews of France was one of peace and prosperity, and R. Nathan and his colleague, Rabenu Tam, were honored at court. The bishop attempted to prove by the passage, "Let us make man in our image," that the Trinity is meant, since the plural is used. R. Nathan's answer was: "Before replying to this, I desire to ask of you a question in law concerning myself. You are aware that I loan no money at interest (this he mentioned because the Jews were then charged with usury). I gave to a friend a sum of money with which to purchase merchandise, and in the profits arising from which I was to share. He transported the goods to Paris, but finding that their market price had greatly diminished, he threw all into the Seine without consulting with me. I am therefore of opinion that I may demand of him to return to me the whole sum; for by what right did he inflict on me a financial loss without first asking my consent?" The bishop replied: "You may without doubt; and according to my opinion you are entitled to additional compensation besides, since how dared he destroy your property?" "If that is so," answered R. Nathan, "you will of course grant that God is at least as just as men, and if, according to you, he had created men with the assistance of the other two Persons of the Trinity, how comes it that he declares, 'I will destroy man whom I have created from the face of the earth?' [Gen. vi. 7], without first consulting the other Persons of the Trinity? They also were entitled to a part in disposing of man." On another occasion, being asked why the Jews were obstinate in refusing to worship Mary, the mother of God, R. Nathan replied: "Tell me, you who are so learned, whether the question never occurred to you: how was it possible that the idea of worshipping the golden calf entered the Jews' minds after they had been witnesses, shortly before, of all the signs and wonders of the Eternal, and the thunders and lightnings on Mount Sinai?" The bishop replied: "True; whenever I read this passage it seems a great problem to me." "But I am not in the least surprised," answered R. Nathan, with hidden irony. "The Jews saw that the gold when thrown into the fire was made into a calf, and they doubted not that the Holy Ghost had clothed itself in this precious metal; but you who affirm that the Holy Ghost became incarnate in a woman must needs remember that when God wished to give to the Israelites the Decalogue he warned them: 'For three days you shall not approach a woman' [Ex. xix. 15]. How, then, can the Jews believe, after this, that when He desired to endow Israel with a new testament, He should himself approach a woman?" Replies of this kind were numerous from R. Nathan, as well as from his sons Joseph and Asher. Thus it is also told of R. Joseph Bchor Shor that to the question, "Why did God choose to appear to Moses in a thorn?" ("bush" in the incorrect version), he replied, "Because from it no image can be made, nor can it be used to form a cross."

These disputes, however, did not bring about the terrible calamities which usually followed those in the Middle Ages, Judith, the Queen of Louis the Saint, protected the Jews and their studies, preventing the priests from taking vengeance for such ironical expressions as those given above. When Bishop Bodo perceived that his aims were not furthered by the disputes, he prohibited altogether such controversies with the hated Jews. A few decades passed, and not only was this prohibition ignored, but the Jews were again constrained to dispute in the presence of Louis IX. and his wife, and the chief civil and ecclesiastical dignitaries, the latter representing Pope Gregory IX. It fell to the lot of the four rabbis, R. Jechiel of Paris, the disciple of Jehudah the Pious; R. Moses of Coucy, the famed travelling lecturer; R. Jehudah b. David of Melon, and R. Solomon b. Samuel, to dispute with the apostate Donin, who took the name of Nicolus. This man while yet a Jew had evinced a tendency, as it appeared to the rabbis, to rebel against Judaism, and therefore they had excommunicated him. In revenge, he went to Rome in 1239, and charged that the Talmud contained sacrilegious sayings as to Jesus Christ and his mother, and so distorted the Scriptures by its interpretations and comments that thereby the Deity was blasphemed. He further charged that it gave license to illegally deprive Gentiles of their property and granted permission to deceive them. The sum of his libel, which contained thirty-five points, was that the Talmud was the enemy of Christian truth and the sole cause of the refusal of the Jews to recognize the divinity of Jesus.

It will be in place here, before further consideration of the character and consequences of this and many other disputes in which Jewish apostates were the accusers and disputants, to speak of the Jews of the Middle Ages, what they were, and, having in view only the truth, to expose their faults. For by their great intolerance, and their conduct towards all who entertained opinions of the least liberality, differing ever so slightly from their own, they brought down upon themselves, as it were by their own hands, terrible calamities. There was at that period, as is well known, a division of opinion among the Rabbis themselves concerning the books of Maimonides. Many Rabbis excommunicated him after his death, and even defaced his epitaph; and the intolerant R. Solomon of Montpelliers, with his colleagues and disciples, resorted to the Flagellants and Dominicans for aid, saying: "Behold, there are among us heretics and infidels, for they were seduced by Moses ben Maimon of Egypt. You who clear your community of heretics, clear ours too" (Karpeles, P. 346). They assented -gladly, and the books of Maimonides were burned at the stake in Paris and Montpelliers. From the conduct of these fanatics towards that lion of Israel (they themselves avowed that he was infinitely superior to them in science and learning) we can conceive their terrible vengeance against an ordinary man or scholar when he ventured to express opinions in any degree at variance with their own, or to transgress the Sabbath by carrying a handkerchief or drinking of Gentile wine, which in their opinion is against the law. Who, then, could resist their terrible weapon of excommunication, which they used for the purpose of making a man a ravenous wolf whom every human being fled from and shunned as though plague-smitten? Many who drank of that bitter cup were driven to the grave, and many others went mad. But woe to the excommunicators if the excommunicated afterward received baptism from the Dominicans I Then the vengeance of those who had been banished was fearful; like serpents they stung their former brethern, and caused misfortunes to thousands of souls who became as sheep for the slaughter.

Thus on the 24th of July, 1240, the complete Talmud was brought by Donin to the royal palace, and R. Jechiel, who, because of the fact that he had disputed with many priests, had been elected head of the disputants, was asked by him, in the presence of the king and the whole assembly, whether he believed in *all* that was written in all these books, now more than four hundred years old. To this R. Jechiel replied, addressing the king: "Our Talmud is not four hundred years old, but more than fifteen hundred, and this alone suffices to prove that the controversy concerning what is *said* in it is superfluous; for up to this time there have been Jewish apostates and many learned Christian priests who were conversant with its contents and found no evil in them. "Hieronymus," continued the Rabbi, "known to all as a wise and devout Christian writer, who was familiar with Jewish literature, much better than this apostate sinner, would doubtless have sought the destruction of the Talmud, if he had found therein such terrible things as this apostate alleges. Therefore I feel sure that this liar, who seeks our lives, will never attain his object; he may indeed deprive us of our lives, but not of our Torah, dear to us as the pupil of our eye. If you vent on us here in France all your anger, still will the Talmud be found in Spain, Greece, Babylon, Media and Mesopotamia, in possession of the Jews of these countries, and there you cannot reach to destroy it." The king was not satisfied with this, but bade R. Jechiel give a direct answer to Donin. To this the rabbi answered that the moral and legal doctrines of the Talmud were held sacred, but that full credence need not be given to the Hagada, which should not be taken too literally, since it is for the most part allegorical. The Ramban gave expression to a like opinion, but it would be superfluous to quote him entire. To the other accusations of Donin, that the Talmud terms the followers of Jesus Christ "Minim" (infidels), that it condemns Jesus, that it allows ill-usage of people of other nationalities, etc., he replied: "In the Talmud there is no mention of Jesus (Jesu) Christ, but only of another Jesus (Jeshua) who was a disciple of R. Joshua b. Prachia, who lived two hundred years before Christ; that the term 'Minim' in the Talmud includes all who deny the Oral Law; that it grants equality before the civil law to all men, idolators included, and commands visitation of sick idolators, support of their poor, and interment of their dead even in Jewish cemeteries. He also proved that according to the Talmud, the Christians are not included among idolators, since the prohibition as to sharing in divine power is directed only to Israel and has not been enjoined on other people; and, moreover, since the Christians abhor idolators, they cannot themselves be counted among them. There is no distinction drawn between them and Jews by the criminal laws of all civilized lands," as well as in the Talmud. (See App. No. 15.)

Thus two days passed in disputing with R. Jechiel, whose replies were written down by a disciple and collected later in a book, "Joseph Ham'qane" (The Zealot). On the third day, R. Jehudah b. David, having been prohibited from holding intercourse with R. Jechiel the first two days, was called to the dispute, and when his assertions were found to agree with those of R. Jechiel, the controversy came to an end.

The second dispute which must be noted is that started by the apostate Pablo Christiani, in July, 1263, with the rabbis of Spain. This was the reverse of the previous dispute, in that the first charged the Talmud with despising Jesus and Christians, while this dispute endeavored to prove from the Talmud itself the Messiahship of Jesus; Pablo claiming that the book contained many such passages. Rabbi Moses ben Nachmani (Ramban) was selected as disputant. This controversy also took place in the royal palace in Barcelona, and lasted four days. The principal topics for discussion were: Whether the Messiah had already appeared or was still expected; whether he would appear as a warrior, to restore the kingdom of the Jews, or as God's son, as Jesus. The passage, "the sceptre shall not depart from Judah until Shiloh come" (which the Jews also understand as referring to a Messiah), Pablo adduced as proof that after the destruction of the Temple and the fall of the Jewish kingdom it must of necessity be considered that the Messiah had arrived. Again, the Talmud itself says, "The Messiah was born when the Temple was destroyed," and "Elijah said to R. Joshua the son of Levi, The Messiah sits at the gates of Rome, among the sick," etc.

Thereupon Nachmani addressed the king. "Know," said he, "we possess three different books; before every other, the Bible, in which we implicitly believe; then the Talmud, which we hold sacred as an indispensable commentary on the biblical laws; but the third book, which we call Midrash, comprises mere sermons or speeches, which are listened to by the Jews but which exercise no authority over them. "The Hagada," he continued, "is, as its name indicates, a mere collection of legends, fiction, a creation of fancy, communicated by one person to another, but not held by the Jews as dogma, and which I myself do not believe." Then turning to Pablo, "I will reply directly to you as to the question at issue. If the Talmud, as you assert, regards the founder of your church as the true Messiah, why have not the Talmudists believed in him? Why did they not avow him, as you, Pablo, have done? For five hundred years have men been at work on the Talmud, and none had been convinced or induced to enter the church. Where," he asked further, "is it to be found in the Bible or the Talmud that the Messiah will suffer at the hands of men? On the contrary, it is said of him, "He will reign from sea to sea," "Dwellers of the desert will kneel before him" and "nations will adore him," which certainly was not the case with your Messiah, who, by the way, was born long before the destruction of the Temple of Jerusalem, and therefore the Talmudic passage can have no reference to him. Rome had not your alleged Messiah to thank for its greatness; on the contrary, its power and dominion gradually declined after his advent, and since the birth of your religion a new creed, the world-dominating Islam, has arisen. Further, were the omens and prophecies of the Messianic time fulfilled? Of this the prophets predicted 'that homicidal war will cease, a universal peace reign in the world; the swords will be beaten ploughshares, the spears into pruning hooks, and the harmless animal will graze by the side of the wild one;' that 'no injustice will occur, a moral elevation will ennoble men, God's spirit will enlighten all peoples, and a universal purified knowledge will be introduced.' But since your Messiah appeared, numberless wars have disturbed mankind, justice, morality, and brotherly love have not yet become the ruling principles of the world, your religious truths have not satisfied the adherents of Islam, and one God does not as yet reign on earth. If you make of your Messiah a God, then we cannot believe at all in him. The Messiah must be, according to the prophets, a man 'out of the stem of Jesse'; he must be sprung a child born of ordinary parents, not a son of God need he be. Nay, the passage in the Talmud which you bring forward as favoring the Messiahship of Jesus, 'that Messiah sits on God's right, and Abraham on his left,' shows him not to be a God, else could not the Talmud say directly after this 'that Abraham's countenance darkened on account of the favor shown the Messiah.' Were he God's son, surely Abraham would have known him as Divinity and have yielded to him, with no feeling of jealousy, the first place. The language of the Talmud is peculiar, and by its assertion that the Messiah was born with the Temple's destruction must be understood the revival among the Jews, through this barbarity and injustice, of the hope of a Messiah. They assuredly do not accept him as Messiah who saw the light of day fully a hundred years before this event, and who, in spite of his sufferings, brought to the world neither salvation nor redemption. And how stands it with your assumption that your Messiah redeemed the world from original sin? The penalties decreed for that sin still exist. Women still suffer pain in childbirth; in the sweat of the brow must the ground be ploughed, and Death still thins the hosts of the living-evils which, according to your construction of the Bible, result only from original sin. As to the passage quoted by you from the Bible, this is its significance: 'The sceptre shall not depart from Judah eternally'--*ad* being equivalent to *load* (forever). The clear meaning of this is that Judah's dependence, if he be condemned to it, will not last forever, for the Messiah will come and restore to him his independence; simply, that he *will* appear, but is not yet come. For the rest," continued Nachmani, "I do not long for the Messiah. With us it is accounted as of greater merit if we, living in foreign lands, among strange people, and under the protection of the king, worship our God, than if we, as free masters, adhere to the law in our own land." Pablo was no match to Nachmani and his striking proofs. The next Sunday, King Jacob I. of Aragon appeared with Peñaforte in the synagogue. The general of the Dominicans resumed the dispute, and sought to prove the Trinity by the simile of wine, which also contains a trinity in it, color, flavor and odor, and yet is one thing. Nachmani, however, refuted him, and demonstrated that to accept this argument would be to assume also a fifth person in God. Peñaforte became perplexed and replied that the Trinity is so deep a mystery that the angels are unable to comprehend it. When Nachmani had asked the modest question, "Why, then, should men raise themselves above the angels to dispute about and to hold fast to so deep a mystery?" The king dismissed him with rich presents, adding these strange words: "I have never yet heard a wrong cause so masterfully defended." Nevertheless, Nachmani was banished, He, did not, as contemporary ecclesiastical chronicles affirm, flee in deep shame, but was expatriated through the intrigues of the clergy, and emigrated to Palestine, which, in his opinion, should be a Mecca for every Jew, and arrived there shortly after Jerusalem had been reduced to ashes by the Mongols. There he continued his labors in behalf of Judaism and compiled his commentary on the Bible. To his disciples whom he left behind it is related that he said, on their asking of him a sign of the day of his death, that his mother's grave stone would be rent in twain.

After seeing, however, that the dispute led to no satisfactory results, and that Nachmani and other Jews were not convinced by the argument of "no salvation outside the church," Peñaforte changed his tactics and impeached the Talmud before Pope Clement IV., claiming that it abused and blasphemed the founder of the church. The Pope appointed a committee to examine the matter, and on their adverse report the obnoxious passages were stricken out, the erasing stylus was drawn through the pages of the Talmud by ignorant Dominicans, and for the first time it was subjected to the judgement of a censor. What a sad concurrence of historic events! Twenty years later the writings of Maimonides were again consigned to the stake at Acco through the efforts of the Kabbalistic fanatic Solomon Petit; in Tiberia the tombstone of Moses b. Maimon, the greatest thinker to whom Judaism had given birth in a thousand years, was shamefully dishonored and its epitaph replaced by the words; "Here rests an excommunicated heretic."

Of far more importance were the attacks on Judaism and the Talmud in the dispute which took place at Tortosa, in, Aragon, in 1413, under the supervision of Pope Benedict XIII., and which required no less than sixty-eight sessions. Long before this time the Jews had held polemics with Christian scholars, and the Jewish literature in defense of the faith which had been current in the thirteenth century, and which included also attacks on Christian dogma, was now in full bloom. Raymond Martin, a Dominican Hebraist and one of the censors of the Talmud appointed by the Pope, who treated the Talmud with comparative leniency, wrote against Judaism two hostile books under the titles "Religious Dagger" (Dagger of Faith) and "Scourge for the Jews," wherein arguments in favor of Christianity were adduced both from Scripture and from rabbinical writings. These books were imposing not less from their powerful logic than from their exhibition of profound scholarship, and the renowned Talmudist, R. Solomon b. Adereth, was called to refute them. The apostate Abner Alfonso Burgensis, a polemic of more danger to Judaism, at the commencement of the fourteenth century, wrote a number of controversial works against his former religion, to whom Isaac Pulgar replied with a trenchant satirical poem as well as an argumentative work. In 1375, Moses Kohen de Tordesillas disputed in the church at Avilla with the renegade John of Valladolid, and soon after this proselytizing cardinal Pedro de Cuna challenged Shem Teb b. Isaac Shoprat to a public religious discussion. The latter published in 1380, a comprehensive defensive work, "Eben Bochan," and also translated the Gospels into Hebrew to enable his co-religionists to arm themselves from the Christian arsenal; they subsequently found themselves obliged to use these weapons only too often. In 1391 occurred the first great persecution of the Jews in Spain, during which many, to escape the sword, embraced Christianity. Whereas the greater part of those who were forced into conversion usually returned to the fold of Judaism, some of these new Christians were, conversely, possessed by a great zeal for proselytizing, as, for example, the physician Astruc Raimuch, and particularly the former rabbi, Paul Burgensis, the latter of whom was a source of much mischief to his people. The satirical poet, Solomon Bonfed, the ingenious thinker Chasdai Crescas, the physician and philosopher, Profiat Duran, indited convincing replies to the attacks of these apostates. But in the foremost rank of these polemic writings stands the circular letter of Joshua Lorqui, which he addressed in an apparently submissive tone to his former teacher, Paul Burgensis, wherein, along with keen attacks on Christian dogma, he tells Burgensis that as a thinking and learned man he could not have accepted Christianity through conviction. When one reads this letter he must hold it almost a psychological impossibility that the man who adopted such an attitude towards Christianity should in later years have gone over to the Christian church and become a scourge to his co-religionists of the Jewish faith; and yet this Joshua Corqui was, with scarcely a doubt, identical with him who later assumed the name of Geronimo, Santa Fe, and came forward to impeach Judaism and the Talmud at the dispute in Tortosa.

Benedict XIII., one of the three popes who were then striving for dominion, had a particular interest in this dispute. This pope had been deposed at the Council of Pisa as a heretic and perjurer, and had been excommunicated; in Spain, however, he was recognized as pope, and from that place he set in motion his plans to make himself universally recognized. If he could succeed in breaking the obstinacy of the Jews and effecting finally their conversion as a people, it would be a great triumph for the church, and for himself personally. From these motives he willingly permitted King Fernando of Aragon to invite Jewish rabbis and scholars to a theological discussion at Tortosa. Sixteen of the most prominent appeared at that memorable dispute, which lasted, with many interruptions, from February, 1413, till November, 1414. The apostate Geronimo, the physician-in-ordinary-of the pope, had arranged previously the following programme for the controversy. First he desired to prove from the Talmud that the Messiah must already have arrived. Should this argument be ineffectual, however, then a war to the death was to be declared against the Talmud, which sustains the Jews in their unbelief. When the Jewish notables appeared in the session hall on the first day, the thousand there assembled, presided over by the pope (who was pompously arrayed and seated on an elevated throne), made upon them an overwhelming impression. The pope himself opened the session with an address, wherein he laid emphasis on the fact that the question now was not as to the truth of Judaism or Christianity; Judaism *once* had been true, but was replaced by the later revelation. The discussion must turn only on the point whether, according to the Talmud, Jesus is the promised Messiah or not. Thereupon, Geronimo delivered a lengthy speech, which he concluded with the text, "If ye be willing and obey, ye shall eat the good of the land; but if ye refuse and rebel, ye shall be devoured by the sword." In his reply, Don Vidal Benvenisti placed the apostate's wickedness in its true light, inasmuch as he had threatened with the sword before any proof for or against had been brought. In the subsequent sessions, Geronimo cited passages, more or less familiar, from the Talmud and Midrash, to prove to the unbelievers that the Talmud itself, when rightly understood, attested Jesus' Messiahship. But as the representatives of the Jews explained these passages according to their real meaning, and at the expiration of sixty-two sessions evinced not the slightest

inclination to be converted, Geronimo, at the pope's bidding, came
forth as impeacher of the Talmud, asserting that it contained blas-
phemies and abominations of all kinds and must therefore be uncon-
ditionally condemned. To prove this, he wickedly or ignorantly
perverted many passages. The Halakha teaches, for example, in relation to the verse in Exodus xxi. 15, "He that smiteth his father or his
mother shall be put to death," that he only is guilty of death who
wounds his parent by beating; from this Geronimo inferred that the
Talmud allows the beating of parents. The Halakha also teaches in
reference to blasphemy that "only he who blasphemes God by his
name of four letters (Jehovah) is guilty of death," and from this
Geronimo concluded that the Talmud permits blasphemy. Geronimo
was also the first to affirm that the Jews may break oaths, in
conformity to the prayer "Kol-Nidre." Every one at all familiar with
this prayer knows that it is for forgiveness for the non-fulfillment of
vows and oaths, taken *unconsciously* or broken through *forgetfulness*,
and is but an argument in favor of the Talmud's scrupulousness in
this matter. The Jewish delegates defended themselves, it is true,
with skill against these accusations, but were finally so hard pressed
that they divided into two parties. Most declared that the passages of
the Hagada brought forward by Geronimo had no authority; whereas
Don Vidal Benvenisti and the religious philosopher Joseph Albo
declared that the Hagada was held by them as of full authority, but
must not be construed literally and then judged. At all events, the
pope did not succeed in causing even one of the delegates to waver or
in effecting the hoped-for general conversion of the Jews. Driven to
anger at his failure, he dismissed them in a very unfriendly manner,
and soon thereafter issued a bull in which he interdicted the reading
or study of the Talmud by the Jews, and ordered that search be made
for copies of the book and they be then destroyed. He also directed
that in Spain the Jews should live separately from the Christians, fill
no official station, practice no trade, nor devote themselves to medicine. Fortunately the hostility of the pope had no effect. The Council
of Costnitz deposed him; his former protectors, King Fernando and
Emperor Sigismund, renounced his cause, and the fanatic Flagellator
and preacher, Vincent Ferrer, preached openly "that such a man as

this pope deserved to be persecuted to the utmost and to be killed by any good Christian." Filled with rage at the issue of the dispute, Geronimo published later a voluminous book against the Talmud, and the apostate Paul Burgensis, who was elevated to the bishopric, composed in his eightieth year, a work hostile to Jews and Judaism. To these and similar attacks the Jews were free as yet to reply without restriction. Answers were published by Joseph Albo, Vidal ibn Lobi, and Joseph ibn Shemtob, defending their own creed and winging arrows at Christian dogmas also. Several decades later the Jews of Spain were attacked not with the pen, but with the fist, not with spiritual weapons, but with physical force, and met with bloody persecutions till finally, in the total exile of 1492, the proud Spanish Jews were compelled to empty the cup of misery to the dregs.

----

1. R. Aqiba with R. Gamaliel, Joshua b. Hanania, Ishmael, Abuhu, and many others.

Chapter 14
The Talmud in the Sixteenth and Seventeenth Centuries

Reuchlin, Pfefferkorn, And The Talmud In The Sixteenth And Seventeenth Centuries.

Joseph or John Pfefferkorn was a German Jew, who lived in the beginning of the sixteenth century. He was ignorant of worldly knowledge, and had but a very limited acquaintance with Jewish literature. He became a Roman Catholic to escape the penalty for a theft. The Dominican monks of Cologne, subordinate to Hochsträter, the judge of the Inquisition, received him into their community with great honor. Hochsträter was a great fanatic and the enemy of every one who bore the name of Jew. His colleagues were Arnold Tangersky and Arthurin Gracia. This latter had committed to a Jewish apostate, Victor Karbensky (1504 A.C.), the task of writing a pamphlet against Judaism. In this pamphlet the author brings various accusations against the Jewish people, the responsibility for which he places on the Talmud. He recounts fabulous charges of Jewish persecution of apostates, and complains that even the poorest and most criminal and hardened Jews subject themselves to all manner of hardships rather than embrace Christianity. The pamphlet concludes with these words: "All this is due to the Talmud, which is the source of all evil, and which the Jews hold in greater reverence than the ten commandments of God." The Dominican monks found that this pamphlet failed of due effect, and asked Pfefferkorn if he could write a better one. He wrote the "Warnungsspiegel" (The Mirror of Warning), wherein he pretended to be a friend of the Jewish people, and, for their own good, desired to introduce Christianity among them. He urged them to convince the Christian world that the Jews do not need Christian blood for their religious rites. He also tried to induce his Christian brethren not to persecute the Jews unto destruction; for, he said, the Jews are also, in a way, human beings. Along with these pretences of friendliness he evinces in the pamphlet the desire (and in this he was seconded by the Dominican monks) to take the Talmud by force from the Jews. "The causes which hinder the Jews from becoming Christians," said Pfefferkorn, "are three: first, usury; second, because they are not compelled to attend Christian churches to hear the sermons; and third, because they honor the Talmud." Therefore he appealed to his co-religionists and the rulers to remove the first two causes; as to the third, he advised the government to take the Talmud from the Jews and burn it. But even this pamphlet was not wholly successful, because the rulers and the people understood that depriving the Jews of the Talmud would inure to the benefit, financially, of the Dominicans; for these latter, being the judges of the Inquisition, possessed the power of declaring the books harmless and of returning them to the Jews for a consideration. Therefore Pfefferkorn hastened to issue another pamphlet, in which he used harsher expressions, and tried to convince the people that the hatred of the Jews for Christianity was due solely to their religious books. He issued also a third pamphlet, on Jewish history, in which he contradicted what he had written in his first pamphlet. He said plainly that every Jew considers it a good deed to kill, or at least to mock, a Christian; therefore he deemed it the duty of all true Christians to expel the Jews from all Christian lands; even if the law should forbid such a deed, they need not heed or obey it in this respect. "It is the duty of the people," he said, "to ask permission of the rulers to take from the Jews all their books except the Bible," as well as all the pledges of Christians to be found in Jewish hands; also, that Jewish children should be taken away from their parents and educated in the

Catholic religion. He concluded his work thus: "Who afflicts the Jews is doing the will of God, and who seeks their benefit will incur damnation."

Although the religious hatred of the times of the Crusades was then far from extinguished, Pfefferkorn's books did not find favor with the rulers, as the Jews were their chief treasurers, from whom they at all times exacted enormous taxes. Therefore they did not desire to drive them from their territories; and to compel them to embrace Christianity did not suit them either, as most of the Christians disliked Jewish apostates and looked upon them disdainfully since they well knew that in most instances they did not accept Christianity through belief in the religion, but from more worldly reasons. In addition to this, all the Jews of Germany, as also the physicians of the rulers, who were for the greater part Jews, did all in their power to prevent Pfefferkorn's advice from being carried into execution. Many Christians, too, asserted that they were convinced that Pfefferkorn was bad at heart, a flatterer, and that his sole object was to enrich himself at the expense of the Jews. Therefore Pfefferkorn wrote a fourth pamphlet, in which he reiterated all he had written previously, and declared that the only way to be rid of the Jews was either to expel or enslave them; the first thing to be done was to collect all the copies of the Talmud found among the Jews and to burn them. Arthurin Gracia, who was the Censor of Art, revised and corrected Pfefferkorn's works and rendered them into Latin and German, and sent them to all the rulers of the period. Besides this, the Dominicans addressed themselves to the sister of the Emperor Maximilian, Princess Kunigunde, who was a nun in a Dominican convent at Munich. They begged her to intercede with the Emperor in behalf of Pfefferkorn. They eulogized Pfefferkorn, telling her of his knowledge of Jewish life and of his good character, and urged her to confide in him. Finally they persuaded her to give a copy of his pamphlet to the emperor, who was then at war in Italy with the Venetians. As a result of all this, Pfefferkorn at once set out for Italy, and succeeded in obtaining from the emperor a decree that all the Jews of Germany should yield up their books to him (Pfefferkorn), to be revised by him; if he should find in them anything relating to

Christianity, it should be destroyed. In this task he was granted the power to call to his assistance, in each city, a priest and two of the civic rulers. The Jews were warned under severe penalty not to resist the royal command.

Pfefferkorn and his party of inquisitors first visited Magdeburg, for in that city dwelt rabbis who were renowned throughout the Jewish world; and although they resorted to every device to prevent the surrender of their literary treasures--even the Bible, the removal of which was not included in the royal mandate, was also taken away--every Jew was compelled to surrender his entire store of religious books.

But many Gentile scholars, to whom Pfefferkorn's conduct did not appeal, assisted the Jews by testifying before the emperor that Pfefferkorn was ignorant on many subjects, and that he wrongfully deprived the Jews of books containing no allusions to Christianity; besides, they referred, in their request to the emperor, to the privileges accorded to the Jews, by previous emperors and popes, of worshiping in their own way. The Elector of Mayence, Archbishop Uriel, enraged at Pfefferkorn's action (we cannot learn why), summoned him to the city of Aschaffenburg, and informed him that the emperor's decree was in opposition to the law of the land, as it made him prosecutor, witness, judge, and executor in one; therefore, the Jews or the people, in disregarding the decree, would be guilty of no crime against the law. He counselled him, in fine, to ask the emperor to alter the mandate to conform with law. Pfefferkorn agreed to do so, and the Dominicans of Cologne advised him to find a prominent Gentile who would actively interest himself in the matter. This man they found in Reuchlin, at that time very popular and respected all over the world. The Dominicans told Pfefferkorn to get a letter from Reuchlin to the emperor, before going again to see the latter.

John Reuchlin, of Paszheim (1455-1522), had a great reputation as a scholar; in addition he had a benevolent heart. He devoted himself especially to the study of Hebrew, in which his interest was enhanced by Count Pick de Marsundella, who opened up to him the study of Kabbala, *i.e.*, Jewish mysticism. Even this did not satisfy his desire to be master of Hebrew. He formed the acquaintance of Jacob

Laanson, a Jewish physician at the Court of Frederick III., from whom he acquired a further knowledge of the language; at this court he came in contact with many Jewish scholars, and attained to such skill in the study that he afterwards wrote a book wherein he praised Hebrew as the best of all languages. He claimed in this work that the dogmas and rites of false religions were due to the ignorance of Hebrew, and to the misconception of the meaning of significant Hebrew terms. As for the Kabbala, he ranked this study with any other branch of learning, and stated that he himself was far from understanding thoroughly its sublime mysteries, for a complete knowledge of which even a lifetime would scarce suffice. Afterwards, when he became the Ambassador of the Elector Palatine to the Court of Pope Alexander VI., he became acquainted with the physician Obadiah Eipminah, the renowned commentator on the Mishna; and it was interesting to see the celebrated German scholar, whose discourses in Italian were greatly admired by the Italians themselves, stooping to ask a Jew to be his teacher of Hebrew literature. It was always his habit, when he came in contact with learned Jews, to obtain some useful knowledge from them.

Nevertheless, Reuchlin was not entirely free from prejudice against those of the Jewish faith. In a letter to a knight who desired to convert the Jews of his dominions to Christianity, he wrote that the whole trouble with the Jews was they were disbelievers, who did not care for Christ and his apostles, and that they held in general contempt all Christians; although it is true that later he repented of having written this letter, as will be seen further on.

The Dominicans relied on Reuchlin, knowing that the words of one so thoroughly acquainted with Hebrew literature would be respected by all the rulers of Germany. But Reuchlin declined to take an active part in the matter, although he commended the project of destroying all books written against Christianity. He also called Pfefferkorn's attention to the injustice of the emperor's decree, and told him it was doubtful whether it could be executed.

Despite his not securing the wished-for testimony, Pfefferkorn succeeded in persuading the emperor to ignore the petitions of the Jews and their defenders, and to give him the power to deprive the

Jews of their books, in a new decree, while harshly reproving them for failing to strictly obey the first. This time the emperor commissioned Archbishop Uriel to carry out the decree. He also ordered him to seek, and to follow the advice of the German universities of Cologne, Mayence, Erfurt and Heidelberg, and also to take counsel with Reuchlin, Victor Karbensky and Hochsträter (although the latter was totally ignorant of Hebrew). Uriel commanded the director of the University of Mayence, Herman Hess, to visit all the cities of Germany, and to remove all the Jewish books. Hess did so. He travelled through Germany accompanied by Pfefferkorn; and in Frankfort alone fifteen hundred manuscripts were taken away (printed books were as yet rare). They did the same in Worms, Lorch, Birgin, Lamuven, Mayence and Dertz. Pfefferkorn said that the Jews, to save their literary treasures, offered to enrich him, but he claimed he did not care to sell his soul and therefore did his duty.

The Jews on the other hand, did not cease in their efforts to prevent their despoliation. They secured testimonials from the more prominent among the Gentiles, and sent a committee to the emperor to petition him to prevent these attacks on their religion. They adduced proofs to show that their books contained nothing against Christian communities. They brought forward the privileges granted to them by former emperors and popes, enabling them to worship their God without the interference of the Church or State. These facts so favorably impressed the emperor that he commanded that all the books should be returned to their owners. The joy of the Jews on learning of this decree cannot be described, since thereby not only were they granted possession of their books, but a peaceful residence in Catholic countries was accorded them.

This joy, however, was only momentary, as both the Dominicans and Pfefferkorn still continued their malevolent activity. To add to the misfortune of the Jews, an event befell which the Dominicans were not slow to utilize as a weapon in their warfare against the faithful, with the aid of which they hoped finally to bring about the latter's destruction. Sacred vessels were stolen from a Christian church by a Gentile, who was arrested and who thereupon confessed that he had sold them to the Jews. As a result, all Jews were severely persecuted by the Bishop of Brandenburg. At the same time, or somewhat later, the Jews were accused of having killed a Christian child in the performance of their religious rites, and at the command of the same bishop the accused Jews were removed to Berlin, and thirty-eight of them were burned at the stake after suffering tortures on the rack.

These events the Dominicans made use of to arouse the fanaticism of the people of Germany. They addressed themselves to the emperor's sister, Kunigunde, to whom they painted these occurrences in the blackest colors, at the same time extolling Pfefferkorn as a converted Jew conversant with Jewish customs and manners. They stated that the Talmud contains the evil teachings which had become rooted in the hearts of the Jews. They represented to her the danger to Catholicism in the latest command of the emperor, and placed all their hopes in her keeping, as she was the only one who could save Catholicism from injury. At the same time they strove to find favor in the eyes of the people who protested against this persecution. A new pamphlet was prepared, in Pfefferkorn's name, which was dedicated to the Emperor Maximilian, praising him for his zeal for the Catholic religion. This pamphlet, after complaining that the Christians do not give full weight to the activity of the Jews against Catholicism, and charging that the whole fault lay with the Talmud, since its teachings prevented the Jews from embracing Christianity and permitted usury, affirmed that the one thing necessary was that the emperor should deprive the Jews of his books, and that it was the duty of all good Christians to help him in this matter, furthermore, that this cause met the approval of the emperor's sister, the nun Kunigunde. It further stated that all Christians who defended Jews should be treated as heretics, and Jewish apostates who did the same should be presumed to have taken up Christianity, not from belief in the Holy Trinity, but for baser reasons. The Princess Kunigunde actually interceded for them, and, presenting herself before the emperor, she begged him on her knees to grant the request of the Dominicans. The emperor again ordered Archbishop Uriel to hasten to seek the advice of the above-mentioned German universities, and especially to get the opinion of Reuchlin, Karbensky and Hochsträter, and transmit the same to him (the emperor), so that he might be prepared to judge whether or not the Talmud should be destroyed.

Reuchlin did not hasten to give his answer, and when, after three months his answer was composed, and delivered to the emperor, it was found to be unfavorable to Pfefferkorn. In this answer he divided Jewish literature into six classes, exclusive of the Bible, as follows: (1) poetry, fable and satire; (2) commentaries; (3) sermons, songs and prayers; (4) philosophy and science; (5) the Talmud, and (6) Kabbala. "In the first class," said Reuchlin, "are to be found books which deny or criticize the Christian religion;" but he could name but two of them of his own knowledge, and these were the pamphlet of Lipman (of the existence of which we have no records) and the life of Jesus. He declared, however, that the Rabbis themselves prohibit the possession of them by Jews and threaten severe penalties upon any one venturing to read them. "It is self-evident," he stated, "that this class of books must be destroyed without scruple."

With regard to the second class, he affirmed that they not only contain nothing harmful to Christianity, but, on the contrary, they are of great value in the interpretation of the Scriptures. Many Gentile scholars, could not, in many cases, fathom the depths of meaning of the Bible, because of insufficient knowledge of Hebrew. "It is true," he said, "that scholars had been heard to declare, we do not care for the Jewish commentaries, as we have a sufficient number by Christians." He compared these same to a person wearing a light garment in cold weather, since the basis for right understanding of the Scriptures is the knowledge of the original language wherein they were written.

"As for books of the third class, it would be an injustice to deprive the Jews of them, because they had received from emperors and popes the privilege of unmolested worship.

"Regarding the fourth class," he said, "they stand on an equal footing with books of the same class in Latin, Greek or German. But of the Talmud I must own that it is to me a sealed book, and it is evident that those who pass judgment upon it have as little knowledge of it as I. They have no idea of its nature; or of its, history; nevertheless they talk as if they knew and understood clearly all that it contains. I can only compare such people to those who would

100

venture to criticise algebra while they are totally ignorant of the rudiments of arithmetic. The fear is expressed that the Talmud might injure Christianity; this is absurd for nothing can withstand the proofs in its favor that are found in the Bible. If the Talmud really were as bad as they affirm, then our ancestors, who were much more religious than we, would long ago have put an end to its existence." He declared that the testimony of Pfefferkorn and Schwartz. against it, being inspired by unworthy motives, should not be given consideration. "Moreover, if we would but study the Talmud we would not destroy it, but rather encourage the Jews to hold it in still greater reverence and study it the more assiduously, for as a consequence there would be copies not alone in Germany, but also in Italy and Turkey, where many colleges for its study exist. To what purpose is the burning of a few copies of the Talmud, if you are unable to annihilate it entirely? Besides, by such action we should commit a breach of faith for we would thus abrogate the privileges granted to them by former emperors and popes."

Regarding the sixth class, he praised the Kabbala in the highest terms, and cited Count Picko de Mirandella, who, he says, induced Pope Sixtus VI. to study it; the latter discovered in it so much in support of Christianity that he translated Kabbalistic books into Latin. Reuchlin concluded that to deprive the Israelites of their books could only be likened to a duke challenging a knight to combat and then taking away his weapons. He advised the German rulers who were desirous of having the Jews embrace Christianity, to establish in all the German universities for a period of ten years, chairs for the study of the Hebrew language; then the students having a thorough knowledge of the language, could convince the Jews, by proofs from their own Bible, of the truths of Christianity. Returning again to the apostates (he plainly referred to Pfefferkorn, though he did not name him), he said: "Of what value is advice given by people who abandon Judaism through jealousy, animosity, fear of persecution, penury, revenge, ambition, love of pleasure, or even through mere recklessness? Such individuals bear the name of Christians, but in heart they are not Christians. I know of some whose faith in both religions, Christianity and Judaism, is weak, and who, if their schemes were brought to naught, would become disciples of Mohammedanism. The Jews have been citizens of Germany for three centuries and should be protected by the law, It would be ridiculous to adjudge them heretics, for they were not born Christians, but have been Jews from a time antecedent to the birth of Christianity.

However, the answer of the German universities was different. The theological faculty of Mayence replied that not only were the Talmud and all rabbinical books full of falsehoods and heresies, as Christian scholars testify (the faculty themselves confessed that they were ignorant of the Talmud and Hebrew), but that the Hebrew Bible also was not altogether free from error on points of Christian doctrine. The faculty deemed it advisable, therefore, that the books be revised by Christian scholars, and if anything be found contrary to Christian belief it should be burned.

The University of Erfurt counselled in like manner, but the Faculty of Heidelberg advised the emperor to select a committee from the faculties of all the universities of Germany to judge the Talmud and all Jewish literature, and let their decision be final.

Reuchlin sent his answer under seal to Archbishop Uriel, but by some means not recorded its contents became known to Pfefferkorn before it reached the emperor. When he and the Dominicans had perused it they were greatly perturbed. They were aware of the esteem in which Reuchlin was held by the emperor, and the weight his answer would be given to by the latter, and resolved to do something to weaken the effect of this answer on the emperor and the public. (In their haste to forestall Reuchlin they did not consider the risk to themselves in making public his answer before it reached the emperor.) A pamphlet was issued under the title of "Handspiegel," in Pfefferkorn's name, couched in flowing sentences, giving prominence to all the weak points in Reuchlin's answer, charging him with ignorance, abusing him and ridiculing his theory and misrepresenting it to the common people. The pamphlet stated that Reuchlin himself understood nothing of the Hebrew language, and that his book on Hebrew grammar was written by other hands; therefore, they asked, how can such a man counsel the emperor in matters of which he himself is ignorant? It stated, further, that Reuchlin's declaration that the Jews must be protected by the law proves the utter absurdity of his whole answer, and that it may be justly suspected he did not do this for nothing. To add force to their contention, they published a letter which Reuchlin himself had written to a knight five years before, and called upon Reuchlin to deny his statement in this letter that the Jews slander Christianity; his refusal to do so would indicate a desire to wantonly mislead the emperor and all good Christians. It said, moreover, that the fact of Reuchlin's renown among the Jews alone showed that he had fallen a victim to their wiles. At the end of the pamphlet, Pfefferkorn charged Reuchlin with having accepted money from the Jews, and blamed him for defending them, since it was his duty to regard them only as heretics. He also charged Reuchlin with countenancing usury (nothing about this was mentioned in Reuchlin's answer).

As Reuchlin was well known and much respected in Germany, this pamphlet made a commotion, and the people evinced a desire to read it, to learn of what Reuchlin was accused, As it was written in the popular jargon, many went on fair days to Frankfort-on-the-Main to purchase the pamphlet from Pfefferkorn. Reuchlin himself was astonished at Pfefferkorn's impertinence, and annoyed at the imputation on his honor; he therefore complained to the emperor. The latter, angry at the action of Pfefferkorn, promised Reuchlin that he would entrust the task of the revision of the Jewish books to the Bishop of Augsburg; but the emperor being at that time deeply occupied with matters of state, this affair was for the moment forgotten. Meanwhile a second fair was held at Frankfort, and Pfefferkorn hoped to distribute the remaining pamphlets among the people. As soon as this point in the contest was reached, Reuchlin resolved, since the quarrel had from a religious become a personal one, to uphold his wounded honor. He wrote a work entitled "Augenspiegel," in which he complained that a Jewish apostate should endeavor to destroy the Talmud. He told the public how Pfefferkorn had come to him, asking his co-operation, and how by despicable means he became aware of the contents of his answer to the emperor, so as to be able to heap more calumnies upon him. He charged that there were thirty-four lies in Pfefferkorn's pamphlet. He said, further, that he had not lost hope of facing Pfefferkorn in court, and that the latter had merited the sentence of death for inciting the people against the Jews. He declared the charge that he had received money from the Jews, a false one, adducing many proofs to show that the Dominicans and Pfefferkorn merely intended to stain his name. He further proved that he himself had written the Hebrew grammar. To the main accusation, that he had learned Hebrew from a Jew, he replied that Christianity did not forbid Christians from having dealings with, or learning from, Jews, especially as this was often productive of good in the conversion of the Jews.

Now, instead of Pfefferkorn's pamphlet, Reuchlin's was distributed at the fair, and was sold in large quantities to the people. The Jews it is fair to believe, greedily bought the work and did their utmost to spread it among the people. A preacher named Peter Mayer, of Frankfort-on-the-Main, while reading Reuchlin's pamphlet in the presence of Pfefferkorn, exclaimed that it ought to be burned at the stake; and, with the sanction of the Archbishop of Mayence, he prohibited its sale. But the priests of Mayence, all friendly to Reuchlin, at their convocation begged the archbishop to recall the prohibition and he consented. In a short time all Germany was in possession of copies of the work, and Reuchlin received many congratulatory letters. However, the strife was not yet over. His enemies did everything they could to overthrow Reuchlin. Paul Mayer, after his attempt to suppress the sale had proved futile, announced that Pfefferkorn would lecture on Reuchlin's books in the Catholic Church during the coming holidays. As Pfefferkorn was a married man, and not a priest, and therefore unable to preach from the pulpit, he lectured in the hall of the church in the popular jargon, holding a cross in his hand. The burden of his lecture was that the Jews should be persecuted unless they accepted Christianity. It was the first time in the history of the church that a Jew had stood in the corridor of a church with a cross in his hand and preached against the Jews.

The monks meanwhile gave Reuchlin's work to Arnold Tangersky for revision, and he naturally, being himself a Dominican, denounced it as heretical. The Dominican, Ulrich of Sternheim, wrote a letter to Reuchlin, in which, speaking as a friend, he says:

"The scholars of Cologne are not yet united in their opinion as to what should be done with your work. Some of them maintain that it should be burned; others say the author should be punished; and still others are stronger in condemnation of it." This letter did not fail of its purpose. Reuchlin understood full well that if the Dominicans openly declared against him, he would be in great peril, since at that time their power was supreme and they were feared even by the emperor himself. The Pope, Alexander VI., himself exercising a power to which kings themselves were subject, declared he would offend a rule sooner than the humblest Dominican. Reuchlin hastened, therefore, to indite, in Latin, a letter to Tangersky, the reviser of the book, in which he modified his previous statements. He said he judged the Talmud, not as a theologian, but as a layman, and he could not know, when writing his book, that the scholars of Cologne, would disagree with him. He also stated that he had not intended to cast blame on any one in his pamphlet, and besought Tangersky to show him his errors in the "Augenspiegel" and not condemn him before doing so. He wrote a letter of a different tenor to his teacher, Koln. In this he ventured to blame the head of the Dominicans, Hochsträter, whom he charged with having written the pamphlet under Pfefferkorn's name, and he begged him to explain his words to the faculty, so that they would see the truth and not blame him (Reuchlin) unjustly. The response to this letter to Koln was not sent to Reuchlin for a long time. The Dominicans obviously sought, by delaying it, to furnish him a pretext for committing an overt act. He finally received together two letters, one from the Cologne students and the other from Koln. The faculty scolded him for interfering in a quarrel which did not concern him, and at the same time preventing the emperor from performing a meritorious act in suppressing the Jewish books. This fact, they claimed and his writing the "Augenspiegel," went far to confirm the suspicion that he inclined to Judaism, and therefore it was their duty to punish him severely. They could not, however, refuse the request of Arnold Tangersky and of Koln to defer punishment until he was given opportunity to write a second pamphlet, retracting all his words in defence of the Talmud and in blame of Pfefferkorn.

Koln wrote him that he should feel grateful to him for inducing the faculty to withhold his sentence and for pacifying the Dominicans. At the same time, he reminded him of the danger which hovered over him, and advised him to hasten and repair his error by another pamphlet, contradicting all his previous statements. As to Reuchlin's accusation that the pamphlet "Handspiegel" was from the pen of Hochsträter he maintained complete silence.

Reuchlin at once answered his enemies in two letters. He thanked them for their intercession in his behalf, but claimed that as a married man (even twice married) he could not be longer counted among theologians, and therefore knew very little of the teachings of faith. He also cited proofs showing that he was not a friend of Judaism or the Jews. Nevertheless he refused to contradict the statements contained in his first pamphlet; on the contrary, he reiterated them, but asserted his willingness to write a commentary on his "Augenspiegel," explaining any ambiguous passages therein. He again urged them to point to him the passages because of which they accused him of heresy, saying that only then could he either defend his assertions or confess that he was in error and revoke them. The Dominicans, seeing that correspondence was of no avail, commanded him, first, to stop the circulation of his pamphlet; secondly, to contradict all he had previously said; thirdly, to restore the lustre of his name by showing himself a good Christian and a persecutor of the Jews and their literature. If he should refuse to do this, he must stand trial before the judges of the Inquisition. Koln also wrote him again, saying that but for this (Koln's) pleading, Reuchlin's pamphlet would long before have been burned and himself brought before the Inquisition; therefore he again urged him to respect the command of the faculty, as, should he fail to accede to their order, he could do nothing more for him.

Reuchlin, seeing that further argument was useless resolved firmly to take up the gage of battle, happen what may. First of all, he replied that he could not stop the circulation of his work, since it was no longer his, but was the property of the publisher. He could only write a commentary as an explanation of doubtful passages. To his supposed friend Koln, he wrote that if the latter had indeed prevented his work from being burned, the faculty should feel grateful to him (Koln) for restraining them from doing wrong, but that he himself entertained no feelings of gratitude for it. He told him he did not fear a contest with the Dominicans, as he had many defenders, men of prominence and power in Germany, and if the matter were attended with any danger it was to his enemies. It was easy, he said, to begin a fight, but much more difficult to gain a victory. He could not understand why his enemies failed to consider how the people would judge them if they took the part of a Jewish apostate against a born Christian and a firm believer in Christianity. He was certain that Pfefferkorn, if thereby he could derive any benefit, would become an apostate even to Mohammedanism or any other religion. To think that Pfefferkorn should preach against the law of the land and calumniate him! The Dominicans, he continued, to seek to accuse him of trivialities, and close their eyes to the many great sins of the apostate. He also said that *poets* and writers of history would stamp with shame the entire faculty, and would make of him (Reuchlin) a martyr for the truth.

Reuchlin kept his promise of writing a commentary to his "Augenspiegel," but it had the effect of adding fuel to the fire. The Dominicans were more than ever enraged, and Tangersky wrote a pamphlet which he dedicated to the emperor, and which contained the following concerning Reuchlin's interference in religious matters which are above his understanding:

In his pamphlet one can see that he favors the Jews, and in keeping with this he has written sentences which border closely on heresies. "The work concludes by saying that it is undoubtedly necessary to put the Talmud to the stake. This pamphlet effected what the author had intended. The emperor, who had hitherto defended Reuchlin, now turned against him, and on his arrival at Cologne he commanded that Reuchlin's pamphlet and commentary should not be circulated. The Elector of Mayence, acting in conjunction with the Archbishop of Cologne, displayed this order on the churches, and threatened the public with excommunication if they did not return Reuchlin's pamphlet to the churches, But even this failed of the desired effect, for Reuchlin's friends were too numerous, greater even in number than those of the Dominicans; the people had but small liking for the latter, and they especially despised the head of the order, Hochsträter. Therefore Pfefferkorn issued a new pamphlet, entitled "Brandspiegel," wherein Reuchlin was accused and debased. Therein he was styled a man who had forsaken the church, and whose hands were sullied with Jewish bribes. As for the Jews Pfefferkorn stated that they ought to be persecuted without pity, and incited the people to plunder them and devote the spoils to convents and hospitals. This was Pfefferkorn's last pamphlet, from this time he ceased to take part in the fight. Reuchlin, under a pseudonym, wrote another pamphlet, "The Defender." In this he says: "If any one asserts that Reuchlin did not, in the Jewish controversy, conduct himself as a true and upright Christian, he utters a falsehood." He attacks all the Cologne scholars, especially Arthur Gracia and Jacob Hochsträter. "Why," he asks, "do they make such an uproar and hold themselves up as greater authorities than other scholars of German universities?" And to the emperor he says: "Permit, your majesty, the Dominicans to judge the Jews by the Inquisition, that will fill their pockets with the gold and silver of the Jews. That is what they want; obtaining it, they will then leave me unmolested." To Arnold Tangersky, who accused him of protecting the Jews, he says: "It is true I am the protector of the Jews. I protect them against false accusations. I know that my assertion that they are citizens of Germany and entitled to the protection of the law, as other citizens are, will excite their enemies; but I say and repeat again, the Jews are our brothers--brothers to Arnold, brothers to the Dominicans, brothers to all the theologians, and the fathers of the Church long ago made alike declaration." To the assertion of the Dominicans that he contradicts what he had written in his former letter, he replies that it is true he had been prejudiced against the Jews until he was convinced of his error. The calumny that Jewish prayers MAINTAIN that all Catholic rulers should be put to death he refutes by quoting a Mishna: "Thou shalt pray for the peace of the kingdom wherever thou abidest."

This pamphlet was sent to the emperor, who received it favorably, and, owing to the complex questions involved, his mind wavered in the course he should pursue. First he assured Reuchlin of protection against the attacks of the Dominicans. Then his father-confessor, an enemy to Reuchlin, spoke in favor of the Dominicans, and the emperor again prohibited the circulation of Reuchlin's work. Finally he commanded both parties to cease their strife. Even this command failed of its purpose. The imperial decree was unheeded by the Dominicans, and the head of the Inquisition, Hochsträter, summoned Reuchlin to appear within six days before the judges of Mayence to defend himself against the charges of heresy and of defending the Jews. This summons was couched in language unprecedented in its insolence. Reuchlin did not appear at the trial, but sent a deputy. Hochsträter opened the court. He was both prosecutor and judge, and was certain that the trial would result in the success of his scheme against Reuchlin, and would cover the latter with ignominy, more especially as he had received favorable opinions from the German universities that had been ordered to afford counsel. The University of Loewen had replied that the pamphlet should be burned, that of Cologne, that besides its misleading nature, it showed decided leanings to heresy; the University of Erfurt gave answer of like import. Those of Heidelberg and Mayence alone did not respond. Hochsträter therefore felt sufficiently supported and certain of winning the trial. He recited a long list of grave accusations against Reuchlin, and gave it to his colleagues of the court, calling upon them to adjudge the defendant guilty and order his pamphlet to be burned. Reuchlin's deputy protested that Hochsträter had no right to be persecutor and judge in one; the less so as he was known to be Reuchlin's bitterest enemy. Seeing, however, that protest was of no avail, he left the court, Hochsträter, hesitating to sentence, contrary to public opinion, one who was not present, posted notices on church doors, requiring Reuchlin's deputy and all who had an interest in him, to appear before the court. He also ordered the public, on the pain of excommunication, to return the copies of the "Augenspiegel" to the judges of the Inquisition. The Dominicans triumphed that day and Reuchlin's defeat was seemingly close at hand. But this triumph was only of brief duration. The people of the better class of the city openly murmured against Hochsträter's proclamation and even the archbishop's colleagues advised that the trial be delayed for a short period, since Reuchlin or his deputies had not undergone examination.

The trial was therefore postponed for two weeks, Hochsträter thinking that Reuchlin would be ashamed to appear in person as a defendant, and feeling certain that at the expiration of two weeks he could be adjudged guilty by default. But Reuchlin did appear in person with the counsellor of the Duke of Württemberg, and that of the Duke of Mayence. The "Kapital" endeavored to make peace between the two parties, but in vain. The inquisitor Hochsträter refused to listen to overtures of peace, and ordered the judges to do their duty. They obeyed and began to write down their judgment, when suddenly a rider appeared with a letter in his hand from Archbishop Uriel. He passed through the crowd and straight to the judges, who were much astonished and anxious to know the contents of the letter. It was read aloud to the assembled people, and was to the effect that Archbishop Uriel commanded the postponement of the trial for one month, and if this command were disobeyed he would declare it a mistrial and dissolve the court. The Dominicans, defeated, left the court amidst the laughter of the people. There was much rejoicing among the Jews, as upon this trial depended their fate; but Reuchlin was not content with the mere postponement of the trial, knowing that the Dominicans would persecute him until they conquered. He determined, therefore, to leave his fate to the decision of Pope Leo X. But, learning that the Dominicans would bribe the advisers of the pope and persuade him to order the trial to be held in Cologne, he wrote a letter in Hebrew to the pope's physician, Bangett Delakes, beseeching his influence to prevent this. Leo, involved just then in grave secular matters--religious questions, for the time being, having no place in his councils--and seeing his quarrel likely to spread over Europe, directed the bishops of Speyer and Worms to end the contest by issuing a decision which should be respected by both parties. These bishops appointed a committee to investigate and report on the matter. The committee, though in awe of the Dominicans, conducted their investigation deliberately, and at the end of a year pronounced the pamphlet "Augenspiegel" free from any heresy, and Reuchlin to have no leanings towards Judaism or the Jews. They therefore

110

permitted its circulation and ordered Hochsträter, on the pain of confinement in a monastery, to pay to Reuchlin 300 gulden as the costs of the trial, and threatened him with excommunication if he disobeyed the order.

Hochsträter then appealed to the pope for an impartial trial, hoping that by a liberal use of the wealth of the Dominicans, since Reuchlin was poor, the latter would suffer defeat. He also sent Reuchlin's "Augenspiegel" to the University of Paris, esteemed the greatest university of the time, urging it to condemn the pamphlet. He appealed also to all of Reuchlin's opponents and all who were zealous for the welfare of the Catholic Church to unite against him. Reuchlin's friends were not idle. Realizing the evil exerted by the Dominicans throughout the world, they, together with a body of Catholics called "Humanists" who sought the reformation of the Church, united under Reuchlin's flag and termed themselves "Reuchlinists." The opposing party adopted the name "Arnoldists." These were the two parties that occupied the public mind before Luther began the Reformation.

Many scholars of young Germany went over to Reuchlin's side, particularly Hermann von Busche, Croates Rinbianes, and the young and sagacious Ulrich von Hutten; also many of the rulers, among whom were Duke Ulrich of Württemberg and all his family, Count Halfenstein of Augsburg, Count von Guernor of Patriz, Welsen, Pirkameier, Neitiger, as well as many Italian priests, notably the General of the Augustinians, Eggodia de Viterba, who loved the Hebrew literature and was at that time engaged in translating the "Zohar." Viterba said in his letter to Reuchlin: "You have saved the books which have spread light all over the world for centuries, and if they were lost, darkness would ensue. And in supporting you, we shield not you but religion; and not the Talmud, but the community of Christ."

The strife spread all over Germany, and there was scarcely a city in which were not to be found either Reuchlinists or Arnoldists--the former, for the preservation of the "Augenspiegel" and the Talmud; the latter, for the destruction of both. The contest became each day more intense, and although the victory was with Reuchlin, he was still anxious as to Hochsträter's appeal to Rome, since the latter had great influence there. His friends therefore advised him to publish all the letters he had received from all parts of Germany and Italy, to convince the pope of the character of the man the Dominicans were persecuting. Among these letters was one from the Emperor Frederick praising Reuchlin in glowing terms and testifying that he was held in honor and respect by the father of the pope, Lorenzo de Medici.

These efforts of Reuchlin and his friends brought about the appointment by the people of Cardinal Gremama, a lover of rabbinical literature and Kabbala, as investigator and judge of the quarrel. The Cardinal summoned Reuchlin and Hochsträter to appear in Rome, and as Reuchlin was very old, he was allowed to send a deputy. Hochsträter, however, appeared in person with all his wealth. This did not, however, disturb Reuchlin, as he had many friends at Rome. Even the Emperor Maximilian interceded for him with the pope. Among his other defenders was the emperor's secretary, Wurke, Duke Ulrich of Württemberg and the Elector of Saxony, Frederick the Wise (later the chief supporter of Luther). Many bishops also defended him, notably those of Strassburg, of Constanz, of Speyer, and numerous other churchmen. Hochsträter spent large sums of money to procure the appointment of Cardinal Bemardine de Santa as assistant to the judge, but, through the influence of the Reuchlinists, Cardinal Pietro Ankenotini de Sant' Isemblia was selected by the pope for this office. The pope's committee forbade any discussion of the matter until the sentence of the judges of Rome was announced. But the Dominicans heeded neither this command nor public opinion, and, in order to influence the pope, they even threatened, should Reuchlin be victor at the trial, to secede from the church and unite with the Hussites of Bohemia. They also, in defiance of the prohibition of discussion, placed hope in the University of Paris, for at that period France and Germany were in conflict in secular matters, it naturally befell that on religious questions also their views were diametrically opposed. So the University of Paris, though in heart and conscience in full accord with Reuchlin, nevertheless, for purely worldly reasons, felt compelled to render an unfavorable opinion of him and of his works, stating that the "Augenspiegel" contained heresy and should be burned, and that its author should be compelled to make full retraction. The Dominicans hastened to published this reply from Paris in a pamphlet entitled "Glocke" (bell), in the name of Pfefferkorn, although for this action Hochsträter was indicted by the Fiscal of the Emperor. The emperor's sister, Kunigunde, again kept Hochsträter from imprisonment. The Dominicans employed every means to delay the trial, so as to increase Reuchlin's expenses, thinking that, since he could not afford the necessary expense attached to it, he would forego trial. Reuchlin's friends represented to the public Hochsträter's evil designs, and at the same time appeared a collection of letters "From the Benighted People." The first volume, written in a satirical style, professed to be from the pen of Krate Rubian of Leipzig, and contained confessions by Dominican monks of their evil deeds since the existence of the Order. These letters were quickly spread throughout the entire west of Europe despite the protests of the Dominicans, which protests, indeed, only furthered their circulation. Hochsträter, fearing lest the trial would end in Reuchlin's favor, demanded that it be given to an international council, since the matter concerned the entire Catholic Church. The pope, who was, as it were, placed between two fires, the German Emperor and rulers, on the one hand, and the King of France and the heir-apparent of Germany (who sided with the Dominicans), on the other, resolved to place it before the Council of the Lateran and all Europe.

Two years passed; the strife had not yet ended, and Reuchlin became sad at heart. He feared that his friends would fall away from him, seeing no immediate prospects of the close of the quarrel; he also feared, as he was advanced in years, lest he should die before its settlement, and the Dominicans win the battle, while his name would become a reproach. These fears were unfounded, as his friends did not weaken in their support of his cause. Finally, on the 2d of July, 1516, the result of the trial was announced at a session of the council, signed by Bishop Gregory Bengiani, as follows: The pamphlet, "Augenspiegel," contained no heresy. The error, in such an assumption, rested with the Paris University, and the other faculties in agree-

ment with it. The Bishop of Malta added that the judge of
the Inquisition, Hochsträter, who considered himself one of the main
pillars of religion, ought to be indicted. Under Bengiani's signature
were written those of the other cardinals, except that of the
Dominican Cardinal, Sylvester Priervis. As the pope himself had not
yet acknowledged or sanctioned the sentence, Hochsträter did not
despair, and, with the aid of his friends, he begged the pope to delay
the execution of the sentence for an indefinite period, hoping to
bring, at a future time, the trial before another council and obtain a
decision in his favor. The pope commanded the parties to terminate
their quarrelings and cease all discussion of the matter, under the
impression that a command from him would put an end to it. He was
mistaken; the strife grew in intensity and spread over Germany. Both
factions were more than ever determined to continue.

When Hochsträter returned from Rome his life was in danger
from the Reuchlinists, and only by the efforts of Reuchlin himself
was bloodshed prevented. The Dominicans lost all favor with the
public. This did not, however, prevent the Dominican, Peter Mayer,
from lecturing in all the great churches against Reuchlin and his
party, and abusing him in the vilest language. Finally, roused to
violence by his words, the Dominicans slew some of the Reuchlinists.
This resulted in a rupture between the pope and the Dominicans.
But when the second volume of "The Benighted" letters appeared,
wherein the Dominicans were painted in the blackest colors, they
begged the pope to shield them from the wrath of the people. This
time he listened to them, and prohibited the circulation of the
pamphlet. This command was unheeded, as the light of knowledge
was beginning to spread over the world, and the satire was read by
many priests and monks of other orders than the Dominicans; and, at
the same time, the Humanists distributed pamphlets and circulars
against the Dominicans.

After no long interval, a second edition of "The Benighted" letters
appeared, to the joy of the Reuchlinists. The Dominican leaders saw
now that there was a rupture in the Catholic Church, and announced
to the pope that the people ridiculed their teachings and would not
obey the doctrines of Catholicism. This time they told the truth.

Hitherto, sufficient credit had not been accorded public opinion by the rulers, although the influence wielded by Luther was almost wholly due to it, and he acknowledged that the controversy between these two great parties had paved the way for the Reformation. After Maximilian's death, the strife became still more intense, and the topics most often heard were those of the Talmud, Reuchlin, Luther, and the Reformation. At the meeting of the electors of Germany, to choose an emperor, they all sanctioned Reuchlin's actions. Ulrich von Hutten persuaded the knight, Franz von Eickingen, to separate himself from the Catholic Church and join Reuchlin and Luther. This knight and his companion, Dalkery, with many other friends of Reuchlin, demanded that Hochsträter pay the sum of 111 gulden to Reuchlin to defray the costs of the trial at Speyer, and also give bonds not to further molest Reuchlin. The Dominicans were fully aware that this command must be obeyed, unlike that of the emperor or the pope, which they would have unhesitatingly disobeyed. They were compelled to pay the above sum, but as the treasury of the government was empty, the sum did not go to Reuchlin, but to the government. Hochsträter was deposed from his post of judge of the Inquisition, and a committee of monks requested the pope to do all in his power to end the strife, and allow Reuchlin to live in peace, since he was a great scholar and a firm believer in Christianity. The Talmud attained new prestige, since henceforth the pope looked upon it with favor, and even persuaded Daniel Bamberg, of Antwerp, a famous printer, to issue a complete edition for the first time in its history. And, so, in the year 1520, the Babylonian Talmud appeared, with all the commentaries, in twelve volumes, and from this all later editions have been copied. Reuchlin in his last years was compelled, like Luther, to leave his home and seek an abiding place where he could live in peace. Later, when Luther sent delegates to the prominent rulers of Germany, the pope was forced to adopt the suggestion of the Dominicans and excommunicate Luther, and at the same time prohibit Reuchlin's works. But both the excommunication and prohibition were publicly burned by Luther on the 10th of December, 1520. From this time on, Luther threw off the chains of the pope, and inaugurated the Reformation. Again, and for the last time, Pfefferkorn appeared with a new pamphlet against Reuchlin, but it received no countenance; on the contrary, he was abused by all factions; and his suggestion to expel the Jews from Frankfort was denounced by all alike. After this event, nothing more was heard of him. As soon as the Reformation was established, Reuchlin was called to take the chair of Hebrew in the University of Tübingen, where be taught many students. He died in 1522, to the great grief of his admirers. Reuchlin was generally credited by the Reformers with being one of the initiators of the Reformation.

Chapter 15
Polemics with Muslims and Frankists

Polemics With Mussulmans And The Disputes With The Frankists

The Jews were not exempt from disputes with scholars of Islam also during the first years of the latter's history, but these disputes differed from those with the Christians in that they did not involve the Jews in calamities. In addition to the oral disputes, many controversial books appeared between the ninth and the sixteenth centuries, among which were the books of Saadiah the Gaon against the Karaites, which the Karaites answered, not with arguments, but with scoffing. A great quantity of books were issued by the Karaites in which they ridiculed the Rabbis, in particular Saadiah the Gaon, who exposed their weaknesses. Like service was performed by the book of Samuel ben Chaphni Hakohen, entitled "To Exalt the Value of Theological Studies," against whom the Karaite Samuel ben Jehudah Eben Agia wrote a pamphlet under the title "Strenuous Denial." R. Jehudah Halevi's "Hakusri" and Maimonides' controversial letters also had for their aim the strengthening of the foundations of the creed.

But the strife raged with the greatest intensity in Spain in the middle of the twelfth century. First appeared the book on "Sepher Habrith" by R. Joseph Kimchi. Following this came controversial works by R. Jacob b. Reuben, R. Moses b. Tikun, and R. Moses b.

Solomon, of Saliri, the title of the latter's book being "A Word of Faith," in which he records disputes with Christians; by R. Jechiel b. Joseph, of Paris, R. Nathan, of Upsala, R. Joseph, and R. Meir b. Simeon, in his book "The Battle of Merit," in which are related his disputes with the Archbishop of Narbonne; and by R. Mordecai b. Tehosaph in his book, "The Strengthener of Faith," written against the Christian, Paul Christianus, who had held many controversies with Ramban and others.

In reply to the book of Abner of Burgos, who adopted the name of Alphonse of Valladolid, and who wrote much that was hostile to Judaism, appeared works by R. Isaac Ebn Palkara, as well as by R. Joseph Shalom, under the title of "A Reply to Alfonso's Writings." How great a degree of tolerance the Jews manifested in this controversy may be seen from what Moses of Narbonne wrote of Abner, his former friend--namely, that he was intelligent and virtuous, but dispairing; unable to endure the calamities heaped upon the Jewish people; not content with the peace to his soul, but seeking also worldly happiness; and, reading in the stars that the Jews destiny was to suffer and bear trials, he fell into the error of thinking that they would never again be strong as a nation, and counselled them as he himself had done, to accept Christianity, not submit to their fate. R. Moses de Torsilla, also wrote a book entitled "Aid to Faith" (1374), consisting of seventeen chapters, in the form of a dialogue between professors of the two religions. In all these books it is declared that the Hagadas of the Talmud are not authoritative but are to be regarded barely as fiction, and as devoid of any sacredness. In Germany also appeared in defense of Judaism the work "Book of Victory" (Sepher Nitzachon), by the excellent writer, R. Lipman of Muelhausen, which appears to have made so deep an impression that the Bishop of Brandenburg, Stephen Batekei, felt it necessary to reply to it.

Lastly may be mentioned the two disputes which took place between the Rabbis and the Frankists in 1756-1757, at the command of Bishops Dembovsky and Micholsky, in Kamenitz, Podolsk and Lemberg, cities of Poland. These terminated the disputes which the Jews were compelled to hold with their opponents in the presence of

the people and dignitaries. They were distinguished by the fact that
the Frankists impeached the authority of the Talmud on the strength
of the Midrash of R. Simeon b. Jochai, termed "Zohar," which they
considered sacred, while they regarded the Talmud as profane. These
disputes were further distinguished by the circumstance that the
founder of the Hasidismus, R. Israel baal Shem Tob, was elected as
the chief disputant to represent the Rabbis, forced to dispute with the
Frankists in Micholsky's presence. The Frankists were an offshoot of
the sect of the false Messiah, Shabattai Zvi, who produced a storm
throughout the whole world in the year 1654. One Jacob Frank, a
Polish Jew, accepted Islamism at Salonica, where he joined the sect of
Shabattai Zvi, who were seeming Mohammedans and were called
Dauma. In 1754 he arrived in Poland and set to work, with the
assistance of two Rabbis, Moses and Nachman, who accompanied
him, to revive the creed of Shabattai Zvi. The followers of Shabattai
Zvi, who still remained in Poland, received him with open arms, and
entered upon an open propagation of the mischievous teachings. The
Jews thereupon informed the ecclesiastical authorities of the country
of their activity, which so alarmed them that they hastened to the
Bishop and asserted their belief in the Trinity, and that they were not
Talmudic Jews, but followers of the Zohar--"Zoharites." They petitioned Bishop Dembovsky of Kamenitz to force the Jews to dispute
with them and thus afford them opportunity to prove that the only
true belief is in one God in three persons, incarnate in the flesh, and
the teaching of the Talmud all vanity, etc., a rehabilitation of all the
old slanderous charges. The Bishop ordered the dispute to begin in
May, 1754; and the Jews, not appearing at the appointed time,
incurred a heavy fine therefor. In June of that year there assembled at
Kamenitz thirty Rabbis, from whom were chosen as disputants R.
Leib Meziboz, R. Bar Jozelovitz, R. Mendel Satanow, and R. Joseph
Kremenetz; and about the same number of Frankists, headed by Leib
Krim of Nadvarna, Soloman Shur of Rahatin and Nachman of
Bushk. The pleading of the Rabbis that in the Zohar and in all the
books of Israel there is no hint of a Trinity, which was purely an
invention of the Frankists themselves, was of no avail, for Dembovsky
decided against the Jews and fined them 5,000 gold guldens, to be

paid to the Frankists, and also directed the Jews to dispute with the latter whenever called upon; one hundred and fifty gold guldens were likewise to be paid by the Jews for the repair of the Christian Cathedral at Kamenitz. All copies of the Talmud were to be burned, although the Jews appealed to the King, August III., against this decree of Dembovsky, claiming that they possessed the right, accorded to them by previous rulers, to print the Talmud; and although they were sustained in this contention by many princes of the kingdom, yet, owing to the political and religious turmoil then existing throughout the kingdom, the king or his minister, could give no heed to the matter, and the Jews were forced to submit to the decree of the bishop. Shortly thereafter, however, Dembovsky died a sudden death (the result of an injury received, it is related, from a fire which consumed the Talmud), and was succeeded by Labinsky, who showed no favor to the Frankists. The Jews, with the help of the government officials and an expenditure of money, effected the expulsion of the Frankists from their residence near Kamenitz, for being neither Jews nor Christians, and they suffered persecutions. They were compelled to shave part of their heads and half of their beard; insults and indignities were heaped upon them, and many fled to Turkey. But even there they found no rest; they were relentlessly persecuted, and Elisha Ratin, one of their leaders, was beaten to death. They therefore betook themselves to the frontiers between Poland and Turkey, in constant peril of their lives from the people of both nations. When their condition became unbearable, they turned again to the king, and begged him to restore to them the freedom granted by Dembovsky. In this they succeeded; the king permitted them in May, 1757, to settle undisturbed in the province of Podalia. And thus they returned to Poland, in poverty and rags. In this state of degradation Frank advised them, in order to better their condition, to embrace Christianity. They therefore, in January, 1758, sent a petition to the Bishop Labinsky by six of their leaders, asking that they be received into the Catholic Church and be granted permission to dispute with the Talmudic Jews, who drink the blood of Christian infants, etc. Labinsky replied that it was not in his power to improve their material condition; their acceptance of Christianity could affect only their spiritual welfare. They again addressed themselves to the king, in May of the same year, but their petition was not answered. Labinsky suddenly resigned his office and Micholsky was chosen his successor. The latter exhibited a great zeal for proselyting, and the Frankists hastened to present their petition to him, requesting permission, before being baptized, to dispute again with the Jews. Perhaps, they urged, they might succeed in convincing the Jews of their great error and madness and in inducing them to accept Christianity too. Micholsky acceded to this request, and ordered the Jewish Rabbis to assemble at Lemberg on a day appointed by him.

At the time set for the dispute there came in sorrow to Lemberg, forty of the chief Rabbis of Poland, at their head Israel Besht of Mezibuz, and chose as disputants three of them--Besht, the Rabbi of the district, Haim Rapoport, and R. Bär Jozelovitz. The disputants for the Frankists were Frank himself, Leib Krim, and Solomon Shur.

The dispute lasted three days, beginning June 23, 1758, and the hopes of the Frankists for a victory were shattered. Though Micholsky and many Polish nobles sided with them, they failed to prove that the Zohar contained anything that favored their religion. The judges, even, utterly disagreed with the distortions to which they subjected the passages of the Zohar and Kabbalistic books. The Jewish Rabbis departed in peace, without being fined, and the petition of their adversaries, that a district in Poland be set apart for their dwelling, was refused, and they were invited to receive baptism. Thus ended favorably for the Jews the last of these peculiar disputes. The Jews made efforts to induce the Frankists to become Christians as soon as possible, that there might in future be no relationship, between them. In this they succeeded, and since that time, between the Frankists, as Christians, and the Jews there has been nothing in common in either religious or secular matters.

Chapter 16
Persecution during the
Seventeenth Century

The Persecutions Of The Seventeenth Century, The Head Of Whom
Was Johann Andreas Eisenmenger.

The victory of Reuchlin, and the establishment of the Reformation by Luther, in the sixteenth century, did not stop the persecution of the Talmud. It was ever renewed by men of rank in the different countries. The most dangerous of them was Johann Andreas Eisenmenger, who spent almost all his lifetime in the destruction of the Talmud and its standard-bearers; and it seems miraculous that he did not succeed.

Eisenmenger was born in 1654, at Manheim. In 1666 he came to Heidelberg where he found grace in the eyes of Prince Carl Ludwig, who was pleased with Eisenmenger's determination to learn the Hebrew language. Prince Carl Ludwig sent him, at his own expense, to travel in different countries to become accomplished in the study of Oriental languages. But when Eisenmenger was about to visit Palestine, the prince died (1680), and he established himself in the City of Amsterdam, where he lived for some time in friendly relations with the Hebrew scholars and with Rabbi David Lida of that city.

At the end of the same year it happened that three Gentiles

circumcised themselves and embraced the Jewish faith. This, according to Eisenmenger's own confession, angered him almost to death. And this occurrence made him determine to write a voluminous book on the "wickedness" of the Talmud, in order (he said) to save Christianity from danger.

He worked hard and successfully for nineteen years; translated into German from 193 different Hebrew books, and a considerable number of pages from various Tracts of the Talmud itself.

This book, which he named "Endecktes Judenthum" (Unveiled Judaism), containing two volumes of more than a thousand pages each, he gave in the year 1700 to the printers of Frankfort-on-the-Main.

The Jews of that city got wind of it, and being afraid that this book would cause a renewal of massacres of Jews, such as took place in the cities of Franken and Bamberg in 1699, where houses and other Jewish property were destroyed by the mob, appealed to Sampson Wertheimer, who was then the banker of Emperor Leopold, that he should point out to the emperor the dangers which such a book would lead to.

Remembering that after the destruction of Jewish property, the mob, in the above-mentioned places, turned to the palaces of the noblemen, the Emperor commanded the Governor of Frankfort to stop the printing of the book, and to conceal all that was printed of the same, until a careful examination of the book by Gentile and Jewish Hebrew scholars would be made.

In spite of the assistance of many prominent men in the German Empire, who petitioned the emperor to release the books, he retained his decision and paid no attention even to the special personal letter from the King of Prussia in behalf of Eisenmenger. When Eisenmenger died in 1704, his books had not yet been redeemed from their captivity; and only in 1711 did Frederick I, King of Prussia, republish the book at his own expense, from a copy which was in the hands of Eisenmenger's heirs, donating all the copies to them. It would take too much space to relate the proceedings of Eisenmenger himself, and those of his heirs against the Jews of Frankfort, and the various decisions of the courts from the time of Leopold to that of the Empress

Maria Theresa. We do not deem it necessary to recount them, since they are in no way related to the subject of the persecution of the Talmud.[1]

We have only to say that in the eleven years since the book was given to the press in Frankfort, until the circulation was permitted in Königsberg, its influence was weakened, so that it did not cause very much harm at that time.

Thereafter, however, many anti-Semites made use of the material gathered in this book, quoting it as being directly from the Talmud without mentioning Eisenmenger; probably because of his notoriety as an enemy of the Jews.

Concerning the book itself, we would refer the reader to Professor Franz Delizeh's book, "Rohling's Talmudjude," sixth edition, 1881, and many other criticisms of Eisenmenger's work by Gentile Hebrew scholars, such as Professor Strack of Berlin and others.

We have refrained from stating our own criticism of the misinterpretation of the quotations from the Talmud, chiefly because we do not deem it necessary to study Eisenmenger's book for criticism. As for the explanation of the Talmud, we do not need to use him as our guide; and also in order to avoid apparent partiality; since we are ourselves the bearers of the Talmud's banner. (See App., No. 16.)

---

1. The details are given in Graetz's ("History of the Jews"), Hamelitz, 1888, by David Kahan.

Chapter 17

Attacks on the Talmud in the Nineteenth Century

The Polemics And The Attacks Upon The Talmud In The Nineteenth Century.

The nineteenth century was the jubilee of the Talmud's 2,000 years since its beginning, and the twelfth century since its conclusion, in which it overcome all attacks directed against it and remained safe, not only bodily but spiritually. This did not prevent the anti-Semites from renewing the persecutions and the accusations of it with increased energy.

Although the accusations were not brought to a public dispute, and to the intervention of the government, still the polemics in books and pamphlets were greatly increased by different persons in different countries. We do not desire to linger on these books, as their discussion would take up too much time and space, still we cannot refrain from mentioning them briefly, as they pertain to the history of the Talmud.

In 1848, A. Büchner, a teacher in Warsaw, printed a book, "Der Talmud in Seine Nichtigkeit," and according to Strack, Jacob Kittseer also printed a volume called "Inhalt des Talmuds und seine Autoritat," etc, both in the German language. The contents of these two books were mainly attacks upon attacks, and accusations upon accusations, rained down upon the Talmud in general and its followers in particular.

At the same time a missionary, McCaul, printed a book in the English language, entitled "The Old Paths," and S. Hoga, an apostate and also a missionary, translated it into Hebrew. The latter edition was distributed gratis and in tens of thousands among the Hebrews. We cannot deny that it was somewhat effective, as it caused many Jews to embrace Christianity.

At about the same time Isaac bär Levinson of Kremenetz, named the Russian Mendelssohn, wrote a book, entitled "Teuda b'Israel," in which he collected all the savings of the Talmud relating to the following topics, (a) that every Jew is obliged to learn the language of his country; (b) to engage in scientific pursuits; (c) that he must learn some trade and occupy himself, if possible, with agriculture, and (d) that be must be patriotic to his country, and must respect the laws of his country just as much as the laws of the "Torah," etc., etc. This book was so excellent that the eye of Nicholas I., Emperor of Russia, was attracted to it and he assisted Levinson both morally and financially. Finally he presented him with 3,000 roubles to enable him to publish his later works, "Zerubbabel," in which he proved the falsehood of the misinterpretations of McCaul in every respect, "Beth Jehuda," and "Efes Damin" (no blood), written against the blood accusation. His books were so effective that as a result McCaul's books were almost ignored.

The later affair in Alexander II.'s reign, however, we intend to elaborate on more fully, as at that time it created a great stir in Russia.

In 1876 a Roman Catholic priest, Lyotostansky by name, who embraced Greek Catholicism, published a book in the Russian language which he entitled, "Upotreblayut li Jewreay christansky Krov?" (Do the Jews need Christian blood for religious purposes?)

This book, which contains about 300 pages, was dedicated to Alexander III., then Crown Prince of Russia. He accepted the dedication with thanks to the author.

Lyotostansky, desiring to have the thanks of the Crown Prince publicly made known, printed posters announcing the Crown

Prince's thanks for the dedication, and set them up everywhere, even on the railroad cars.

The dailies and periodicals in Russia also announced the works favorably owing to the fact that the book found favor in the eyes of his highness, the Crown Prince. The contents of the book are chiefly attacks upon the Talmud, accusing it of being the source of all the bad customs of the Jews, etc.

A meeting of the prominent Jews was then called and resolutions were passed as follows:

First, that Lyotostansky's attacks upon the Talmud itself should be silently ignored, for a debate on this subject in Russia would do the Jews more harm than good.

Second, to republish and distribute the voluminous book of Prof. Chwolson, who was a Christian, which defends the Talmud in general, and conclusively proves, both theoretically and practically, that the blood accusation is a trumped-up affair, and that all investigations in many countries have shown that no instance occurred in which the Jews used Christian blood.

Third, to republish the "Ukase" (decree) of Nicholas I., which declared that no blood accusation for religious purposes should be directed against the Jews as a people, and that if it should happen that a Jew be accused of murdering a Christian, he should be tried as an individual merely.

As is well known, there are people who endeavor to benefit themselves from all current calamities, and to announce themselves as leaders without considering that from such actions the calamity or affliction may become still greater.

At that time there were two such men, one in Russia and one in Austria, who desiring to make themselves popular, endeavored to place themselves in the front ranks of the defenders of Judaism for their own benefit.

In Russia there was Alexander Zederbaum, publisher of the periodical "Hamelitz" in St. Petersburg, a man of little knowledge, and who was never fitted for a public debate. He challenged Lyotostansky to a public debate, which, however, the latter declined to accept.

The real leaders of Israel, like the well known S. I. Fünn of Wilna and Perez Smolensky, editor of the "Hashachar" in Vienna, and others, were angry because of Zederbaum's challenge, believing that such a challenge had caused an extremely unfavorable impression upon the Russian people, especially as the newspapers declared that Lyotostansky's declination was due to the fact that the alleged leader of the Russian Jews was an ignoramus.

The very learned Lazar Zweifel, teacher of the Rabbinical Seminary in Zhitomir, who, besides publishing a great book in Hebrew, entitled "The Defender," against Lyotostansky's book, appealed in our periodical "Hakol," Vol. I. No's 27 to 31, to his co-religionists in Russia that they should appoint a committee to petition the Czar, Alexander II., to forbid all polemics about the blood accusation in newspapers, books or pamphlets, for such incitations always do harm to the government itself.

However, Zweifel's appeal was a voice in the desert, as the attempts upon the life of the Czar, in which, to our sorrow, some of our race took part at that time, made it impossible to bother the Czar with such petitions.

We may say, however, that even in this case the Talmud itself was saved, and the government did not stop the publication and circulation of it in Russia and even the study of it in the Jewish schools and institutions. Even in the curriculums of the institutes for Hebrew teachers, established by the government, some tracts of the Talmud were inserted.

Alas, we cannot say that the blood accusation by Lyotostansky had no effect; as in 1882, there were massacres in many cities where Jews dwelt. Although these were secretly instigated by the government itself from a political standpoint, the provoking of the mob was on the basis of the blood accusation.[1]

---

1. In all probability the discussion in this chapter will seem very brief and almost inadequate, but the reason for this is that most of the details of this chapter are related at length in our weekly "Hakol" of 1877. Then, again, the entire matter is not so interesting or so important to warrant giving it more space here. Of far more interest is the works of Professor Rohlings and their results to which we shall give

considerable space in our next chapter, especially as we ourselves were greatly taken up with this affair and were compelled by the circumstances to write four books bout this affair, three in Hebrew and one in German.

Chapter 18
The Affair of Rohling-Bloch

The Affair Of Rohling-Bloch.

D r. August Rohling, professor in Prague, wrote a pamphlet, the "Talmudjude," sixth edition, 1877, in the German language, the previous editions of which were translated into many languages, in which he painted the Talmud itself and all past Talmudical laws in very black colors. The material in all Rohling's writings (which are named in the previously mentioned introduction of Strack) were taken from Eisenmenger, and from other men hired by him, as will be seen further on. Although the above pamphlet was received with great joy by the enemies of the Jews, who quoted him as a great authority, nevertheless, it would have been nothing more than a mere piece of literary work which could create no harm to the Jews had not something unusual occurred which put a different aspect to the affair.

Joseph Samuel Bloch who was at that time a Rabbi in a small town of "Florisdorf," and who was anxious to get a name for himself, considered all Rohling's work as a means of attaining his desire. He understood that if he should challenge Rohling to a debate and should accuse him of perjury and falsehood, and thus compel Rohling to sue him for libel and insult, this would give him a great name and the Jewish congregations of Austria, and especially of Vienna, would be compelled to defend Bloch with all their power, for the case would not be Bloch *vs.* Rohling, but the Talmud *vs.* Rohling.

Notwithstanding that at this time the Israelite congregation of Vienna was full of great men and scholars like the famous Dr. Jellinek, Chief Rabbi Güdemann, etc., etc., who deemed it better to pay no attention at all to Rohling's work, considering it as a mere literary piece of work, and the criticism of which they thought better to leave to Gentile Hebrew scholars such as Delitzsch, Strack, etc., who had already criticized Rohlings works. Bloch wrote an article in a weekly paper attacking Rohling most furiously and reviling him terribly with every possible epithet, including the charge of perjury.

Bloch's desire was then realized, for Rohling not being able to remain silent, secured the services of the very great lawyer, Robert Pattai, M.P., and brought suit against Bloch for libel.

The Israelite congregation of Vienna, although they were very much incensed at Bloch for his deed, nevertheless felt themselves compelled to secure a lawyer of equal ability to Pattai for the defense of Bloch, the result of which will be seen further on.

Circumstances helped Rohling to find an apostate Jew named Ahron Briman, pseudonym Dr. Justus, who wrote a book for him named, "Judenspiegel," composed of 100 passages alleged to be found in the Jewish code, "Schulchan Aruch," according to the ordinances of the Talmud against Christianity, and asserted that the whole Talmud consists of such passages.

This book naturally created a tremendously unfavorable impression upon the whole Christian world, and several papers that were anti-Semitically inclined announced the *contents* of the book. One of these papers was "Die Merkur," in the City of Munster, which quoted many passages of the book and at the same time inserting a glaring editorial against the Jews. The District Attorney finding this article to be an incitation against a race, brought suit against the editor of the paper. This trial occurred December, 1883, and in order that the reader may have some idea of the proceedings, we translate in our Appendix some pages of our German work, "Der Schulchan Aruch und seine Beziehungen zu den Juden und Nicht juden." (See Appendix, No. 20.)

To illustrate who the person Ahron Briman the assistant of Rohling was, we have only to translate a few lines written by us about him in our "Hakol," No. 191, page 117, March 19, 1885:[1] "Anti-Semitism was stricken very hard this year. All their leaders are taken one by one to the prison, and they will have to give an account for their deeds to the judges. With the imprisonment of Briman, Rohling's sources were revealed and annulled, as his right hand, Briman, or Dr. Brimanus, or Justus, all of which names are identical, is now behind the bars, and the newspapers are now recounting his sins one by one.

We, however, say that he and all his literature are not worthy of such an honor. There is no doctor, nor learned man, no distinguished being, no Satan, but a simple, ordinary swindler, who endeavors by everything that comes to his hand to deceive the people. He (according to his biography which is published in the dailies of this week) has made a study of the Talmud and the Schulchan Aruch only that they might serve as his business schemes. He was a student in the college of Hildesheimer, where it was easy to imbibe sanctifica-tion and really become sanctified in the city of Hague. To be still more purified he washed himself in the holy waters of Protestantism. Seeing, however, that this act would not bring him much fruit, for to be a "Pfarrer" (minister) one must labor diligently, and this he would not do, he set all this deed aside at one stroke and swerved over to the Catholic faith.

And then he followed his nature to catch in his net some young girls, who had confidence in him, and going further in this way the attention of the police was called to this, who put a stop to him.

For whom then such a fuss? We are neither a prophet nor the son of a prophet, but nevertheless we recognized his character from his so-called literature even as far back as 1883. As the following are our words in our pamphlet "Kritischer Ueberblick uber den Judenspiegel-prozess in Munster," December, 1884, page 8, footnote 11, (when we were not aware who the author was): "If such would be written by a Jew he would be named criminal, deceiver, misanthrope, etc." True,

132

that when we wrote this, we did not know that he was a Jew, and now we see that he was. For this, however, we have only to be grateful to him because he left the Jewish fight before he wrote his hateful "Judenspiegel," and also before he gave his miserable material to Rohling. This, because the anti-Semites can. no longer blame the Jews on account of this person as they brought him over to become their ally.

But what became of the suit of Rohling against Bloch? We have to give the full credit to Dr. Kopp who forced Rohling to withdraw his complaint seeing that according to the testimony of his co-religionist scholars he could not win his case. And this may be seen from the book which Kopp has published in Leipzig, 1886, second edition. We, however, deem it necessary to give the details of this book, in order to defend the Talmud, as this will throw light upon all past and present accusations against the Talmud. As we have done this in our Hebrew monthly "Morgenblitze," Vienna, 1886, we have only to translate here a part of our review to the book of Kopp named "Zur Judenfrage nach den Akten des Prozesses Rohling-Bloch von Dr. Joseph Kopp Hofgerichtsadovkat Zu Wien," Leipzig, 1886:

"Many books are lying before us for review or for announcement. However, the book named above is unique in every respect. It cannot be criticised either way, and the same is true of the author of this book as he himself does not give his own opinion concerning the subject matter of the book. Nevertheless, we may fully say that it is a scientific book in every respect.

"The author of this book is a Gentile, a prominent member of the bar in Vienna, and, according to his own testimony, he knows neither the Hebrew language nor the talmudic and post-talmudic literature at all. Notwithstanding this, the book, as a whole, sanctifies the Talmud and all post-talmudical literature.

It can not be taken as a defender of the Talmud because of arguments, as the whole book contains merely facts which can never be denied and which prove clearly that the Talmud and its bannerbearers are clear of every accusation and of every suspicion concerning the love of man, be he who he may, even according to the present laws and established etiquette."

The above facts were not given by the author himself, but by two well-known Gentile Hebrew scholars, upon whom the Supreme Court of Vienna threw the burden of translating four hundred passages and quotations. These the Jew-haters have used as a sample of the wretchedness of the Jewish literature. The chief aim of the Jew-haters was to belittle the Talmud, which is the pillar of the Jewish race.

The author of this work, whom the Israelite congregation of Vienna choose to defend Bloch in the case of Rohling-Bloch, has done his work well. He gathered all the quotations quoted by Rohling in his writings from both the Talmud itself as well as from post-talmudical literature, those which were written in the Hebrew language and also in other languages, by converted Jews who reached then the dignity of Catholic priests. All these quotations he divided into two groups, (*a*) the quotations in Hebrew he brought before the Supreme Court, who appointed Gentile Hebrew scholars to translate them correctly under oath, into the German language; (*b*) the quotations in the living languages he examined himself. However, when he found a quotation in another language besides German he submitted it to the sworn interpreter of the Supreme Court for translation. Then, when both the translations of the quotations by the Jew-haters and the translations of the same by those who were appointed by the Court appeared before the court, it was revealed that the alleged quotations of Rohling were not quotations of the Talmud at all, but merely falsehoods. And thus was it proved that every line written by Rohling in his "Talmudjude," "Antichrist and Das Ende der Welt," "The Catechism des 19 Jahrhundert fur Juden und Protestanten" (in which he praises the Spanish Inquisition, declaring it holy to the Lord and to the Catholic Church), "Das Salomonische Spruchbuch," "Meine Antworten an die Rabbiner," "Die Polemik und die Menschenopfer des Rabbinismus," and also in his letter to Ghetza Anhadi of June 19, 1883, were all fabrications which never existed since the creation of the world.

"If such a falsehood would not be revealed by the learned Christians under oath it would be impossible to believe that a man whose dignity came from a professorship of a university should act so. The contents of this book are as follows: All quotations which were translated by the experts as well as those which Rohling himself falsely quoted,[2] Dr. Kopp arranged them thus, preface, instruction, the story proceeding the trial, the proceedings of the trial, the conclusion derived from the true testimony which was obtained from non-Jews; *i.e.*, the Bishop of Leon Agobardus, Paul Medriki, Rabbi Maldava, Rabbi Mendel, August Fabius, Gerhard Tickson, Franz Delitzsch and August Wunsche.

"After sub-dividing the answers of the above scholars in two parts, (*a*) those which are mentioned in the Talmud, etc., in general, and (*b*) where it speaks of the subjects in particular, and this he again sub-divided into nine groups; *i.e.*, (1) about injuring of Gentile property, (2) harming their lives, (3) partiality in cases where Christians come before Jewish judges, (4) the application of animals' and beasts' names to Christians by Jews, (5) about the oath of the Jews, (6) about Jewish witnesses, (7) the Jews against the Christians in the laws of slaughtering cattle, (8) about the flattering and deceiving practised by Jews: divided into two paragraphs, (*a*) the non-responsibility of the Jews (see Appendix No. 19), (*b*) about the infallibility of the Rabbis concerning the blood accusation, and (9) the conclusion of the author himself. All these comprise 196 royal octavo pages.

"It is self-evident that such a book is above criticism, for, as we said before, the book contains only facts, viz: (1) the translations under oath of the well-known Christian scholars, and (2) the falsehood of Rohling's quotations translated into German when compared with the text, and this is all the more evident when it is known that Rohling, after seeing all these facts, not only withdrew his complaint but pardoned even the most rigorous accusation of perjury which Bloch accused him of in the past, saying that he was always ready to swear falsely at any time if only it would cause harm to the Jews."

---

1. At the time he was imprisoned for many crimes and the dailies wrote continuously about this in long articles.
2. The author Kopp points out also many quotations quoted by Rohling from books which never existed.

Chapter 19
Exilarchs, Talmud at the Stake and Its Development at the Present Time

Since the colleges were open in Palestine and Babylon, after the destruction of the Temple, there were two kinds of rulers: the Palestinian were called princes (Nassies), and the Babylonian were called Exilarchs (Rashee Hagula). The former are well known to the students, as every one of them is mentioned in the Talmud, and their biographical sketches are written in many books by modern historians, also in our historical and literary introduction to our new edition.

The Exilarchs, however, who are seldom mentioned in the Talmud, are almost forgotten by the historians. Notwithstanding that the duration of their reign is about 450 years, no arrangement of their names and times is to be found in their history.

It is true that some of their names are mentioned in Seder Ualam Zuta," "Machzor Witree" and "Yuchssin," but it is so confused that no order can be found out.

We have to be grateful to the learned Abraham Krochmal, who first took up this matter, and wrote an excellent long article of seventy-three pages in his "Scholein zum babylonischen Talmud."

His suggestions, however, though of a great genius, are scholastical and were criticised by many in periodicals and pamphlets. Finally Felix Lazarus, in the "Jahrbücher" of N. Brill, issued a separate pamphlet about this subject, the result of which the reader will find in a list further on.

And as many of the Exilarchs were the heads of the colleges in Sura, Pumbeditha and Nehardea and took a great part in the development of the Talmud, they must not be omitted from the History of the Talmud.

LIST OF EXILARCHS.[1]

- Nahum Johanan Shepot - 140-170
- Huna I - 170-210
- Uqba I - 210-240
- Huna H., his son - 240-260
- Nathan I. b'Huna - 260-270
- Nehemiah I - 270-313
- Mar Uqba II - 313-337
- Huna III., his brother - 337-350
- Aba Mari, his son - 350-370
- Nathan II - 370-400
- Chanan, son of Aba Mari. - 400-415
- Huna IV - 415-442
- Mar Zutra I., son of Chanan - 442-455
- Chanan II - 455-460
- Huna V., son of Zutra - 465-475
- Huna VI., son of Chanan - 484-508
- Mar Zutra II. (Achunai) - 508-520
- Huna Mar Chanan - 520-560
- Kafnai - 560-580
- Chanini - 580-590
- Bostanai - -660

With the conclusion of the first volume of this work at the beginning of the twentieth century, we would invite the reader to take only a glance over the past of the Talmud, in which he will see that in almost every century and place of the different countries in Europe, the Talmud was condemned to the stake. By a glance over the present time, however, he will see that not only was the Talmud not destroyed, but was so saved that not even a single letter of it is missing; and now it is flourishing to such a degree as cannot be found in its past history, as will be seen further on.

The details of all the persecutions of the Talmud were given in the preceding chapters. Here we give a list of the places and dates in which it was at the stake, as well as the names of the persecutors.

THE TALMUD AT THE STAKE.

Time. - Place. - Persecutor.

1244 - Paris - King Louis IX

1244 - Rome - Innocent IV.

1248 - Paris - Cardinal Legate Odo

1299 - Paris - Philip the Fair

1309 - Paris - Philip the Fair

1319 - Toulouse – Lous

1322.--Burned in Rome by order of Pope John XXII., and accompanied by robbery and murder of the Jews by the mob.

1553.--Rome: Pope Julius III.--Similar burnings by the same order took place in *Barcelona, Venice, Romagna, Urbino* and *Pesaro*.

Here three wagons full of books were burned; but first they were carried through the streets of the city, while royal officers proclaimed publicly that their condemnation was due to the insults to Christianity which they contained.

1554.--Burned by hundreds and thousands in *Ancona, Ferrara, Mantua, Padua, Candia* and *Ravenna*.

1558.--Rome: Cardinal Ghislieri.

1559.--Rome: Sextus Sinensis.

1557.--Poland: Talmud burned because of the charge made against the Jews that they used the blood of Christian children in their ceremonies. This occurred during the Frankist disturbances.

Such was the past of the Talmud which we hope will never be repeated. Now a glance at the end of the last century and the beginning of this one.

The colleges for the study of the Talmud are increasing almost in every place where Israel dwells, especially in this country where millions are gathered for the funds of the two great colleges, the Hebrew Union College of Cincinnati and the Jewish Theological Seminary of America in New York, in which the chief study is the Talmud and its post-talmudical literature. The heads of these colleges are of the most learned scholars of their time, who are very careful in selecting the professors and instructors for these institutions of learning. We were honored to be present at some lectures which the late great Talmudist, Professor Mielziner, delivered before the senior class in Cincinnati, from which we derived great pleasure and, we may also say that in some instances they were to a degree instructive to us in our task of translating the Talmud.

What concerns the theological seminary in our own city, in which we were not permitted (see App. No. 20) to hear the lectures on the Talmud, we are also in the full belief that it will do much for the study and development of the Talmud in this and in future generations. We use the statement of the Talmud, "One may be certain that a master will not leave out from his hand a thing imperfect," and as the dean of this faculty is not only a learned man but also an experienced teacher, there is great hope that he will do all in his power to select instructors and perfect lecturers for this institution.

There are also in our city houses of learning (Jeshibath) for the study of the Talmud in the lower East Side, where many young men are studying the Talmud every day.

We are also glad to notice that among Gentiles the study of the Talmud is more or less spreading, as we have the experience that a great number of Gentiles and almost all the theological seminaries and public libraries subscribed to the Talmud, and also many queries concerning it frequently came to us from Gentiles. This all shows that the study of the Talmud among Gentiles is not very rare.

The Jewish Encyclopædia (see App. 21) which is in progress now is also a great help to the study and development of the Talmud, as all the treatises of the Talmud are and will be separately named, with many particulars which will cause many readers to study the Talmud itself.

———————————————————

1. We are unable to give their biographical sketches in a clear way, as in many instances we agree with Krochmal, whose arrangement is much different from Lazarus's list and the discussion would take up too much space, which we cannot spare. We have only to say that many of the Exilarchs were only holding their offices, but were not so learned as to take part in the colleges. They were appointed by inheritance and according to the excellence of their morality. All of them were descendants of David's kingdom, direct from Solomon. The Princes of Palestine, who were also descendants of the same kingdom, were only from their mother's side descended from Shepetiah b' Abital.

Appendix A

No. 1. In the history of the "Oral Law," Part I., by I. H. Weiss, the reader will find an account of the deeds of the Samaritans in detail, though only a few instances are dealt with.

No. 2. We may refer the reader to the book, "Maamar Haishuth," by Holdheim, Berlin, who explains the belief of the Sadducees, and their opposition to the Pharisees.

No. 3. We agree with those who say that the tearing of the skin at the performance of circumcision was discovered since the Israelites had begun to undo circumcision; at the time when the theatres were opened by Nero, and the Jews who had to go naked there to wrestle with the beasts, were ashamed to be distinguished by this peculiarity. For this purpose the tearing of the skin was devised. (See Tract Sabbath, p. 307, in the Mishna: "One who was circumcised without having had the skin torn open is considered uncircumcised.") To this there is neither any source in the Scriptures nor any tradition mentioned in the Gemara. Some scholars don't agree with us. (See the letter of A. Bernstein in Tract Roshhoshonah, in the first edition). We, however, base our opinion on the fact that we doubt whether Antiochus Epiphanes would have prohibited a circumcision, customary then among the neighboring nations; and therefore it seems to us that he prohibited only the tearing of the skin which had been ordained by the Pharisees.

No. 4. See our brief introduction in Tract Sabbath. Our opinion is that some written Mishnayoth had been in existence long before. Also *Jellinek's Kuntres Haklalim*, Note 4, for the opinion of the French and Spanish scholars about it. Also I. H. Weiss and our "Hakol," Vol. VI., p. 11.

The London Athenæum, VI., 808, has cited our statement in the general brief introduction, p. 15: "Most of the Mishnayoth date from a very early period, and originated with the students of the Jewish Academies which existed since the days of Jehoshaphat, King of Judah [2 Chron. xxii., 9]: 'And they thought in Judah, and with them was the book of the law of the Lord, and they moved about through all the cities of Judah and taught the people,'" as ridiculous. This, however, does not terrify us, as notes of commentaries on the text of the Scriptures, the whole or in part, have been found in the hands of students from the time colleges had, been founded; and this opinion of ours has met with approval from many contemporary scholars.

No. 5. See our "Hakol," Vol. VI., in which we state that the Gentiles who desired to embrace Judaism, asking Hillel to convert them, were men of rank, for a common man would not dare to make such a stipulation as to be a high priest in Israel.

No. 6. The belief in the divinity of Jesus became acute at a much, later period, when the heathens accepted this fight according to all modem scholars.[1]

No. 7. (See App. No. 4.) We shall also come to this matter in our later notes.

No. 8. In our translation we have added the Tract Ebel Rabbathi, or Sema'Hoth, as the law of mourning was taken from this, tract. We have, therefore, added it to the tract "Minor Festivals," which also treats of mourning on the festival days. What concerns the beginning of "Section of Seeds" with the tract "Benedictions,", see I. H. Weiss for another reason which does not seem probable, to us.

The names of all the treatises of the tracts of each section, and, of their chapters in detail, the reader will find in books written, for this purpose by Strack, Mielziner, and also in the encyclopædias, especially in the Jewish Encyclopædia.[2] We deem it not necessary to name them here as we give at the end of Vol II. the synopsis of each tract, translated and published up to date.

No. 9. Details will be given in the second volume of this book in the introduction to our new edition.

No. 10. In our book mentioned, we also show additions made by the opponents of the Talmud for the purpose of degrading it. For examples, see Vol. II., Part III.[3]

No. 11. We shall come to this matter in the second volume of this book, in the chapter devoted to the Ethics of the Talmud.

No. 12. Almost all ritual poets composed after the Talmudic Hagada. Sometimes comments will be found, by a critical eye, there on the Hagada or even Halakha, as the ritual poems relating to Passover, contain almost all the laws of Passover.

No. 13. His decree was only for the German, French and Polish Jews, and extended only until the end of the five thousandth years after creation. However, the above-named Jews accepted his decree as extending indefinitely. In Syria and in Palestine, however, where his decree was not accepted, some of the Portuguese Jews, known there as Franks, marry two wives even at the present time in such cases when the first wife is barren.

No. 14. See "Measseph Nidachim," Vol. X., by A. E. Harkavy, where he proves that in Spain had existed houses of learning from ancient times and that the Gaonim of Babylonia had relations with them; and in many places they tried to follow their customs. (See there).

No. 15. As to what were these places, and who the disputants, whether only Messianists or also Persians and idolaters, the opinions of modern scholars differ. To us it seems that the Messianists possessed only the house of Abidan, and the Persians and Magians that of Nitzraphi. Rabh refused absolutely to dispute with the first, but was forced to do so with the latter, perhaps by his proximity to the government. Of the house of Abiani scholars say it was composed of Messianists.

No. 16. As his interpretation of the text, "it shall be a sign unto thee upon thy hand, and for a memorial between thy eyes," that it is a figure of speech, it shall be memored as if written on thy hand, as, "set me as a seal upon thy breast," [Song of Solomon, vii. 6]: "between thy eyes," as an ornament which it is customary to put on the brow, and there is no mention of the use of Phylacteriens in his whole commentary, though the Talmud based the custom of Phylacteriens only on these texts. We have spoken already of this in our work on Phylacteriens.

No. 17. In the excellent work, "Kritische Geschichte der Talmud Übersetzungen," by Dr. Erich Bischof, we read, p. 67: Trotzdem heute der frühr überschätzte Eisenmenger allzusehr unterschätzt wird, weil er noch nicht den historisch--Kritischen Blick unserer Tage besass lässt sich doch gegen seine--Übersetzunger der genanten[4] Stellen nichts Erhebliches mit Fug einwenden sie sind vielmehr fast stets richtig, etc.

We may say that though we respect very much the above-mentioned work as one whose opinions in general are correct, we would like to call the attention of the learned author to the following facts:

(*a*) Notwithstanding the fact that in a period of eight centuries over a thousand persons of varying opinions were engaged in the compiling of the Talmud, in the edition lying before us there is not to be found any designation as to time, and in many places, even the author of that saying is not mentioned, Eisenmenger gives the sentence, calling it literal translation, as if it were said by one person at a given time. It is self-evident, however, that such literal translation changes the meaning entirely.

(*b*) An opinion of an individual concerning Gentiles, he quotes it in the name of the Talmud, in spite that this saying is immediately opposed by the Gemara.

(*c*) He erred even in the literal translation, *e.g.*, "*Margela be Pume de Abye*," this paragraph is translated by us in third part of Vol. II. of this book. He translates, "A pearl was in the mouth of A."; while the literal translation of the word Margela is, "It was used," *i.e.*, Abye "used" to repeat this saying very often. At another place he asks why should the "Talmud" be called great, while the word "Talmud" in that sentence means "teaching," *i.e.*, the teaching is greater than action; for teaching causes action. And we wonder how Dr. Bischoff can say of such, "it is rather correct."

No. 18. Concerning the pamphlets and books against the Talmud, written by apostate Jews, see Strack, page 95.

No. 19. Rohling declares that the Rabbis had concluded that all the sins of a Jew, be it against heaven or against man, are forgiven him if he only remains a Jew. He also declares that every Rabbi considers himself infallible concerning the laws of non-Jewish blood.

The conclusion o our review of this book seems to us of interest to the reader, and therefore we translate it here: "The Lord hath made all things for himself: yea, even the wicked for the day of evil" [Proverbs, xvi. 4]. If we will look with an open eye into the history of Israel, we shall find that at all times, when characterless men arose to accuse and oppress Jews because of jealousy or animosity (except in cases where a man fights for his livelihood, which is natural), their opponents who fought them openly were equal to them in every respect. As the poet says, "Also unto thee, O Lord belongeth mercy for thou renderest to every man according to his *deeds*" [Ps. lxiv. 131. If these words should be explained according to their literal meaning the question would arise why *mercy* if to every one is rendered according to his deeds. Therefore it is to be explained thus: "mercy belongeth to thee that thou repayest the wicked man for his evil deeds by one who is equal in *deeds* to him."

Similarly did it happen in the time of the judges when Sisera oppressed the Jews terribly, providence transferred him to a prostitute, Jael, who rebelled against her husband and also against her lover (Sisera), who thought to be saved, being between her knees, and was slain by her [Judges, v. 27].

Haman, the Agagi whom Harbonah had assisted in creating the gallows to hang Mordecai, was transferred to Harbonah's hands and was hanged by him who was equally devoid of character. Hadrian who decreed that the Jews should not circumcise their children under the penalty of capital punishment, and Simon b. 'Yohaie who was going to Rome to petition the Caesar to abolish this decree, the miracle occurred through Ben Tmalion (a devil). Notwithstanding that Simon wept saying, "To the servant of my grandfather (Hagar), when she was in need, an angel appeared three times [Genesis, xvi. 7-12], and to me who am troubled with the needs of all Israel, an angel did not appear, even one time, but only a devil" [Me-ila, 17, b], it did not help him, for who of the angels would lower himself to appear before such a low person who desires to oppress humanity without any reason but merely on account of their religion.

In reality it is revealed before Him, who said a Word and the World was created, that a man of delicate nature would dislike to come in contact with men of doubtful character, and would not fight with a dirty man; as there is a rule that he who fights bodily with a dirty man must become dirty himself. Therefore the Lord has created the wicked and characterless men for the purposes of such an evil day that he should conquer his opponent, who is equal to him in every respect.

Our sages seem to be aware of this, as we find that when a dispute was needed on subjects concerning Israel, they selected a common man (see Sanhedrin, page 270), and similarly to this, we have seen last year when the measure of the renowned Stoecker's deeds were full, his comrade, Greenberg, who exchanged his needle for a scribe's pen, and when driven out from the Socialists in Berlin, became a comrade of Stoecker, and finally his secretary, and later sold him with all his writings for ten German *thalers*, so that it became known who the Preacher of the Royal Court was, and a case identical to that of Rohling-Bloch, that he (Rohling) fell into the hands of a equally characterless man, Bloch,[5] whom God had created for this dark day, as said above that from all the great Jewish men of Vienna, not one of them humiliated himself to enter into a fight with Rohling. However, if there is need for a miracle to occur, it matters little from whence it comes, and after all, we have to praise Bloch that he was the cause for the appearance of such a book, just as the prophetess Deborah praised the prostitute *Jael* [judges, v. .24]: "Blessed shall she be of the women of the *tent*."

No. 20. The following is a translation of a few pages of the beginning of our pamphlet, "Der Schulchan Aruch und seine Beziehungen zu den Juden und Nichtjuden." "On the 10th of December, 1883, a trial came before the 'Landesgerichte,' at Münster, which created a great commotion in all Germany" . . . viz., "one of the anti-Semites, named Dr. Justus, published a pamphlet in Paderborn under the name 'Judenspiegel' containing 100 law paragraphs of the 'Schulchan Aruch,' concerning the treatment of 'Akum,' abbreviation of three words, 'Obde Kochabim Umazoleth,' literally, 'worshipper of stars and planets.' However, the author, Justus, put the word 'Christians' instead of 'Akum' in every place in the text. The editor of 'The Merkin' in Münster quoted many passages of this pamphlet with a glaring editorial, and the district-attorney, who considered such as an incitation against a race, made him responsible for this. The 'Landesgerichte' appointed two experts, one a Jew, Dr. Treu, a Hebrew teacher in the 'royal gymnasium,' and a Gentile, Dr. Ecker, an instructor in Semitic languages."[6]

Dr. Ecker Privatdocent at the royal academy of this place declares, that having devoted the last ten years exclusively to the study of Semitica, he is in a position to express an opinion. He then goes on to say:

"In the first place, I feel it my duty to point out that I can in no way agree with the conclusions arrived at by my esteemed colleague, Treu, and that concerning the essential point I entertain a conviction the very opposite of his. Three questions are here concerned which I am to answer:

(1) Is the 'Schulchan Aruch' vested with legal sanction?

(2) Does the word 'Akum' mean also Christians?

(3) Are the quotations of Dr. Justus in agreement with the original text."

As his answer to the first question treats about the "Schulchan Aruch" only, and also whether the Jews at *that* time are to be named Schulchan Aruch Jews or Talmud Jews, we omit it as it does not belong to the purpose of our history. We begin therefore with the second point.

"As to the second point, whether the word Akum comprises also

Christians, I do not see how this can be denied. It is my firm conviction that Akum is nothing less nor more than non-Jews. And I believe that the Christians too belong to this class. Thus a law book that has appeared in the middle of the sixteenth century in *Krakau* should contain laws regulating the behavior of Jews (1) towards Jews, (2) toward planet-worshippers who live hundreds of miles away? This is indeed ridiculous. Gentlemen, allow me to draw a comparison. Suppose, here in Munster, a Jew would conceive a notion to sit down and write a new law book in which there are but two classes of laws, how the Jews should behave toward Jews and toward--well, for my part let him call them what be may, it means after all non-Jews; suppose further that the prescribed behavior toward non-Jews is very rude and inhuman, and the author is held responsible for so treating the Christians, the learned Jew says: Ye Christians of Munster are not at all included in the class of non-Jews, which class has reference to the--Hottentots!

"Now, gentlemen, it is just as ridiculous to assert that in the sixteenth century there have appeared laws in Krakau regulating the behavior of Jews toward planet worshippers, and the Christians are nowhere mentioned. And, gentlemen, since this point has received no emphasis on the part of my esteemed colleague, it is important to call attention to it! If Akum does not comprise Christians, then laws against Christians are wholly missing. In the 'Shulchan Aruch' there are mentioned only Jews and Akum; we Christians are surely not Jews, hence we are *beyond all doubt confused in the term Akum.*

"I repeat once more, Akum is congruent with non-Jews. The Rabbis them. selves prove this. I have in my possession a recent Wilna edition of the 'Shulchan Aruch,' in which not infrequently the word Akum of the older editions is substituted by *Eno Ichudi, i.e.* non-Jew. The fear for the censor prompted many to an alteration, but in this case it has rather been an unhappy one, since the publishers themselves say that Akum is synonymous with non-Jew."

We are in a position to meet also this issue of the Herr Expert. The term non-Jews is by no means generic for the term Christian. In order to fully perceive the truth of this statement, it remains for the learned doctor to merely cross the channel over to England. This great world dominating nation consists in its overwhelming majority of pious and strict Christians. They sacrifice millions for the propagation of the Christian creed, and the evangelic writings all over the world. However, they call themselves with self-gratification, "The genuine Jews, sons of *The New Union.*" They pretend to be the descendants of the enigmatically vanished ten tribes of Israel, and to still be Jews, body and soul. Very often you find on their worship places and educational institutions inscriptions in both English and Hebrew. Here you read in strikingly large letters: *"Chapel of the Jews-Christians," "Jewish-Nazaric School."* In the cosmopolis London the most influential princes and the highest state officers call themselves with self-consciousness, *"Jew-Christians."* What then is the decisive trait that makes the Christian a non-Jew? Furthermore, the theologically educated Expert can hardly be believed to be ignorant of the fact that the first adherents of Christianity in its *statu nascendi* had preserved the name Jews for a long period, had remained piously obedient to the customs, precepts and tenets of the Jews, and had in their outward apparel distinguished themselves in nothing from their former brethren in creed. Notwithstanding their sincere devotion to the new movement, they still called themselves, *"devout sons of Israel"*; only few were they who assumed an outspoken antagonistic position with regard to the customary Rabbinic or Pharisaic ordinances, and were on this account stigmatized by the Talmud as "Min," "Apikores." Now, has non-Jews always been identical with Christian? Aside from this the first edition of the "Schulchan Aruch" was printed in Adrianople (Turkey), where the most inhabitants were Mussulmans.

Such falsifications of the text in more recent editions have perplexed me to some extent, when I investigated the laws of Justus. The fourth law reads: 'When a Jew is met by an Akum (Christian) with a cross in his hand, the Jew is strictly prohibited from bowing his head.' However, in my Wilna edition I find instead of Akum the word *adam, i.e.* man. I then compared a new Stettin edition, and there I even find: 'When an *obed kochabim* (star worshipper) with *abodath kochabim* (idol) in hand meet,' whence nothing could, of course, be proved. Only in an older edition I have found the original: 'When an Akum meets you with a *sheti vaereb* (*i.e.* woof and warp = *cross*).' And, gentlemen, this proof is incontrovertible. It is known to everybody that *no heathen reveres the cross*. Akum here *must* mean a Christian."

One moment, profound Herr Dr. Ecker, the case appears after all to be very far from being so manifest and ultimately settled. During their existence, extending over thousands of years, the Jews had experienced among the various nations many a thing of which many a sage can not even dream and which seems unknown also to Dr. Ecker, the theologian, who bears even the title Doctor. As there is in general *nothing new under the sun*, the consecration of the cross in Christianity was not a wholly new creation. In the Brahman religion the cross had enjoyed great esteem some six centuries B.C. The Hindu symbolized therein the space relations of the universe. According to accounts relating to those times, the Fakirs would stand motionless, their hands stretched crosswise, for days or, as some would have it, even for weeks until the nails on their fingers would grow to be inches long. By thus blunting their bodily sensibility they endeavored to give palpable expression to the negation of man's earthly existence. The commentary to Eben Ezra, *mekor chaim*, gives in the book *Margalioth* an account of this custom. Accordingly, it is by no means so incredible nor could have been so infrequent that a Jew should have met a heathen with a cross. The assumption is therefore plausible that the Talmud had in view such heathens. However, we admit that this is merely an hypothesis, and that Shulchan Aruch was no more familiar with Indian mythology than Dr. Ecker appears to be. We aim solely at showing that it is possible for one impelled by judophobic purposes to carry on the study of Semitica for ten years, and yet exhibit drastic ignorance here and there--all diluted eloquence and vain presumptions notwithstanding--and that it is altogether ill-becoming to venture upon expressing a competent opinion on Jewish laws that have arisen in ancient times. It is of this that we wanted to remind Herr Dr. Ecker and his anti-Semitic commilitants.

"In conclusion one more proof that will of necessity convince everybody. We all know that the Jews do not eat meat unless it has been slaughtered by a Jew. Meat slaughtered by Christians is not 'kosher,' and yet the 'Shulchan Aruch' says that meat slaughtered by an Akum is not kosher; hence Akum means also the Christian."

Patience, Herr Dr. Ecker. Also this your far-fetched remark deserves an answer, and such that will remove the scales off your eyes. How indeed is it possible that a theologian who has been exploring Jewish literature for ten years should exhibit such salient gaps? The most ignorant Jew could beat you in this point. Who does not know that only a trained slaughterer examined and supplied with a diploma is allowed to slaughter? Any other Jew, and he that the most enlightened and distinguished among the Rabbis themselves, is not entitled to slaughter, and were he to do it the meat of this animal would be unallowable and regarded as though the animal had been torn to pieces by a beast of prey, and is therefore "*Terefa*," (torn.) And upon this case Dr. Ecker bases his deduction that Akum is absolutely a Christian, for the cattle slaughtered by an Akum is not kosher? How ridiculous! Is it kosher if slaughtered by a Jew not in possession of the right to slaughter?

"Now comes the important third question: Are the laws of Dr. Justus really contained in the 'Shulchan Aruch'? Herr Colleague Treu has made the utterance that many a point of these laws is not contained in the 'Shulchan Aruch.' Particular stress was apparently laid on this remark. The case is not set down with precision I compared all the laws with the original text and reached the following result should simply sign my name under all these 100 laws from A to Z, you require of me. In their main substance they are correctly contained in the 'Shulchan Aruch,' but the foundations of some single laws are borrowed by the author somewhere else; on the whole, however, well grounded. I admit, and this is natural enough, that the laws are *poignantly* formulated, and in some cases in a manner which I should not approve of. We read, *e.g.*, in law 79: 'The Jew is allowed to eat unclean in case of a dangerous sickness . . . however, he is not allowed even in this case to use for his cure something that belongs (in the opinion of the Jews) to the most-unclean, viz., to a Christian Church.' As already observed, no mention is made of Christians, and also here in the text it reads 'idol worship.' Of course Christian Church too belongs here. Thus, the case is not untrue, yet in its formulation the law sounds sharper and Dr. Justus should have left the text also unaltered and added Christian Church' in parentheses."

Truly, we are at a loss to find the proper expression that might appropriately characterize this expert deposition of a theologically educated priest. Let us in the first place inquire somewhat more closely into the law in question, which in its formulation is in neither the Talmud nor the Shulchan Aruch. In the former we read: "If a man is seized with bulimy he may be fed with unclean food, till his eyes become clear" (Yoma, 125) . Here no mention is made of either Akum or idol worship. In the Shulchan Aruch the same law is worded as follows: It is allowed to give the dangerously sick *prohibited* food to eat (Orach Chaim, 6 18, 9). Here again the word unclean has been eliminated. Still another passage treating of the same subject reads: "For curing purposes all is allowed to be used but the wood of an Ashera, Astrate, that what was in Phœnician an unchaste phallus-idol." We read further in the same place: "With all things it is permitted to cure one's self except by means of idolatry, adultery and shedding of blood." (Pesachim, 36.) The word Tumah = unclean is not met here at all. In the Shulchan Aruch this law is restated as follows: "It is not allowed to seek convalescence in the name of idols" (Yoreh dea, 155.) Neither is here the word Tumah to be found. It thus remains an enigma where Dr. Justus may have borrowed the expression *"the most unclean,"* which is to Dr. Ecker of course synonymous with the *Christian Church*, since the word is not at all used in the original text in connection with *this* law! But we must do justice to Dr. Ecker; he possesses a highly cunning method of polemizing; he displays admirable dexterity in securing for his comrade Dr. Justus an open back-door. Yes, indeed, Dr. Ecker is master of his art, he leaves far behind that so-called "Jewish method of polemizing," which has been according to the "Germania" revealed in this action. Herr Dr. Ecker makes notably the statement that Dr. Justus has taken his law from the Shulchan Aruch, their interpretations, however, he has borrowed from *somewhere* else. This open admission manifests the intention of false conception. Dr. Justus has namely borrowed that marked, or to use the language of Dr. Ecker, "*poignant*" expression from a place that has absolutely nothing in common with the law in question. Aboda Zara, *i.e.* idol worship, is termed in the Talmud the father of uncleanness: Abh hatumah, which defiles by touch (Sabbath, Aboda Zara.) Now Dr. Justus resorts to the following stratagem; he renders Abh hathmah with "the most unclean," substitutes Aboda Zara, idol worship, by "Christian Church," then he fabricates a law under the label of the Shulchan Aruch which has never had any thing of the kind, and in the name of this firm sends it out into the wide world. Dr. Ecker, it is true, finds that such method of procedure is "poignant," but on the whole correct and to the point. What may criticism say on such an escapade? If a Jew had the mishap of venturing upon such a shaky ground, the whole stock of degrading names, such as rogue, rascal, impostor, misanthrope, etc., would not suffice to stigmatize so shameless a forger. Indeed it requires very little originality and still less sagacity or witchcraft to pick out phrases from places that stand in no relation to one another, and compile them with a view of criminating whomever it may be. Dr. Justus has done such a work, and a Catholic priest, a custodian of the church who should adhere to truth, right and peace, has the impudence to assert that this work is in substance *correct*, though *poignant* because "Christian Church" should have been enclosed in parentheses; as if then the falsehood would turn to truth! Can a theologian bear such false testimony, a priest who declares himself to be well versed in the Hebrew and hence competent to pass judgment on Rabbinical literature?

Let us now examine somewhat more closely the Hebrew concept, "*Tumah*," In default of a corresponding similarly expressive German word, one is of necessity prompted to render it with "unclean." In reality, however, the Biblical and Rabbinical "Tumah," is *toto cælo* different from the current notion unclean. The German "unclean" is synonymous with the dirt and filth, which is in no way the case with Tumah. According to the Mosaic law, a human corpse is the very origin, the progenitor of all Tumah, "*Abhi aboth hatumah*." In Dr. Ecker's German this could be styled "the most unclean." The tent, the room that shelters a corpse, with all the utensils therein, is permeated with the fluid of *Tumah*, uncleanness. Whoever lingers, sits or sleeps there, whoever touches the corpse, is infected with the *Tumah* and becomes in turn "Abh hatumah," the father of uncleanness, and he who touches the Abh hatumah is called "*Rishon lettimah*," the first of uncleanness; he is prohibited for seven days from entering the sanctuary or from approaching the altar. He imparts *Tumah* to him who may happen to touch him. It is here absolutely immaterial whether the corpse was, when alive, sheltering the divine spirit of Moses, of the crowned bard of the unparalleled psalm songster David, or of one of the lowliest in the Jewish nation. The assertion that the corpse of Moses, David, etc., is the most unclean would be a sure symptom of insanity. Are the two words Tumah and unclean congruent? The religious law of *Tumah* is laid down in the Torah without foundation at all, and belongs to those laws concerning which we venture to speculate, yet are unable to warrant their validity. Now, the Rabbis, eager to keep the Jews from following idolatry of those times, to prevent all contact therewith, were therefore teaching: "An idol defiles by touch; it is not allowed even for curing purposes." However, it was not the material part of the idol that was prohibited, such as the wood, the stone, the dust (for the use of all this was allowed in case of danger), but the prohibition is to be conceived of in the following sense. If one were to whisper in the ear of a dangerously sick person: "I will in your behalf invoke the help of this or that idol," as such was really the case with Ben Dama, the nephew of R. Ismael (Aboda Zara, 27), it is such a medicinal use of the idol that one is energetically warned against. Supposing now that the emblems of Christianity too are actually subsumed under the category of idols, which is by no means the case, supposing further that it is prohibited to seek recovery by their help, even then there would be no way of justifying a rationally thinking person in his attempting to refer such a prohibition to the Christian Church, or to go further yet, and assert that the latter is in the mind of the Jews *unclean*, or, according to Dr. Ecker, altogether *the most unclean*.

As an illustration of how the Rabbinical school used to term *Tumah*, we quote an eloquent account of the Mishnah [Iodaim, 4]: "The Sadducees were once deriding their antagonists, the Pharisees, as follows: 'How amazingly absurd is your procedure in establishing laws! the writings of Homer are not defiling while the sacred books of the Bible should be subject of defiling; is it not the height of absurdity?' Hereupon replied R. Johanan b. Zakai: You could adduce against us yet other analogous but more drastic facts; the bones of an ass are not defiling while those of the high-priest Johann Hyrcan do defile! How would you solve this paradox?" Whereupon the Sadducees answered: "This is obvious. The position one holds when alive is in direct ratio with the uncleanness after death; the more revered and beloved one was when alive, the more defiling is his corpse." Now you see, said R. Johanan b. Zakai, this speaks as well as for us, I could turn the very same weapons unto ye! the profane writings of Homer--that are not our favorite--are indifferent to us, they do not defile; the sacred books which we revere and love are subjects of defiling the hands that touch them!

Now, if according to Dr. Ecker's and Justus's literary artifice, the Christian Church too belongs *"of course,"* to the *most unclean,* is it not possible in the rabbinical sense to construe on the contrary a consecration, a proof of superior esteem for the church? Ye gentlemen Doctors, where is your wisdom?

Artifices of this kind can be brought about only by a Dr. Justus, who, impregnated with malice and Jew-hatred, misuses ink and paper to openly and scornfully defy the truth. And a consecrated priest, an academic teacher, stamps his approval upon his tricky work and in a sacred place where justice is being administered, whither he, credited agreeably to his sect and position, was summoned to conscientiously elucidate the truth, where he might have been made to confirm under oath the veracity of his conviction! Verily, Dr. Ecker has badly sinned, not only against the Jewish people, but also against Christian Germany! Is then in our age the Hebrew literature a book sealed with seven seals? Are not there in Germany also Christian savants who could detect this arbitrary procedure, who could trace to its source such a groundless absurdity? Would that he may perceive the opinion of the Christian professors, Delitzsch, Cassel, etc., expressed with reference to his expert opinion, he would see then whether they regard his depositions as actually impartial, or as of a wholly different nature, he would learn whether they agree with him in that the Christian Church too belongs *of course* to the most unclean! This is, honorable priest of the church, your impartiality, such is it prima facie!

"I should like yet to touch here upon the point which was thought to be important when Herr Colleague Treu has pointed out that he has nowhere read in the 'Shulchan Aruch' that Christians are worse than dogs. To be sure, it is manifest that a law book is not the place to state that the Christians are worse than dogs; but it is perverse to infer from here that Dr. Justus has falsified the text. This sentence was namely brought forth as a foundation of law 31, where note 3 remarks, however, that it is borrowed from the renowned exegete Rashi."

We do not know the passage attributed to Rashi. However, places of this nature are not rare in the Talmud. Let us quote such a passage. The question was discussed, for whom it is allowed to prepare food on a holiday; in this connection it reads: "What causes you to exclude the Akum. from, and to introduce the dogs into, the law? The dogs depend on you in their food and rearing, therefore I treat of them in the law, but the Akum. I exclude, for no one is obliged to take care of him," (Betza, 21b). Rashi has surely commented on such a place in the Talmud, and Dr. Justus was dexterous enough to forge thereof a poisoned arrow and to direct it as best it suits his instincts. But is here even a particle of insinuating contempt and depreciation of *an Akum* or a Christian? In the foregoing quotation the question is discussed as to the preparing of food on such holidays that do not coincide with the Sabbath, which preparing is allowed only for such persons and animals that depend on others in their food. We refer yet the reader to our next observation.

"Another point was contended against by Herr Treu, in law 17, which treats of the case that the Jews pray when the plague rages in their midst, but not when the plague is among animals. Here it reads further: 'But they do (pray) when the plague is among *swine*, as their intestines resembles those of man, *likewise* when the plague is among Akum (Christians).' I agree with Herr Treu that in lieu of 'likewise' should be 'the more so,' and therewith the law loses its poignancy, but

156

it looks suspicious all the same that in one and the same line the *Akum are coupled together with swine."*

The Herr Privatdocent of the royal academy displayed masterly skill to excite his audience, and to unbridle the passions of hatred. Verily, also we must make an extraordinary effort to control our agitated mind. The reasons, however, lie by no means in the affected depreciation of the human dignity in general, or of that of the Akum in particular, no matter who is meant thereby as ascertained by the Expert, but in the boundless ignorance of this theological doctor, which is truly astonishing, nay startling. And yet he asserts to have been studying Semitica for ten years! David, the King of Israel, was considered by the older Rabbis, the highest unattainable authority, the ideal of the Jewish people. As far as rank and merits are concerned, they put him above the Patriarchs Moses and Joshua, each of whom, they tell us, had his hands stained in one way or other, wherefore none of them was honored with saying the benediction over the goblet. David, however, was found wholly stainless, the goblet was predestined for him, and only he was allowed to grasp it and praise therewith the Omnipotent! This legend is to be found in Talmud (Pesachim, 119). But the very same so highly revered David is somewhere else coupled together with dogs, and, in defiance of all shame and discretion, treated even worse than a dog-- in the sense of Justus and Ecker. It is namely recorded: David died, and his son and successor to the throne, Solomon, had his messenger ask in the college as follows: "The remains of my royal father are exposed to the scorching sun rays, the dogs of my father's household are hungry and menace them, may I in view of all this touch on the day of Sabbath the remains, and have them sheltered?" Hereupon came the answer: "First of all satisfy the hunger of the dogs by having a carcass cut to them; thereafter put upon your father's corpse a loaf of bread or a child, then you may have it removed into the shade." Contemplating this, Solomon made in his later years the utterance: "Truly the living dog is better than the dead lion." Thus reads the legend in the Talmud (Sabbath, 32). And more yet; of their own people the sages say: "Three are insolent, Israel among the nations, the dog among the animals, the cock among the birds"

(Betza, 25). Who would assert that in these passages David and Israel are depreciated? This elementary point should not have escaped the consciousness of a theologian trained in the Hebrew and Rabbinical literature, viz., that expressions of this kind were current among the law teachers of those days, without, however, any intention on their part to either elevate or degrade any one! Again, we read in the Talmud (Pesach, 112): "The rabbis taught, there are three who hate one another: the dogs, the cocks, and the sages." Others add yet the rival women, still others also the teachers at the Babylonian academies. Well, Dr. Ecker, what would you say to this point? Could the sages find no better company than the dogs, cocks and rivals? And again, are the Evangelists more moderate in their language? Does not Matthew also call the nations *dogs and swine?* (Mat., 6, 7). Where then is here room for indignation? The patriarch Jacob on his death-bed blesses his sons who surround him. Their characteristic merits and defects he designates by animal forms which they resemble. Jehudah he calls a young lion, Naftali a bitch, Issachar an ass, Dan a serpent, Benjamin, his youngest favorite, a rending wolf. Moses, too, calls in his farewell blessing the tribe of Joseph, "a first-born ox." Should these two reverend old men have had the malicious intention, at the most serious moment when they were preparing to part with life, to revile and insult? Here is a point for Herr Dr. Ecker to meditate on![7]

No. 21. As we are lacking in time we requested the dean of this faculty to send us a copy of the curriculum with an admission card, so that we might arrive at the exact hour appointed for some lectures on the Talmud and on theology which we saw announced in the programme; to which we received the following letter:

THE JEWISH THEOLOGICAL
SEMINARY OF AMERICA.
NEW YORK, *January* 5, 1903.

Dear Sir.--Your letter of the 21st ult. is just before me. I have not yet been able to send you a copy of the curriculum, which I shall be very glad to do when it is printed. Whilst a weekly curriculum has been adopted for the year, some of its provisions are still under advisement, and I have not deemed it wise to put it in print.

I have not at the moment any copy of the hours of the lectures either, nor do I really think it would be profitable for you to attend an occasional lecture, as you suggest. You realize, too, that the classes must necessarily consist of young men, that practically every hour involves a certain amount of recitation, and that the students will feel awkward, or necessarily ill at ease, in the presence of some one older than themselves.

Yours very truly,

S. SCHECHTER,

President of the Faculty.
Michael L. Rodkinson, Esq.,

No. 22. The Jewish Encyclopædia is undoubtedly a monumental work and most eminent scholars in both continents are taking part in it, and there a great many scientific articles which are instructive to the students and also many laymen are pleased by reading a great deal of articles in every branch. (True, that some articles though scientific would be better if omitted in the encyclopædia. We refer to Dr. P. Mendus' message to the Union Orthodox congregations which took place recently.) However, because it is a monumental work, we cannot restrain ourselves from remarking that the editors should be more careful in their revision of the articles. In Appendix No. 8, we show that the bibliographies are not complete and now we will remark that the editors are not careful in their biographies.

There is a short biographical sketch in Vol. I., p. 16, of Aaron Ha-Levi Ben Moses of Staroselye, who was our mother's father. In the *American Hebrew*, June 28, 1901, we have already remarked that his family name was Hurwitz, which he received from his ancestor, the famous Ishiah Halevi Hurivitz, known by the name Shelaw, the author of "Snee Luchoth Habrith," and this was omitted.

We have then overlooked that his main and wonderful work,

"Sharee Haychud ve Haemuna" (Gates of the Unity (of God) and its Creed) is not mentioned. This great work has surprised not only the Cabbalists and Chasidim, but also the Maskilim like Sneier Zachs and Lazar Zwefel. The former mentioned it in his well-known "Hathchia" thus: "and the wonderful work by Aaron Hurivitz" and so also the latter in his "Solom Al Israel," who speaks of it enthusiastically and at length. Remarkable it is that in the bibliography of the sketch is mentioned Rodkinson's "Toldath Amude Hachabad" and in this book his family name as well as the above-mentioned work with more particulars are to be found. By this we see that the editor of this subject did not care to look up the bibliography at least to make it correct. He should at least have seen Fünns' "Kneset Israel," in which the name and the books are mentioned.

All this concerns the incorrect biography. Should we count the omissions of the names of very great men, even only of Aaron and Abraham of all classes, who ought to be mentioned in the encyclopædia, who played a great rôle in Israel, it would take too much space and time. A glance into our *Biographie sämmtlicher Rabbiner der Gouvernments Vollhynien, Podolien, Ukraine, Gross- Klein-Polen und Galizien von Jahre 1695 bis 1876 (Konigsberg 1876)*, pp. 30-34, will convince the reader of this.

---

1. What concerns Ben Zakkai, according to Heilprin, in his "Seder Hadoroth," and other authorities, Johanan b. Zakkai died 72 years A. C., that is, about forty years after the death of Jesus, at which time the followers of the latter had already begun to dispute with their Jewish colleagues. We also find a disciple of Johanan b. Zakkai whom he very much respected, very friendly to, and pleased with, Jacob of the village Sachnon, who was one of the first disciples of Jesus. Hence our conjecture.

2. Speaking of the encyclopædias, we are sorry to say that in spite of the advertising of their completeness, with all additional information in every branch up to the time of publication, one can not rely upon them. It seems to us that they omit the mention of books of great interest. According to our knowledge, books the subject of which is interesting to most students, not to speak of whether they are well done or not, ought to be mentioned and, if necessary, with a remark about the quality of the books. Now take the "Century Encyclopedia-Dictionary and Atlas," which is advertised as the best of its kind and which is published in New York City, and if we look under the subject "Talmud," the fourteen or fifteen volumes of the *first* English translation of the "Talmud" by Michael L. Rodkinson, published

in the, same city, are not to be found, although about 175 daily papers and periodicals, here and abroad, noticed and reviewed the publication. The same is the case with Appleton's new encyclopædia under the same title "Talmud." Here also Rodkinson's translation is not mentioned, though some small tracts which were translated into German are mentioned. Still more remarkable is it, that the reviser of this article p. 123 on the "Talmud" was Dr. Richard Gottheil, who is one of the editors of the Jewish Encyclopædia, and who himself wrote a criticism in "The Bookman" in 1897 upon this translation. What concerns the Jewish Encyclopædia, which is devoted only to matters relating to the Jews, one is still more astonished on examining its bibliographies. On pages 390 and 394 of vol. ii., etc., etc., the contents of Tracts Baba Batra Metzia and Kama are explained. In the bibliography of this article are neither mentioned the excellent translation into French by 1. M. Rabbinowicz nor the translation into English by Michael L. Rodkinson. The same is the case with vol. iv., Page 526, etc., concerning the tracts "Derekh-Erez Rabba" and "Zuta," for in the bibliography there is not mentioned its translation in vol. i. (ix.) into English by the same M. L. Rodkinson, together with Abot de Rabbi Nathan, which is mentioned in the first volume, page 82. Here the bibliography reads: "An English version is given by M. L. Rodkinson in his translation of the Babylonian Talmud, I. (IX.), New York, 1900." We cannot find any excuse for such a sin of the bibliographer unless we ascribe it to the carelessness of the editors, for even if the authors of the articles were ignorant of it, in spite of the fact that this translation is to be found in almost all the libraries of the cities and countries, still the editors ought not to have been so.

3. To the critics who will try to find fault with us because of the article by Prof. Schechter in the *Westminster Review* of January and April, we will say that in spite of the respect which we feel for the article and the author, we do not agree with it on many points. Therefore, without any controversies, we state here what seems reasonable to us, leaving it to the reader to judge.

4. He quotes namely, the places of the Talmud which were translated by him.

5. In our pamphlet "Barquai," Vienna, 1886, all Bloch's proceedings as well as his character are related.

6. The testimonies of Dr. Treu, who was a Jew, we do not deem necessary to translate, especially as they may be understood from the answers of Dr. Ecker. However, the latter's testimony and our replies we translate literally for the purpose of enlightening such passages which are to be found in the Talmud.

7. We are convinced that many, yes, *very* many, offensive passages in the Talmud are traceable to the Jews-Christians among the Rabbis. For a long time theme Jews-Christians remained in close relations with their Jewish brethren, refrained from ostentatiously manifesting their belief in the messianism of Jesus; however, in their innermost selves they entertained and nourished a more and more unfolding rancor against the teachings as well as against the authority of the law teachers, who would by means of all imaginable contrivances interfere with their clandestine plans to carry on propaganda for their idea. Jacob from Kefar Sekania and Jacob Minaah (Megila, 23) are mentioned as such, and there must have been many of this class. It is to these Jews-Christians that we attribute the authorship of some of the above-cited sentences that sound in a measure defamatory to the Rabbis. In like manner the foregoing David legend may have originated in these circles. Indeed, David was far from being stainless; he himself was conscious of it and expressed it in a penitential psalm to which we refer (Psalm 51). But as the

pretended ancestor of Jesus the adherents of the latter surrounded him with dazzling though undeserved glory. (We, in our new edition of the Talmud have omitted both legends concerning David, as we are certain they are not to be ascribed to the Rabbis of the Talmud; see also our edition [Betza, 491 footnotes. We have omitted the whole saying but Maelits, for the same reason.) In this, our pamphlet, from page 35 on, we explain all the passages where *Akum* is mentioned and what it signifies, not by suppositions but by facts, and as it is written in the German language, we may refer the reader, who would like to know this, to them.

Appendix B

Criticism To Chapter VII (Karaites). The Belief Of Sadducees, Karaites, And Of The Reformed Jews.

DR. MICHAEL L. RODKINSON.

Sir:--Having read your article about the "The Karaites" in *The American Hebrew* (23-24), though in general I have found therein likely and probable things, I cannot forbear from calling your attention to several points on which, in my opinion, it behooves not a man like you to take a partial view, while presenting to the readers a historic account. It is the duty of every fair writer of history to give an account of the facts without any personal bias, and where there is a difference of opinion, without sufficient evidence for demonstrating the truth of any, then it is the duty of the historian to state as much, and if he is able to decide between them, he should give his opinion also; if not, he shall leave the task of deciding to some of the readers who might be able, perhaps, to do so. But you have not done so.

You have written (p. 685) that when Anan saw, etc., and have ignored, or are unaware of, what the head of our poets, R. Jehudah Halevi, wrote in his "Cuzari," III., 65, that in the time of Jehudah b. Tabi and Simon b. Shetah Karaism commenced an account of what happened between the Sages and the King Janæus, etc., see carefully that passage, you will find there that R. Jehudah Halevi admits that the doctrine of the Karaites is an ancient one. And you ought to mention this fact.

So also I do not agree with you in what you say, that at present are found only 4--5,000 Karaites in the world. For, in my opinion, the Reformers in Europe and America must be regarded as Karaites, as they decided at their Congress at that they do not consider the Talmud as authoritative, and that only the Pentateuch is the basis of their doctrines. If it is so, then they are evidently also Karaites. And if in some ceremonies they differ from the contemporary Karaites, for this reason cannot separate them from them. You yourself enumerate sects among the distinguished from each other in their ceremonies, and yet they all avow the to be Karaites.

This is what I have wanted to remark, and if you are conscientious, you will modify this, not to mislead the future generations who will read your history, and thereby you will insure yourself against critics, who condemn a whole book when they find in it one thing which is not quite right.

Your obedient servant,
ISAAC LEVI SHALIT.

Answer.

With many thanks for your ingenious remarks, and for your love of truth and eagerness to save me from unfair critics, I state at your desire what I have to say in reply, and what I have omitted in the article itself, viz.:

First--let it be known that I am not writing the history of the Karaites, but that of the Talmud, and mention those who have contributed to its extension and diffusion, as well as those who persecuted it, from the time it had begun to develop till to-day. For this purpose it does not matter whether Karaites were an old or a new sect, from the time of Anan, as all admit that they persecuted the Talmud to the utmost. And I, who have been, obliged to give briefly the history of the Karaites for the reason that they persecuted the Talmud, used as authorities the latest historians who have treated this subject, as Pinsker, Graetz, Fürst, Geiger and Gottlober, who have all decided that it was an invention of Anan himself. But out of respect to truth, I am bound to tell you that I was not unaware of, nor did I conceal, what is written about the Karaite sect in the "Cuzari." For of this has the head of the reformed rabbis, the learned scholar Holdheim, written long ago, in his book "Maamar Haishuth," as much as it is worth, and philosophized about the assertions in the "Chasar," but he also found that be had been mistaken in this (or that he was compelled to write this, for reasons unknown to us at the present day; I myself say, he wrote thus because in his days the Chasars were reported to also be Karaites, and he who made his book in the form of a controversy between a Karaite and Rabbi did not want to charge it with being a new sect, but admitting one point, namely, that it is an old sect, he still urged that there is no foundation for it). And to make you, and those who entertain the same opinion, to cease to think that the reformers of the present time are "Karaites," and also that the readers may know what the Karaites plead; that the Karaite sect has been from the time of Moses, who was himself a Karaite, and the Rabbinical innovation dates from Jeroboam b. Nebat, we have only to quote from the above-mentioned book of Holdheim, p. 117, etc., and also what he wrote to refute their assertions, p. 122, and also what we will find to remark on his words.

[1]It is known that according to the opinion of the Karaites themselves in their books, their belief and their tradition is identical with the Pentateuch. Together with the body of the Pentateuch, the Lord communicated to Moses an oral comment, and he communicated to his contemporaries, who transmitted it to the succeeding generations till the death of Solomon. When the people was split into two parties, one adhered to Rehoboam, and the other followed Jeroboam, who sinned and led his party into sin. The Karaites named their traditions the inherited yoke and burden, and according to them there was during all that time only one Torah for the whole people, as one God, and the text and its interpretation were inseparable and sprung from the same source, the father of the Karaites being Moses himself, the trusted pastor who carried all his people on his shoulders. As Jeroboam was one of those who had received the tradition transmitted from age to age as above-mentioned, and one of the men of the

Great Sanhedrin, fearing that the royal power should be recovered by David's dynasty, he invented strange and spurious interpretations of the Torah to replace the good ones and true ones which the Sanhedrin had by tradition. He presented it to the people, whom he misled, and brought to evil. The nation believed him, followed in his footsteps, exchanged most commandments of the Torah for others, subtracted, added, at their pleasure. Since then Israel was divided into two sects, and the Torah became two rival and hostile Torahs. Judea kept the law according to the ancient custom received from Moses without any change, addition or subtraction, Karaism. being the modern continuation thereof. Israel, on the other hand, observed the laws according to the new manner, with alterations, additions and subtractions invented by Jeroboam, and Rabbinism is its continuation; later false prophets rose in Israel, and, claiming divine inspiration, misguided them, and even some of Judea, etc. But Judea, nevertheless, continued to be the seat of the Mosaic tradition, as the majority adhering most to the truth. However, as the Temple was demolished, most prophets, priests, Levites and Sanhedrin were slain, while those left alive were mostly of the sinners. Therefore at the restoration of the second Temple, even while there still were prophets, who are called the "good figs," there were two sects and two separate Torahs. After the cessation of prophetic inspiration this split grew and widened. The party holding by the truth said the Torah was only that one written by Moses and given to Israel; the party believing in the falsehood said there were two Torahs, written and oral, invented by Jeroboam and the false prophets, and which they also referred to Moses, who received it (according to them) from the Lord. Thus it continued till the time of Matthew, the Hasmonean (Maccabee), when Antiochus the Wicked, wishing to suppress altogether the Jewish lore, in which time of calamities all great sages of the Sanhedrin who had the true tradition of the comment and the Torah were all murdered, and the tradition till then transmitted, was now severed, and the greater part of the comment and the Torah was lost and forgotten, only an infinitesimal fraction being left. This fact took place in the year 3560 after creation.

As Matthew triumphed, and peace was restored in the land, the men of intellect sat down to learn the Torah and understand it with the aid of their reason. But owing to its great depth, they could not comprehend it, and many diverse opinions existed. Thus the differences between sects, Karaite as well as Rabbinical, arose, and persist to these days.

The quarrel between the two sects grew in violence till the time of the king and high-priest Janeus was reached, and something happened between the sages and him, as is well known, so that be massacred all the sages in his anger, and none remained except one great man of each sect, Jehudah b. Tabai, who held the truth, and Simeon b. Shetah, drawn after the false doctrine of Jeroboam b. Nebat and the false prophets. The king, wishing to kill both, Jehudah b. Tabai hid in Jerusalem, and Simeon b. Shetah was the queen's brother, who facilitated his escape to Egypt, where he stayed three years; being there, he learned from the Israelite sages found there since the destruction of the first Temple, and the days of Jeremiah, all the strange comments invented by Jeroboam and the false prophets. Simeon b. Shetah added thereto some of his own, and built there a great temple and sacrificed there, though it was not the chosen place; and after his return to Jerusalem he wanted to be a great lord in Israel, and taught, therefore, the people what he had acquired in Egypt, as the oral law communicated to Moses, and transmitted by him; and, because he was the king's brother-in-law and had much influence at the court, his false doctrines became popular among Israel, who received the false Torah instead of the true one.

After that Israel was divided into two parties, and the quarrel commenced also in the Sanhedrin, the heads of the nation, and heirs and teachers of the Torah. One sect went after R. Jehudah b. Tabai and was called Sadducees (Zadikim) (Upright), from the phrase "hearken unto me, ye that pursue righteousness" (Zadik) [Is. li., i.], and their justice is everlasting justice, and their Torah is truth; Karaism is a continuation thereof. The second sect followed Simeon b. Shetah, and were called Pharisees (Parushim), separatists, for separating themselves from the old faith of Israel. This state of things continued from 3650 after creation, from the time of Jehudah b. Tabai, till the ruin of the second Temple, year 3828. At that epoch, the majority of

the Sadducees were slain, but the Pharisees mostly survived, for
which there were two causes: first, because those of the Sadducaic
party were the political and warlike men, while the Pharisees were
humble and were students; secondly, because the Sadducees were
stricter in observing the duties, and their conduct was of much holiness and purity, and had seen that if they were to be exiled, being an
unclean earth, and without water for removing the uncleanness, they
could not keep the law as it ought to be; therefore they were martyrs,
choosing to be murdered rather than live, and all were killed for the
sanctification of the Lord. Put the Pharisees who were not strict, and
were not afraid of the ruin of the Temple or exile, and chose life
rather than death, and went out to Titus, the Wicked, and, surrender-
ing, were all left alive. Therefore, after the ruin of the Temple the
Pharisees rose in power, whereas the Sadducees declined. Thus it
continued till R. Jehudah the Nassi, the editor of the Mishna. He
collected all comments, good and bad, true and false, ancient and
recent, all together; he wrote them down in a book without making
distinctions between the sacred and profane, unclean and clean; he
decided and declared that they are all Sinaic. This occurred in 3945.

After the conclusion of the Mishna, rose up those who composed
the Palestinian and Babylonian Talmuds, and from that time on the
quarrel grew in force, and the hate, rivalry and jealousy grew
between the two sects, the Sadducees and Pharisees. For the
Sadducees held the true Torah, written by Moses our teacher, and
those few true comments that have been left from many; but the
Pharisees abandoned the written Torah and ignored it as of subordinate importance, and clung to the oral law, that is, the Mishna and
the Talmud, making it the thing of the first importance, saying that
tradition will be victorious. They said every one who studies the
written law has fulfilled only partially his obligations, but every one
who studies Mishna or Talmud he has completely discharged his
obligations; every one who trangresses the written law is culpable of
stripes, who transgresses the words of the sages is guilty of capital
punishment, and that one should not object even if they say to you of
the right that it is the left, and of the left that it is the right and similar
erroneous teachings. Thus it continued to be till the time of Anan the

Nassi, the Holy and the Saint, the son of David the Nassi, in the year 4400 after the creation. Anan[2] lived in Babylonia and was of the Sadducees, and for his great wisdom Israel, Sadducees as well as Pharisees, chose him as Nassi, as the head of Beth Din and Exilarch. After his instalment as Nassi and head of Beth Din by the sanction of the Arabian monarch, and the will of all Israel, he became zealous for God and his Torah, and wished to restore it to its primitive purity; he commenced to plead against the oral law, *i.e.*, the Mishna, and deny and declare it as nought. When the Pharisaic sect perceived all this, they rose upon him and devised stratagems to kill him. But out of fear of the king, they did not lay their hands on him, but denounced him to the king that he had rebelled against the law of the government, but the king pitied him and saved him from them, and so he was left alive. When Anan perceived that the Pharisees did not want to return to the truth, he was disgusted with being a Nassi, left his house and possessions in Babylonia, and departed with his sons and disciples to Jerusalem, the Sacred City. He built there a synagogue, "The Temple of God," to pray and to weep morning, noon and evening; and perceiving that the Pharisees were increasing, and that the Sadducees decreased, and fearing lest the true Torah be forgotten entirely, and lest the Sadducees be absorbed in time by the Pharisees, he commanded his disciples, friends and acquaintances, to keep themselves apart from the sect of the Pharisees wholly and with the utmost possible strictness. He forbade them to eat *their* foods, for *they* are not careful about all kinds of uncleanness, and eat carcasses and tallow prohibited by the Torah. So also he forbade them to intermarry with them, because they had trespassed the barriers of consanguinity. And Anan interpreted the Torah and commandments according to the true comment, as he had received it from his fathers and masters by tradition, who belonged to the sect of Sadducees, continuing from the oldest times; and as the whole Sadducean doctrine is founded on the text of the Holy Scriptures, Pentateuch, Prophets and Hagiographas, therefore Anan the Nassi called the Sadducean sect "Karaites," (Karaim), that is, who are *called* and go in their simplicity. (Ba'ale Mikre): and as the whole object of the Pharisees was to pursue high positions and *lordliness*, and also because they are *many* in comparison with the few Karaites, he called them "Rabbanim," (lords, many), that is, the adherents of the Mishna and Talmud. . . .

This is the opinion of the Karaites themselves about their history, and that every one who wishes to know and understand all the errors of the Rabbis (according to them), should see the Book of God's Wars, ("Sepher Milhamoth Adonai"), by Salman b. Jerucham I and the Admonitory letter ("Igereth Hatochachath"), by Sahal Hakohen, and "Eshkol Hakopher," by Jehudah Hadasi Haabel (the Mourner), he called himself thus for mourning, and "Apiryon Asah," and "L'hem Sheorim," by R. Solomon the Turk, also the "Asara Maamaroth," of Elijah the Jerusalemite, and the "Amuna Omen" by Abraham b. Joshua the Jerusalemite, all which books are written to refute the false Rabbinical laws; and of the Rabbinical sages after Anan they say that when they saw that the plain and just truth is evidently on the side of the Sadducees, they invented about them calumnies, that they were Sadducees, and Bithusiaus followers of Zaduk and Bithus, the infidels, and their glory they confounded with shame by conscious falsehood for whereas they had been called Tzadikim from ancient times, they altered their name to Tzadukim (Sadducees, Zadukim), followers of Tsaduk, etc., etc."

. . . [3] Here we have given to the reader what we have briefly quoted so far as needful for our purpose, and to spare much of our own discussion by citing the words of another. From "Orah Tzadikim" treating of the split between the Karaites and Rabbis, written by the scholarly rabbi, Sim'ha Isaac of Lutzki in 550. And we, desiring to call the attention of scholars and thinkers to the affirmations of the Karaites themselves about their ancient history, both their charges against us and their justifications of themselves, have abridged their statements, for it is our duty to hear what they say for themselves, and try to separate the truths from the falsehoods as impartial judges, not as advocates.

And, before all, I say, the man is dreaming who speaks that the difference between the Karaites and Rabbis began in the time of Rehoboam; the son of Solomon, and of Jeroboam, the son of Nebat, when Israel revolted against David's dynasty. And if the Rabbi, were to make such a senseless assertion, that the rebels against David's dynasty were the same that the Karaites are, beyond doubt the Karaites would say that they pervert the words of the living God and deny what is written in the Prophets, that Jeroboam led a away the people from the worship of the true God who had protected them from the times of Egypt till then, to serve golden calves which he had made, and made a festival in a wrong month which he invented that the people should not go to celebrate the holidays at Jerusalem, and the royalty not be restored to David's house. The Karaites state here a strange fiction, which is ridiculed by every one who has any knowledge of books.

Besides that, any one who has eyes to see, ears to hear, and a palate to taste, that which is written in the Scriptures, is aware that during all the time of the prophets till the exile of Israel and Judea from their land and captivity in the land of their enemies, the quarrel between the parties was not about the interpretation of the Torah, or about the reasons of the commandments, but about the Torah itself, between those who knew it and those who did not know it, between the worshippers of the true God and the idolators. The prophets of the true God, and the best element of the people who followed them, have served God and loved him, and were his true servants, adhered to him and observed his commandments and his law. But the king and the common people devoted themselves to drink, to idolatry, adultery, and other uncleanness of the other nations of their time.

And truly, the author of the "Orach Zadikim," as well as the writers whom he quotes, have not adhered to the truth but indulged in falsehoods, by fixing the beginning of this quarrel at a time which it was impossible to have begun. And if the author and his co-religionists fully believe that the present Pentateuch was known to and in the possession of the names in the days of David and Solomon, Rehoboam and Jeroboam, and that, together with the written Torah and its commentaries,--it was in the possession of the Sanhedrin and the members of the great and small Beth Din of those days, as the same belief was entertained by the Pharisees from the written Torah and its commentaries, we will not plead with them to question or reflect upon this belief, and state from the investigations of the modern as well as the ancient critics, that the Pentateuch was at that time of recent date and no one knew of it because it had been written only in the days of Solomon, and no one had seen it,--for it would be unfair to refute a warranted belief on one hand by a total denial on the other. But we will argue from the standpoint of the Karaites themselves, who adhere to the text and deny the commentaries which are conflicting with the ordinary interpretation of the Scripture. For they themselves have interpreted the Scripture wrongly, and ascribed to it a meaning which has never been intended, by stating that the quarrel between Israel and Judea, or between Jeroboam and Rehoboam, has caused a quarrel, in no way or manner resembling it, between the Karaites and the Rabbis regarding the interpretation of the Scripture. This is one of those falsehoods which have absolutely no foundation whatever, and are shunned by those who are able to distinguish between truth and falsehood.

The statement that the difference between the Karaites and Rabbis dates from the time the difference between Jehudah b. Tabai and Simeon b. Shetah broke out, etc., is nothing but a net spread out by the Karaites to catch therein the people of Israel, etc. But it is up to date not known who is the author of this statement and who circulated it among the Karaites that they might make it the foundation of their structure, which foundation, if demolished, would cause the ruin of the whole structure.

There is no doubt in our mind that the Karaites have borrowed this statement from the Pharisees when endeavoring to separate from the Sadducees, whom they also considered as infidels, and to erect a new edifice for themselves, for the Pharisees also consider Simeon b. Shetah to have restored the Torah to her old .glory, as they state in the mentioned Boraitha: "The world was embarrassed until Simeon b. Shetah appeared and restored the Torah to her former state." And here they found an opportunity to use the Pharisees' arguments against them. The Pharisees say that after the massacre of the sages and those learned in the traditional law by Johanan Hyrcanus, the oral law was forgotten in Israel till Simeon b. Shetah came and restored it. By oral law is meant that traditional comment on the Torah as it was afterward written down and concluded by R. Jehudah-the Nasi and his successors in the Mishna and Talmud against which the Karaites protest. Now, the difference between restoration and innovation is insignificant, and what the Pharisees and Rabbis term restoration the Karaites name innovation, and maintain that Simeon b. Shetah made a new law, that is the oral law which was unknown previously, and had not descended to them from their forefathers: and from this new law a new quarrel sprung forth among those who believed in tradition, which quarrel has no connection whatever with the old controversy between the disciples of Sadduk and Bithus, the infidels, and the Josees, the believers, on whom all Israel leant.

As for the statement of the Karaites above mentioned that their belief dates from the time of the second Temple, etc., and that only Anan brought it to light again, after it had disappeared, the same was very ably criticised by the scholarly rabbi, S. J. Rapaport ("Kerem Hemed," p. 200), by laying out his own plan for the investigation of the causes of the Karaite history; he says, namely: "The activity of Anan was not isolated in its kind, but it war, only a link in the chain of the history of the nations of those days. For there existed religious differences among the Arabians, some holding only the Koran and what Mahomet communicated to his son-in-law Eli, and who are known as the Shitin; while some held the traditions communicated by Mahomet, his wife and son-in-law, his sons, and many disciples, who are known as the Shonin."

And it seems that this religious quarrel has, to our shame, infected the Jews; Anan and Saul, his sons, tried to establish a new sect in Israel similar to the Shitin, for they thought that the Arabian high officers would assist them, for they would be at one with them in taking for the basis of their belief only what is written in the text, and to deny tradition. And how many times have religious movements, similar to those, taken place among the nations among which we live, even in our own times.

Having thus laid before the reader the views of the Karaites themselves, *i.e.*, of those later Karaites who endeavored to justify Anan for his complete separation from the Rabbanism, although Anan himself was very far from doing so, as can easily be seen by every one who has some sense of his own, from the statement of Anan: "And I will prepare you a Mishna and Talmud myself," (*vide supra*, 27), and also some of the opinions of the scholars Holdheim and Rapaport, we wish to submit our own opinion in regard to this matter.

In our judgment they all erred in making the following two assertions, viz: that the Sadducees did not believe in retribution in the world to come; and that the Talmudists had no knowledge of a sect naming itself, or which was named by others, Karaites. The error in making these assertions caused them to draw farfetched inferences and to write a number of articles, which will not stand any proper criticism. For Holdheim, in refuting upon the assertion of the Karaites that their sect was founded in the days of Jehudah b. Tobai, fixes their origin at a much prior date, by stating that the Sadducees and Karaites are one and the same sect, and that the latter name was adopted by them at a later date, but at the time of the Talmud they were known by the former name, and that accounts for not finding the name Karaites in the Talmud, basing his assertions on Maimonidus and Abraham b. David of Paskira. Some of these assertions may be found in Rapaport, although he tries to reconcile both sides. And because the Karaites differed from the Sadducees in that the latter did not believe in resurrection, and, according to him, also not in retribution after death, Holdheim asserts that the Karaites, who are the same as the Sadducees, have adopted that belief only at a later date, when that belief has already been adopted by all other nations and religions.

And coming to such conclusion he justifies the Sadducees and their views, and gives them preference over the Rabbanism and *their* views, which constitutes almost the whole subject of his book. But we will prove his error, and therefore most of his assertions will prove of no value, and the Talmudists and their views and teachings will remain true and everlasting.

But before attempting to explain ourselves in more detail we feel it our duty to say a few words in regard to Resurrection, which is the basis of the whole contention between the scholars above mentioned and the sects themselves.

The first Mishna in Chapt. Halek (Sanhedrin) reads: "The following have no share in the world to come: the one who says the Resurrection does not originate from the Pentateuch," which is explained by Rashi as follows: "*i.e.*, he who does not believe in the inferences drawn later on in the German that resurrection originates from the Bible; and even if he does believe in resurrection, but says that it does not originate from the Pentateuch, he is an infidel, for if he does not believe in its origin from the Bible what do we care for him or his belief? Wherefrom does he know that so it is? He is, therefore, a perfect infidel." And although some doubt whether these quoted words came from the pen of Rashi, because it was not Rashi's way to enter into lengthy explanations, still all concede that it expresses the true meaning of the Mishna.

Now, if we will take the true intent of the Talmudists, that although one believes in resurrection he is an infidel, if he does not believe that its origin is from the Pentateuch, we will at once conceive that when the latter belief began to circulate among all nations and among the masses of Israel to such an extent that, it was considered an essential element of the belief in God, and that any religion which did not consider it one of its dogmas, was not worthy of being ranked as a religion at all, the Talmudists endeavored to prove the origin of this belief from the Pentateuch and that other nations and religions borrowed it from *that* source, in order to refute those who asserted that its origin was in the New Testament and, therefore, the latter was the principal religion and the former ceased to exist.

We will now take up another Mishna in Tract Berachoth, P. 54a: "Since the Sadducees have perversely taught that there is only one state of existence, it was ordained that it shall be pronounced: 'From Eternity to Eternity,'" which Rashi explains, *i.e.*, "that they denied resurrection." Rashi again diverts the Mishna from its plain meaning, that the Sadducees did not admit the existence of the world to come, *i.e.*, retribution after the soul separates from the body, and limited their disbelief to resurrection only; (and that the meaning of "perversely taught" means that they perverted from their own opinions and taught the masses that belief).

It is self-evident that the perversion of the Sadducees consisted, according to Rashi, only in denying the inferences drawn to establish the origin of resurrection in the Pentateuch. But from the dispute of the Sadducees with the founder of the Christian religion, or with his disciples, and from the derisive question, "whom of them a widow of seven brothers will marry after resurrection," which is quoted in the work of Azariah Di Rossi, we can easily see that the Sadducees did not believe in resurrection *at all*.

If we will examine carefully the interpretations of the Talmudists in desiring to find a hint for resurrection in the Pentateuch, and that they did not infer it from the plain statement (Deutr. xxxli. 39): "*I alone kill and I make alive*; I wound and I heal," which, on every occasion they explained to mean "as the healing follows the wound, so also does life follow death" (see Ben Ezra), but resorted to far-fetched interpretations instead, we will clearly see that the Talmudists did not wish to state that resurrection is *expressly* stated in the Pentateuch, for in such case they would, of necessity, have to admit that this belief was known and circulating at the time the Pentateuch was given. They only wanted to find some slight reference to it in the Pentateuch, and were of the opinion that the belief in resurrection was known only to a limited number of select men, but not to the masses, from whom it was kept secret, for fear that they might as well believe in "familiar spirits" and "wizards ("Ob and Yaduni"), or in "inquiring of the dead." But only after this belief has been borrowed from the neighboring nations and has been adopted by the masses, the Talmudists found it necessary to find some source for it in the Pentateuch in order to strengthen the latter, although not explicitly stated therein.

It follows from all this that at the time the Mosaic Law was proclaimed, that belief was not only not obligatory, but on the contrary every effort was made to keep it from the masses, and, therefore, no promises were made as to resurrection, but only as to longevity and tranquillity during life-time.

When, however, the founder of Christianity made this belief one of its dogmas and minimized the Old Testament, the Talmudists made it obligatory to believe that its source is in the Pentateuch. And the Sadducees who rejected this belief at all were considered as disbelievers.

But we find nowhere that the Sadducees ever denied the immortality of the soul or that they ever denied the belief in retribution after death, for according to all opinions the Sadducees were not the disciples of Autigonus of Socho, Zaduck and Bithus, who, according to a statement in Aboth d'Rabbi Nathan, rejected the belief in retribution. The name Sadducees, as we have said in the beginning of this article, had its origin from Zaduck the high priest of David, according to Geiger's opinion. Or, perhaps, Holdheim's opinion is the correct one, viz.: that in the beginning they were surnamed "Zadikim," as Simon the high priest was surnamed the "Zadik."

Neither do we find anywhere that the Sadducees repulsed the statement of the Talmudists, to wit: "In order that thy days may be prolonged" (Deutr. v. 16), that means in the world to come which is prolonged (endless), and as the simple proof, if one say to his son: "go up on the roof and examine the bird's nest, and take the young ones, and send away the mother, in both of which (sending away the mother and honoring the father) longevity is the promised compensation in the Pentateuch; and the son in doing so fell and was killed; how can the promise be fulfilled? We must, therefore, say that the promised longevity has reference to life after death." Nor is it anywhere found that the Sadducees refuted the statement of the Talmudists: "That person shall be cut off" (Numb. xv. 31); that it means, he should be cut off from this world as well as from the world to come."

The assertion of those who consider themselves competent to make it, that there is no basis in the Pentateuch for the immortality of the soul, is not correct, for besides the many plain passages indicating. that, the same can also be established from the necessity of the marrying the widow of the deceased childless brother, for if the soul is mortal what is the benefit of "raising up the deceased's name?" So, also, greatly err those who, from this very passage, draw a contrary conclusion, *i.e.*, by asserting that because the soul dies together with the body the Pentateuch commanded that decedent's name be raised up if he die childless, for if the soul dies as does the body, why all that trouble of marrying the widow, or the ceremony of the "Chalitza," and spitting out before the one who refuses to marry the widow of his deceased childless brother, as commanded by the Pentateuch? If the soul derives no benefit therefrom, why all that? There is no honor in all that either for the dead or for the living, and it is very well known that this custom of raising up the name of the deceased on his estates was known and observed in ancient times, and the family that did not observe this custom incurred disrespect.

Thus far as to the Pentateuch, but as regards the prophets or Hygiogropha only a blind man can fail to find in them retribution and immortality of the soul after death. The whole book of Isaiah is full of that, and it says plainly (Isa. lvi. 4-5): "For thus saith the Lord concerning the eunuchs (those who die childless) I will indeed give unto them, in my house and within my walls, a place and a name better than sons and daughters, an eternal name--they shall not be cut off." And not to mention about the early and the later Hygiogropha (Ps., xvi. 10): "Thou will not abandon my soul to the grave," and also (ibid. xxvii. 13): "Unless I had believed to see the goodness of the Lord in the Land of life." And it is also explicitly stated, (ibid. xxv. 13): "His *soul* shall abide in happiness; and his *descendants* shall inherit the land." Now, how can it enter the mind that the Sadducees, who, according to Holdheim, are the Karaites, whose only endeavor was to give the whole Scripture, not only the Pentateuch, the illiteral meaning of the words will deviate from the literal meaning, and explain all those passages as referring only to this earthly life? We can also see from the fact that the Sadducees were more strict as to purification than the Pharisees in going as far as saying that profane writings (the book of Homer) make the hands unclean, to such an extent that if they touch Terumah the latter must not be eaten; that they believed in immortality of the soul, which they considered to such an extent clean that they will not tolerate the least uncleanliness in a sacred thing. And how much did the Sadducees sacrifice themselves in order to prevent the enemy from defiling the sanctuary? How much did they sacrifice themselves for the sake of the Holy name (קידושהשם), which no one who does not believe in immortality would do? But Holdheim seems to advance a strange assertion, viz., that the Sadducees believed in immortality of the soul and nevertheless denied retribution, which we can by no means understand, because what is the benefit of immortality if there is no retribution? If all are equal and alike after death, the righteous and the wicked, the wise and the fool? (The philosophy of Aristotle concedes at least that the soul of the right-eous unite with the (שכלהפועל) after death, but according to Hold-heim there is absolutely no preference to the human soul over that of the animal). It is true that we heard some few years ago (in 1885) in Leipsic, at a meeting of spiritualists, in company of the late Dr. Mandelkern, a professor, state in his lecture that the spirit of a certain man who, during his lifetime was one of the easy-minded, rested upon his shoulders for about two weeks, and that he was then of the same disposition as before death, and from this he drew the conclusion that the soul remains the same after death, in the spiritual world, as during the lifetime, but we hardly believe Holdheim ever entertained this belief, which is contrary to common sense, and still more, he endeavors to make his beloved Sadducees entertain such belief.

Dr. Geiger's opinion that the whole contention between the Sadducees and Pharisees was originally over political affairs, the former struggling to have the control over such affairs, because of their descent from prominent families, and the latter not desiring to submit, and from this the contention extended to civil and religious matters; the Pharisees being extremely faithful to their traditions saw in everything the Sadducees differed from them, a denial in tradi-tion;--seems to be more correct, as being also supported by history. The same theory is followed by I. H. Weiss in his work "Dor Dor V'dorshow," who proves conclusively that the Pharisees always laid down their decisions in direct opposition to that of the Sadducees in order to prevent the masses from joining the ranks of the latter. In fact, we see that the differences between the two sects, mentioned in the Talmud, were as to minor things which have very little to do with religious dogmas. We also have proved at the end of Tract Sabbath of our new edition, from page 381 on, that all the eighteen precau-tionary measures adopted by the Pharisees at the attic of Hananiah, were directed against the priests who mostly belonged to the Sadducees.

We do not mean to rebuke the Pharisees for having acted thus, for they did so of necessity, because the Sadducees endeavored to transplant Hellenism into the Hebrew religion in such a manner that it should not be noticed, and in order to guard against this they opposed the decisions of the Sadducees even when the latter were not contrary to thee true teachings of the Torah, for (Ps. cxix. 126): "It is time to act for the Lord: they have broken thy law."

It is very probable that because the belief in resurrection was so deeply rooted among the masses, because it is very natural that cue should desire to meet again his relatives alive after they had once died, and the Sadducees have opposed this belief and ridiculed it, the Pharisees assigned so much importance to it and endeavored to find some source for it in the Scripture, in order to prevent the names from adhering to the teachings of the Sadducees and thereby preventing the transplanting of Hellenism into the Hebrew faith, although in the very beginning of its development this belief was kept secret from the masses.

The result of what has been stated is that the Sadducees as well as the Pharisees, have expounded the Scripture according to tradition and have believed in the immortality of the soul and retribution after death. And the animosity of those two sects grew from the desire of each of them to have the control over political affairs. Therefore, when the Pharisees in the end gained the overhand, the first thing for Simeon b. Shetah to do was to remove the Sadducees from the Sanhedrin, in which he was very successful. But after the quarrel was carried on for several centuries, and almost during the whole time of the existence of the second Temple, and during that time more than once the danger was imminent that the teachings of the Pharisees should be swallowed up by Hellenism, and especially so during the time of Johanan the high priest and king, during whose reign the Pharisees were executed by the hundreds, and many emigrated to Egypt and Babylonia, the animosity and hatred assumed such proportions that the name "Sadducee" alone was contemptible. Still more, when after the Pharisees had already been successful they were

compelled to have public debates with them in religious matters, for
their teachings have been deeply rooted among the masses and could
not easily be rooted out.

This animosity assumed still greater proportions when Christianity began to develop; for the latter has confirmed many of the
teachings of the Sadducees, although not directly still indirectly, and
has opposed those of the Pharisees, although they did not differ to a
considerable extent from the latter in religious matters and principles,
the masses adhering to the teachings of the Pharisees, have greatly
despised the Sadducees, and considered them infidels and disbelievers in retribution and immortality of the soul, and in the
appearing of a personal Messiah from the houses of David and
Joseph, which belief has been circulating among the masses during
the last days of existence of the second Temple, and they endeavored,
with all their might, to obliterate their teachings. Those few
Sadducees who lived after the destruction of the second Temple
gathered up all the courage they could and entered into public
debates with R. Johanan b. Zakkai, R. Jose, etc., but seeing that their
hope was forlorn, and that they would not be able to rise again, they
gave up the battle publicly, although they did not renounce their
beliefs, or abandon their hatred, and tried to continue the same
against the teachings of the Pharisees secretly. At least, during the
second century we hear nothing of them publicly.

Now we will stop for a moment to see who the Karaite sect was.
There is no doubt that there existed a sect by this name in the days of
the Talmudists, for they are mentioned several times in the Talmud
under the name "Adherers to the Scripture," (בנימקרא), and in one
place it is plainly stated "the Karaites added" (Pesachim, p. 117; our
edition, p. 246, see foot note 3). Neither is there any doubt that they
were not favored by the Talmudists, as we find in many places in the
Talmud remarks reflecting on them, as *f.i.*: "They who occupy themselves with the study of Scripture are not to be blamed, but, on the
other hand, not to be praised" (Baba Metzia, 79), and in Hagiga, it
states plainly; Rabh said: "If a man goes out from the study of the
Mishna to read the verses of the Bible, this man can have no more
peace." And there is no doubt that many similar remarks found in the

Talmud have reference to this sect. But we can not, with exactness, fix the time when and to what extent this sect openly declared against the teachings of the Talmudists. However, we do not hesitate for one moment to state that during all that time this sect has brooded an intense hatred to every Israelite who has not followed them, although at times they were compelled to conceal their hatred.

One penetrating glance into the history of the Samaritans and into that of the Karaites; one penetrating glance into the literature of the former and into that of the latter; the curses pronounced by both of those sects against the followers of the Rabbanism; the beliefs and principles common to the religion of both (although differing slightly ceremonially), will suffice to induce one to agree with us that the Karaites, whose sect was established in the days of Anan, and a few of whom are living in our own time, have not only borrowed from the Samaritans their teachings, but that the Karaites are the former Samaritans and that even up to date they have changed slightly only in their outward appearance and in name, but not intrinsically.

From the whole sect we will pick out only Anan, who descended from the family of the Exilarch, who came from the house of David (and perhaps was his mother or grandmother of Samaritan descent), and who, from jealously having scorned and despised the traditional teachings, had gathered the remainder of the Samaritans, who had long ago changed their name and tendency, had become their chief to fight their battles and to separate completely from the house of Israel, for he could afford doing so, being a descendant from a prominent family. But we do not in the least intimate that Anan founded a new sect with new principles.

This, our present view, is not unfounded, but is based on historical facts, for we do not find anywhere in history any such intense, unchangeable, everlasting and unfounded hatred as that of the Samaritans and Karaites toward the house of Israel.

Whenever we find in history that any ill-feelings or hatred existed between two nations it is easy to find the reason for such feelings or hatred; it was either the craving for subjugation of foreign countries, or the desire to reign supreme over others, or, in very ancient times also the desire to prove the supremacy of one nation's idols over those of the other, and many other reasons, which provoked one nation to go to war with another and to take vengeance of one another. But we find no such reason for the hatred of the Samaritans toward the house of Israel, yet when the latter returned from Babylonia and intended to build the Temple, no plausible reason can be found for the endeavoring of the Samaritans to mislead the Israelites whenever they tried to establish the new moon. (See Rosh Hashana, Chap. II., our Hebrew edition, p. 25; English, p. 38.) Neither can there be assigned a reason for the custom of the Samaritans to pronounce curses over Ezra the Scribe, at the time of the opening of the ark of scrolls every Sabbath, which prevails up to date. (See our "The Pentateuch, its Character," etc., as well as for many other things which the reader may find in the Talmud and Apokrypha, and in Graetz's History of the Jews, which, if quoted here would occupy a full volume.) In a word, there can be found no substantial reason or ground for these things, except that they blindly hated the house of Israel. Neither do we find any reason for the slandering and reviling by the Karaites of the Rabbanism in general, and of Rabh Saadiah Gaon in particular, nor for all the false accusations and malicious charges and denunciations against the Rabbanism. contained in the extensive literature of the Karaites.

History shows us that nations who hated each other to the extreme have in course of time laid the weapons aside and made up. History records numerous instances, that sects between whom differences existed, and which even reached such a degree that they resulted in actual fight, have in course of time become reconciled and associated with each other, and intermarried, and the former hatred and quarrels were wholly forgotten. We will not cite as an example the Beth Shammai and the Beth Hillel, who, although widely differing from each other in their opinions, still intermarried, as found in the Talmud; but even the Sadducees and the Pharisees, did they there decline to eat and drink with each other, or intermarry? We do not find that anywhere.[4] The Samaritans, however, and Karaites are singular instances in this respect in history. Although most of them have already intermingled with other nations, not a single instance can be pointed out that they have intermarried with an Israelite or have partaken of his food or drink.

The toleration of the Pharisees and of their teachings is well known. The disciples of the Beth Hillel have done all that lay in their power to bring them into the house of Israel: they credited them in regard to purification; they permitted them to be counted in the number of three for the benediction over the meal (זיטון) and in the number of ten for prayer in the prayer house (מנין עשרה) and in fact, wanted to consider them as Israelites for all purposes, but their animosity and trickery increased to such an extent that they could no more be tolerated, and therefore, the leaders of Israel were compelled to regard them in all respects as idolators, and prohibited their bread, wine, and oil. Exactly the same thing happened with the Karaites whom the Rabbanism endeavored, with all their might, to draw near them and debate with them, until they convinced themselves that their hatred toward Israel is so great that they said "הקרעים אינן מתאחין לעולם"(the rents will never be sewed together), "the Karaites will never make up with us," and they are up to date regarded as idolators.

We know well that we are too brief in this article and that we ought to adduce at length all the facts to prove that all that the Samaritans and Karaites have done unto Israel was not to derive any benefit therefrom, or with a view of subduing them, for they well knew that this was an impossibility, but only out of blind hatred deeply rooted in them, which descends from generation to generation. We know this very well, but we can not enter here into such details, as it would exceed the limits of an article, and would comprise a whole book in itself. We, therefore, rely upon the intelligence and knowledge of the reader that be will know where to find those if needed.

Even in our own times, when the Karaites number only a few thousands, which accounts for their enjoying equal rights with the natives, since Emperor Nicholas of Russia, they make no secret of their hatred toward Israel. When the anti-Jewish disorders broke out in Russia some few years ago, and many of our co-religionists were exiled from the Middle States of the Russian Empire, the latter have petitioned the Russian Government to be permitted to embrace

Karaitism. The Minister of the Interior has expressed his willingness to grant their petition if the Karaites will consent to receive them into their midst, and directed an inquiry to this effect to their Hacham in *Odessa*, but the latter answered that there is no desire on the part of the Karaites to receive the Jews as their co-religionists.

These facts need hardly any comment; they speak for themselves. In fact, during all the long period since the year 760, it has not as yet happened that even a few individual Karaites should intermarry with our co-religionists, or should in any way associate with us. (Even in business affairs they do it only with great reluctance and very seldom.) Is there any stronger proof necessary of this race-hatred? No other race or nation, no matter how great their hatred may be, will ever decline to receive into their midst a Jew, if he only wishes to gain their faith, and will never refuse to associate with him; and the masses, as well as the intelligent classes, have always been favorably inclined toward the Jews. But this hatred of the Karaites has no equal among other nations in any generation.

As the Samaritans have forged and falsified the Pentateuch, as is now well established, so also did the Karaites forge and falsify the Talmud. And we hereby reproach the writers of the history of the Karaites, who without much deliberations wrote; For Saadiah the Gaon, when king, unable to assign any good reason for a statement found in the Talmud (Jerushalmi), that the Beth Shammai have killed some of the Beth Hillel, and *vice versa*, has denied the existence of such a statement at all; and Sahl, the son of Matzliah, his opponent, in order to prove to the world the delinquency of R. Saadiah, has descended from Palestine to Babylonia with the Jerusalem Talmud in his hand! And they did not conceive that Sahl himself has forged the manuscript of the Talmud by writing in this statement, and he was not the first one to do so, but was probably preceded by others, as we have remarked in the introduction to our edition of Rosh Hoshana. In fact, we are surprised at those who are handling the Karaite literature that they have not perceived it. Why should more evidence be given to Sahl the forger, than to Rabh Saadiah, who states positively that such a statement did not exist in the Talmud? Why should we not be-lieve R. Saadiah that in his manuscript such a statement was not in existence? (To our regret this statement was added to, and remains in the Talmud through the fault of the printers.) Especially so that even now in our own days the Karaites continue to forge and falsify, as proved by many modern scholars at the head of which is Abraham Harkawy, by exposing the falsifications of Abraham Firkowitz, the Karaite Hacham, in all his writings.

The result of all that stated is that from the similarity of action, in all details, of the Karaites and Samaritans we can logically arrive at the conclusion that the Karaites were doing nothing new, but only stepping in the shoes of their ancestors, the Samaritans, who they were, only under a different name, and being so they never descended from Israel. And all that Anan did was to gather the scattered Samaritans and encourage them to continue their fight against Israel, which has been hitherto conducted by them secretly, openly and publicly and with more vigor and animosity.

And if we will examine with a critical eye the literature of the Karaites we will easily see that they are none others than the Samaritans. And in vain has Dr. Holdheim held up as a striking proof the "laws of divorce," saying that such were the opinions of the Sadducees, and that the Karaites who were none else but the Sadducees clung to their old laws. No divorce was granted under the teaching of the Samaritans, unless on the ground of adultery. And as to this also the Talmud bears testimony in stating (as quoted above), "The Beth Shammai are as the Kuthaiz, *i.e.*, the Beth Shammai who prohibited a divorce unless on the ground of adultery, agree with the Samaritans who taught the same thing, and so also are the laws of the Karaites (even in regard to this has Dr. Holdheim blamed the teachings of the Pharisees without any foundation, for formerly even the Pharisees did not allow a divorce unless on the above-stated grounds, and all the leniency as to divorce which was afterwards decreed by the Beth Hillel, of whom R. Aqiba was one, was only introduced because the exigencies of the time required it, for it was at the time the New Testament began to gain strength and become popular, which declared every one who married a divorced woman to be an adulterer; as proved by I. H. Weiss in his work, and all other laws of the Karaites"). The strict observance of the Sabbath, etc., is nothing else but the laws of the Samaritans, and the slight difference in the ceremonies of these two sects is only because the former lived much later than the latter, and had to struggle with other sects who were their superiors, and to submit to them, and therefore many ceremonies were forgotten altogether. As to principles and dogmas, we have never heard that the Samaritans have ever rejected the belief in resurrection or in the world to come. On the contrary, as the belief in resurrection has circulated among all nations, and as the Samaritans have produced no great and learned men, and being widely separated from Israel, it is very natural that they did believe in resurrection as did their descendants the Karaites.

Another proof can be adduced that the Karaites are the descendants of the Samaritans; namely, that the Karaites mourn much more over the destruction of the Temple (and some of their Hachams have even adapted the name "Mourner" or "Mourners"), than we do, because, as the Samaritans they mourn over the loss of their temple on the Mount Gerisim which was destroyed by Janai, and continue to curse him up to date in their prayers.

We could adduce numerous other proofs taken from both the extensive literature of the Karaites and the inextensive literature of the Samaritans, to show that we did not in the least exaggerate our opinion as to the origin of the Karaites, but this article has taken up much more space than we expected and we are unable to give them here to the reader.

Before closing this article we find it our duty to answer the gentleman who put the question to us: "What are the reformers of our times, if not Karaites?"

A careful examination of the literature of the reformers in Europe, as Holdheim, Geiger, Ritter, etc.; of the prayer books of the reformers in this country, and of the sermons of their preachers all over the world, we will at once recognize in them the early Sadducees, with all their particularities. They (generally, not considering here and there an exception) believe in immortality of the soul, in retribution after death and in many Talmudical traditions, as can be shown by the fact that they observe the holidays as established by the Talmudists; but they do not believe in resurrection, neither in the coming of a personal Messiah, and do not recognize the Talmud as final authority in all matters; and self-understood those rules and regulations established subsequent to the close of the Talmud but in its spirit, the same thing did the former Sadducees.

But as our present reformers are descendants of the Pharisees, and the Sadducees being no more in existence, therefore they also have in many things adopted a new form, and recognize the teachings of the Pharisees (as for instance the observance of the sixth day of Sivan as Pentecost) as indisputable laws. But we can by no means accuse the reformers in not believing in tradition generally, as we cannot well accuse of that the former Sadducees. (Even those reformers who have changed the Sabbath, for even this can be explained in accordance with the general rule of the Talmud which sanctifies the seventh day, but not the Sabbath itself, and for this reason the Talmud decreed that in case one forgets which day is the Sabbath, he shall count six days and observe the seventh as Sabbath, see our article in the Deborah, 1894.) Should the reader put the question to us whether the reformers are not to be charged with transplanting Christianity into Judaism, and whether there is no danger that in course of time Christianity will swallow up Judaism altogether, as the Unitarism of our own days, as such danger has already threatened Judaism during the early Sadducees, we will say that this question requires a deliberate answer, and cannot be answered by "yes" or "no" offhand.

We can only state that we have devoted much of our attention to this question, and with a penetrating eye have followed the work of the reformers of the School of Holdheim, Ritter and their companions, in Berlin, of the school of Isaac Wise in Cincinnati, and of the teaching of Emil G. Hirch in Chicago, and having collected considerable data of their past, and having bestowed much deliberation upon their future, we consider ourselves competent to give our opinion about Otis matter. In fact we have prepared a long article dealing specially with the following questions: (1) Does the Hebrew religion require any reforms? (2) If it does, what are they and on what basis can we introduce them? (3) What are the re. reforms introduced by the conservative reformers, and what are those of the radical reformers? (4) What benefit resulted from these reforms in general and in particular? (5) The result of the reforms of Cincinnati and of those of Hirch, and (6) What is the meaning of the name "Orthodox," and to whom shall it be applied? This article we are willing to submit to the readers (after accomplishing our task of the translation) if desired.

END OF VOLUME I.

---

1. Translated almost verbatim from Mamar Haishuth.
2. It is well known that the Karaites make Anan's life date 100 years earlier than in reality, *i.e.*, 4400. But S. L. Rapoport, in his "Kerem Chemed," p. 203, has explained and proved their mistake, from the testimony of Sherira the Gaon, and the "Book of Tradition," by Abraham b. David, that Anan rose in the age of Jehuda the Gaon, who was a Gaon from 4516 to 4529 1/2.
3. Page 122, Holdheim's opinion.
4. An example may be given of the last century when a new sect (*Chasidim*) established themselves. The greatest authority, at least in Russia and Poland, Eliah Wilna, called the "Wilner Gaon" in conjunction with all the Rabbis, excommunicated the whole sect, prohibited their eatings and beverages and intermarriage with them. Moreover he allowed any one to denounce the new sect, and their rabbis were imprisoned by the government. But what was the end? Nothing at all. All the excommunications, prohibitions, prosecutions, etc., were abolished, without even the result of a meeting, and as soon as the quarrel was over, not one of either party hesitated to mingle with the opposite sect. All are called Israel, all are Israelites, and at the present time nobody gives any attention to all that happened then.

Historical and Literary Introduction to the New Edition of the Talmud

Chapter 1
The Combination of the Gemara, The Sophrim and the Eshcalath

Voluminous books were written about the text of the Mishna and Talmud in almost every language, besides valuable articles by very scholarly men in different books and periodicals. In the bibliography the reader will find all modern works arranged with various references to subjects. We shall only point out the special books on this subject, viz., "Darkhe Hamishnah," (The Ways of the Mishna), by Zachariah Frankel, "The Introduction to the Mishna," by Jacob Brill, 1876, "The Tradition of the Oral Law," by H. Weiss, and "Toldat Hamishnah," (History of the Mishna), by Haim Oppenheim, all in Hebrew; "Jahrbücher," by Dr. N. Brill, Frankfort, A. M., "Real Encyclopædie," by J. Hamburger, "Die Lehrer der Mishna," by M. Braunschweiger, and Graetz's "History of the Jews," all in German. Finally three special introductions were written (1) "Einleitung in den Talmud," Leipzig, 1894, second edition, by Dr. Herman Strack, in German; (2) "Introduction to the Talmud," 1891 and 1894, second edition, by Dr. M. Mielziner, in English, and (3) "Introduction to the Mishna," in the Russian language, by N. Perferkowitz.[1]

In these introductions are mentioned also the different translations of the Mishnayoth and Talmud in all the languages up to the time these works were written. Finally, Dr. Erick Bischoff wrote a special book named "Kritische Geschichte der Talmud-Überzetzungen aller Zeiten und Zungen," Frankfort, a. M., 1899. All the above mentioned introductions explain the terms of the text of the Mishna and Talmud, their abbreviations and the method of both Talmuds, to enable those who desire to study the text in the original. We, however, who wish to give an introduction to our English translation of the Talmud, deem it not necessary to trouble the English reader with the explanations of the text, and shall give only what pertains to our new edition.

We have already mentioned in our brief introduction to *Sabbath* that the Talmud, in general, is composed of *Mishna* and *Gemara*. In this introduction, however, we shall give all the particulars pointed out by Strack and Mielziner which we deem of interest to the English reader. As a text we took Mielziner's "Introduction," which is an excellent work, omitting what seems to us not necessary for the reader, supplying it with necessary remarks and additions.

(1.)

The Talmud is a combination of *Mishna* and *Gemara*, the latter is a collection of *Mishnayoth, Tosephtas, Mechilta, Siphra, Siphre* and *Boraithas*, all of these, interpreted and discussed by the Amoraim, Salboraim, and also Gaonim at a later period. "The Mishna is the authorized codification of the oral or unwritten law, which on the basis of the written law contained in Pentateuch, developed during the second Temple, and down to the end of the second century of the common era." The author of which was R. Jehuda, the prince named "Rabbi" (flourishing toward the end of the second century), taking the unfinished work of R. Akiba and R. Meir as basis.[2]

(2.)

"The word Tosephta means Addition, Supplement, and, as indicated by this name, the work is intended to complete deficiencies of the Mishna.[3] It is divided into Masechtoth, generally corresponding

194

to those of the Mishna, but differing from them in the arrangement of their subject, and in the division of their Perakim. The latter are not subdivided into paragraphs. There are in all sixty Masechtoth and 452 Perakim. The Tosephta contains mainly the remnants of the earlier compilations of the Halacha made by R. Akiba, R. Meir, R. Nehemia, and others not adopted in the Mishna, and, besides additions made after R. Jehuda Hanasi's death by his disciples, R. Chiya, R. Oshaya, Bar Kappara and others. But we find in that work also many sayings and decisions of later Amoraim of the Babylonian and Palestinian schools. In its present shape it belongs to the fifth or sixth century."[4]

(3.)

"The Mechilta, the Siphra and the Siphre have this in common, that they treat of the oral law not according to well arranged subjects, as is the case with the Mishna and the Tosephta, but rather in the form of a running commentary and discussion on the biblical passages from which the law is deduced or on which it is based.

"The Siphra, also called Torath Cohanin, is a collection of traditional interpretations of the whole book of Leviticus, introduced by an exposition of R. Ishmael's thirteen hermeneutic rules."

(4.)

"The Siphre, or, as its fuller title reads, the books of the school of Rab, comprises the traditional interpretations of the book of Numbers, beginning with Chapter V., and of the whole book of Deuteronomy. The author of the Siphre on Numbers was evidently not the same as the author of that on the last book of the Pentateuch. The style of the former, being more argumentative and discursive, often resembles that of the Siphra, while Siphre on Deuteronomy is generally brief, bearing more resemblance to the Mechilta." The author of it is said to be R. Simeon b. Johai.

Besides the Tosephta, the Mechilta, the Siphra and the Siphre just described, other collections of a similar character existed during

195

the Talmudical period. In the course of time they perished, but many hundred fragmentary passages thereof are quoted in all parts of the Palestinian and Babylonian Gemara. Such a passage quoted from those lost collections as well as from the Tosephta, Mechilta, Siphra and Siphre was termed *Boraitha*, or *Mathnitha Boraitha*, meaning *extraneous* Mishna. This term was used in order to distinguish those passages from passages in *our Mishna*, that is, the authorized Mishna of R. Jehuda Hanasi, compared with which they had but a subordinate value. The Baraithoth are often found to be conflicting with each other or with the authorized Mishna, and in this case the Gemara usually displays great ingenuity and subtility in the attempt to reconcile them. In some instances, however, one or the other Boraitha is declared to be spurious.[5]

The authorities mentioned in the Mishna and Boraitha[6] as having transmitted and developed the oral law belong to three different periods; namely: (1) The period of Sopherim. (Scribes); (2) The period of Zugoth; (3) The period of Tanaim.

(*a*) Sopherim or Scribes were the learned men who succeeded Ezra during a period of about two hundred years. To them many institutions and extensions of the Mosaic law are ascribed. The Sopherim. are also called collectively "the men of the Great Assembly (Synod)." According to tradition, this Synod consisted of 120 members, but we have no record of their names with the exception of *Ezra*, its founder, and of *Simon the Upright* (*Just*), (the high priest Simon I., between 310-292, or his grandson Simon II., between 220-202 B.C.), who is said to have been one of the last members of the Great Assembly.

Antigonos of Socho, a disciple of Simon the Just, was the connecting link between this and the following period.

(*b*) The word *Eshcalath* (*Zugoth*), meaning the pairs (duumviri), is the appellation of the leading teachers from Jose ben Joezer till Hillel, of whom always two, at the same time, stood at the head of the Sanhedrin, one as president (Nasi), and the other as vice-president (Ab beth din).

The succession of these Zugoth was:

(1) *Jose ben Joezer* and *Jose ben Jochanan*, flourishing at the time of the Maccabean wars of independence.

(2) *Joshua b. Perachia* and *Nitai of Arbela*, flourishing at the time of John Hyrcan.

(3) *Juda b. Tabai* and *Simon b. Shetach*, flourishing at the time of Alexander Janai and Queen Salome.

(4) *Shemaiah* and *Abtalion*, flourishing at the time of Hyrcan II.

(5) Hillel and Shamai, flourishing at the time of King Herod.

(c) With the disciples of Hillel and Shamai begins the period of Tanaim, which lasted about 210 years (from 10 to 220 Ch. Era). With the beginning of this period the title Rabbi (teacher) for the ordained teachers, and the title Rabban (our teacher) for the president of the Sanhedrin came in use.

In the Mishna, the term Tana, meaning a teacher of the oral law, does not yet occur. Those teachers are there signified by generally adding the title of *Rabbi* to their names, or by calling them collectively the Sages, while the authorities of the preceding period are occasionally designated "the former elders." It is first in the Gemara that the term *Tana* is applied to a teacher mentioned in the Mishna and Boraitha, in contradistinction to the *Amoraim*, expounders of the Mishna, as the teachers after R. Jehuda Hanasi are called. (In Babylonian Talmud: in Palestinian, however, the Amoraim are also called Rabbis.)

The period of the Tanaim is generally divided into five or six minor sections or generations. The purpose of this division is to show which teachers developed their principal activity contemporaneously, though the actual lifetime of some of them extended to more than one generation. The following chronological tables contain the names only of the more prominent[7] teachers of each generation. Every table is followed by short biographical sketches of the teachers mentioned therein.[8]

---

1. This work, which is the first of its kind in the Russian language, is also worthy to be considered.
2. The meaning of the word Mishna is already explained by us in the first volume of this work, as well as its division into sections. In Mielziner's "Introduction," pp. 18-

21, the reader will find all the details about Mechilta Siphra and Siphre and Boraitha, which we deem it not necessary to repeat as they are not of importance to the reader.

3. See also our brief general introduction, vol. i.

4. The Tosephta is usually printed as an appendix to Alphasi's compendium of the Talmud. In the Vienna edition of the Babylonian Talmud (1860-72) the Masechtoth of the Tosephta are appended to the corresponding Masechtoth of the Talmud. A separate revised edition of the whole Tosephta was published by Dr. Zuckermandel (Pasewalk and Treves, 1877-82). Dr. Adolph Schwartz is publishing a new edition of the Tosephta, with notes and text corrections, of which the first volume is out, Wilna, 1891. Critical researches on the Tosephta are foul) din Frankel's "Darke Hamishna," pp. 304-307, and in I. H. Weiss's "Dor Dor," etc., II., pp. 217-225; also in I. H. Duenner's "Wesen und Ursprung der Tosephta," Amsterdam, 1874.

5. Some critical researches on the Boraitha are found in Frankel's "Darke Hamishna," pp. 311-313, and in I. H. Weiss's "Dor Dor," II., pp. 239-244.

6. We do not find the *Zugoth* to be mentioned in the Boraitha. However, we do not cancel it as it is so written by Mielziner.

7. We do not understand very well what the learned Doctor Mielziner means by the word *prominent*, as it seems that the Tanaim whom he omitted were not less prominent than those whom he mentioned. On the contrary, some of them were even more prominent. We are sorry that our work was delayed until after the departure of the learned doctor, who was our friend and whose loss we greatly lament, so that we cannot ask him the reason as we always meant to do. (See our remarks further on.)

8. Fuller characteristics of the lives and teachings of the principal Tanaim are given in the following works:

   Graetz, "History of the Jews," Vol. IV.

   Z. Frankel, "Darke Hamishna."

   I. H. Weiss, Zur Geschichte der juedischen Tradition," Vols. I. and II.

   Jacob Bruell, "Mebo Hamishna," Vol. I.

   J. Hamburger, "Real Encyclopaedie," Vol. II. "Die Talmudischen Artikel." M. Braunschweiger, "Die Lehrer der Mishnah."

   H. Strack, "Einleitung in den Talmud."

   N. Perferkowitz, Talmud, Part I.

Chapter 2
The Generations of the Tanaim

FIRST GENERATION.

The principal Tanaim of the first generation, which lasted about seventy years, from 10 to 80, Ch. Era,[1] are: (1) The School of Shamai and the School of Hillel; (2) Akabia ben Mahalalel; (3) Rabban Gamaliel the Elder; (4) Rabbi Chanina, Chief of the Priests; (5) R. Simon ben Gamaliel; (6) R. Jochanan ben Zakkai. (Strack adds to this first generation [10-90] the judges), (7) Admon, and (8) Hannan; (9) Nachum the Madaith; (10) Eliezer b. Jacob I; (11) Haninah b. Dosa; (12) Nechunyah b. Hakanah; and (13) Zadock.

Mielziner counts Adman, Hannan and Nachum of Madaith at the end of this paragraph, not numbering them among the first generation, so also he did with some others in the succeeding generations.

Characteristics and Biographical Sketches.

1. *The School of Shamai* and the *School of Hillel* were. founded by the disciples of the great teachers whose names they bear. Following the principles of their masters,[2] they differed widely in their opinions on many legal questions; the School of Shamai, in general, taking a rigorous, and the School of Hillel a more lenient view of the question. In their frequent controversies the School of Shamai, having been founded already during the lifetime of Hillel, is

199

always mentioned first. Of individual teachers belonging to either of these two schools only a very few are occasionally mentioned by name. Both schools existed during the whole period of the first generation, and the antagonism of their followers extended even to the middle of the subsequent generation.

2. *Akabia ben Mahalalel*. Of this teacher who flourished shortly after Hillel only a few opinions and traditions are recorded. According to what is related of him in Mishna Eduyoth, V., 6, 7, he was a noble character with unyielding principles.

3. *Rabban Gamaliel the Elder*. He was a son of R. Simon, and grandson of Hillel, whom he succeeded in the office of Nasi. Many important ordinances (תקנות) of the Rabbinical law are ascribed to him. He died eighteen years before the destruction of Jerusalem. The epithet "the Elder" generally added to his name, is to distinguish him from his grandson Gamaliel of Jabne, who flourished in the following generation.

4. *Rabbi Chanina, Chief of the Priests*, or the proxy of the high-priest. He, as well as "the court of Priests," is incidentally mentioned in the Mishna in connection with laws concerning the sacrifices and the Temple service.

5. *R. Simon ben Gamaliel*. He was the son and successor of Rabban Gamaliel the Elder, and was executed by the Romans in the time of the destruction of Jerusalem. Belonging to the School of Hillel, his individual opinions in questions of law are but rarely recorded in the Mishna. He must not be confounded with his grandson who had the same name and belonged to the fourth generation of Tanaim.

6. *R. Jochanan b. Zakkai*. This distinguished teacher was one of the youngest disciples of Hillel, occupied a high position already before the destruction of Jerusalem, and afterwards became the founder and head of the celebrated academy of Jabne (Jamnia).

SECOND GENERATION.

This generation lasted about forty years, from 80 to 120. The principal Tanaim belonging to it are:

200

(1) Rabban Gamaliel II., (of Jabne); (2) Rabbi Zadok., (3) R. Dosa (b. Harchinas); (4) R. Eliezer b. Jacob;[3] (5) R. Eliezer (b. Hyrkanos); (6) R. Joshua (b. Chanania); (7) R. Elazar b. Azaria; (8) Elasar b. Arach;[4] (9) R. Juda b. Bathyra. (According to Strack), (10) Papias; (11) Alazar b. Zadock; (12) Samuel the Little; (13) Nachum of Gimzu; (14) Ben Paturi; (15) Jose the Priest; (16) Elazar of Modium.

We refrain from giving the sketches of those who were added by Strack and others, as they would take up too much space. The reader who is interested in them can easily find them in the reference books pointed out by Strack, who gives to each of them the sources in the German language from which he draws.

Characteristics and Biographical Sketches.

1. *Rabban Gamaliel II.* He was a grandson of Gamaliel the Elder; after the death of R. Johanan b. Zakkai he became president of the academy of Jabne, and like his ancestors, he bore the title Nasi (Prince); with the Romans, Patriarch, In order to distinguish him from his grandfather, he received the surname *Gamaliel of Jabne*, or the Second.

2. R. Zadok. Of him it is related that he, in anticipation of the destruction of the Temple, fasted for forty successive years. He then removed to Jabne where he as well as his son, R. Eliezar b. Zadok, belonged to the distinguished teachers.

3. *R. Dosa b. Harchinas* belonged to the school of Hillel, and removed with R. Jochanan b. Zakkai from Jerusalem to Jabne, where he reached a very old age. He stood in such high esteem that his most distinguished colleagues appealed to his opinion in doubtful cases.

4. *R. Eliezer b. Jacob* was head of a school, and in possession of traditions concerning the structure and interior arrangements of the Temple. He is also mentioned with commendation as to his method of instruction, which was "concise and clear." There was also another Tana by a similar name who flourished in the fourth generation.

5. *R. Eliezer b. Hyrkanos*, in the Mishna called simply R. Eliezer, was one of the most distinguished disciples of R. Jochanan b. Zakkai, who characterized him as "the lime-cemented cistern that does not lose a drop." He was a faithful conservator of handed-down decisions and opposed to their slightest modification and to any new deduc-

tions to be made therefrom. His school was in Lydda, in South Judea. Though formerly a disciple of the Hillelites, he inclined to the views of the Shamaites and consequently came in conflict with his colleagues. Being persistent in his opinion, and conforming to it even in practice, he was excommunicated by his own brother-in-law, the patriarch Gamaliel II.

6. R. *Joshua b. Chanania*, in general called simply R. Joshua, was likewise one of the favored disciples of R. Jochanan b. Zakkai. Shortly before the destruction of the Temple he left Jerusalem with his teacher, after whose death he founded a separate school in *Bekiin*. As member of the Sanhedrin in Jabne, he participated conspicuously in its deliberations and debates. His discussions were mostly with R. *Eliezer*, to whose unyielding conservatism he formed a striking contrast, as he represented the more rational and conciliatory element of that generation, and combined with great learning the amiable virtues of gentleness, modesty and placability which characterized the Hillelites. As he, on several occasions, was humiliated by the Nasi Gamaliel II., with whom he differed on some questions, the members of the Sanhedrin resented this insult of their esteemed colleague by deposing the offender from his dignity and electing another president. It was only through the interference of the appeased R. Joshua that R. Gamaliel, who apologized for his conduct, was again restored to his office.

7. R. *Elazar b. Azaria* descended from a noble family whose pedigree was traced up to Ezra the Scribe. Already while a young man, he enjoyed such a reputation for his great learning that he was made president of the academy at Jabne in place of the deposed R. Gamaliel. When the latter was reinstated, R. Elazar was appointed as vice-president. His controversies were mostly with R. Joshua, R. Tarphon, R. Ishmael and R. Akiba. On account of the noble virtues which he combined with his great learning he was compared to "a vessel filled with aromatic spices," and R. Joshua said of him: "a generation having a man like R. Elazar b. Azaria, is not orphaned."

8. *Elazar b. Arach*, of whom it is said (Aboth, p. 61), "If all the wise of Israel were in a scale of the balance and Eliezer b. Hyrkanos

with them, and Elazar b. Arach in the other scale, he would outweigh them all."

9. *R. Juda b. Bathyra* had a school in *Nisibis* (in Assyria), already at the time when the Temple of Jerusalem was still in existence. He was probably a descendant of the family Bene Bathyra, who were leaders of the Sanhedrin under King Herod, and who resigned that office in favor of Hillel. Several other Tanaim had the same family name, as R. Joshua b. Bathyra, R. Simon b. Bathyra and one called simply Ben Bathyra.

THIRD GENERATION.

Several Teachers of the third generation, which lasted from the year 120 till about 139 (130-160, Strack), flourished already in the preceding one. The principal teachers are:

(1) R. Tarphon; (2) R. Ishmael; (3) R. Aqiba; (4) R. Jochanan b. Nuri; (5) R. Jose the Galilean; (6) R. Simon b. Nanos; (7) R. Juda b. Baba; (8) R. Jochanan b. Broka. Strack counts all the above-mentioned in the second generation, with the addition of, (9) Papus b. Jehuda; (10) Elazar b. Chasma; (11) Jose of Damascus; (12) Hananya b. Trodyan; (13) Jos b. Kisma; (14) Elazar b. Parta; (15) Simeon b. Azai; (16) Simeon b. Zoma; (17) Elisha b. Abuyah; (18) Chaninah b. Gamaliel; (19) Chaninah b. Antigonos; (20) Elazar of Bartutha; (21) Simeon of Taimon; (22) Chananiah, the son of Jechosua's brother; (23) Jehuda b. Buthyra; (24) Matyah b. Cheris;[5] (25) Chittkah; (26) Simeon the Shakmone; (27) Chananiah b. Chakniel.

Characteristics and Biographical Sketches.

1. *R. Tarphon*, or Tryphon, of Lydda. He is said to have been inclined to the views of the School of Shamai. On account of his great learning he was called "the teacher of Israel"; besides, he was praised for his great charitable works. His legal discussions were mostly with his colleague R. Akiba.

2. *R. Ishmael* (b. Elisha) was probably a grandson of the high-priest Ishmael b. Elisha who was condemned to death by Titus, together with the patriarch Simon b, Gamaliel I. When still a boy, he

was made a captive and brought to Rome, where R. Joshua who happened to come there on a mission, redeemed him at a high ransom and brought him back to Palestine. R. Nechunia b. Hakana is mentioned as one of his principal teachers. When grown to manhood, he became a member of the Sanhedrin and was highly revered by his colleagues. He is named among those who emigrated with the Sanhedrin from *Jabne* to *Usha*. His residence was in South Judea in a place called Kephar Aziz. His academical controversies were mostly with R. Akiba, to whose artificial methods of interpreting the law he was strongly opposed, on the principle that the Torah, being composed in the usual language of man, must be interpreted in a plain and rational way. As guiding rules of interpretation he accepted only the seven logical rules which had been laid down by Hillel, which he, however, by some modifications and subdivisions, enlarged to thirteen. A separate school which he founded was continued after his death by his disciples and was known by the name of "Be R. Ishmael." Of the book *Mechilta* which is ascribed to R. Ishmael.

3. *R. Aqiba* (b. Joseph) was the most prominent among the Tanaim. He is said to have descended from a proselyte family, and to have been altogether illiterate up to the age of his manhood. Filled with the desire to acquire the knowledge of the law, he entered a school and attended the lectures of the distinguished teachers of that time, especially of R. Eliezer b. Hyrkanos, R. Joshua b. Chanania, and of Nachum of Gimzu. Subsequently he founded a school in B'ne Brak, near Jabne, and became a member of the Sanhedrin in the last-mentioned city. Through his keen intellect, his vast learning and his energetic activity he wielded a great influence in developing and diffusing the traditional law. He arranged the accumulated material of that law in a proper system and methodical order, and enriched its substance with many valuable deductions of his own. His methodical arrangement and division of that material was completed by his disciple R. Meir, and later on became the groundwork of the Mishna compiled by R. Jehuda Hanasi. Besides, he introduced a new method of interpreting the Scriptures, which enabled him to find a biblical basis for almost every provision of the oral law. This ingenious method was admired by his contemporaries, and notwithstanding the

opposition of some of his colleagues, generally adopted in addition to the thirteen hermeneutic rules of R. I Ishmael. R. Akiba's legal opinions are very frequently recorded in all parts of the Mishna and in the kindred works. His academical discussions are mostly with his former teachers, R. Eliezer, R. Joshua, and with his colleagues, R. Tarphon, R. Jochanan b. Nuri, R. Jose the Galilean and others.

R. Akiba died a martyr to religion and patriotism. Having been a stout supporter of the cause of Bar Cochba, he was cruelly executed by the Romans for publicly teaching the Law, contrary to the edict of the emperor Hadrian. (See Aboth, p. 2 8.)

4. *R. Jochanan b. Nuri* was a colleague of R. Akiba, with whom he frequently differed on questions of the law. In his youth he seems to have been a disciple of R. Gamaliel II., for whose memory he always retained a warm veneration. He presided over a college in Beth Shearim, a place near Sepphoris in Galilee.

5. *R. Jose the Galilean* was a very distinguished teacher. Of his youth and education nothing is known. At his first appearance in the Sanhedrin of Jabne, he participated in a debate with R. Tarphon and With R. Akiba, and displayed such great learning and sagacity that he attracted general attention. From this debate his reputation as a teacher was established. He was an authority especially in the laws concerning the sacrifices and the Temple service. His discussions were mostly with R. Akiba, R. Tarphon, and R. Elazar b. Azariah. Of his domestic life it is related that he had the bad fortune of having an ill-tempered wife, who treated him so meanly that he was compelled to divorce her, but learning that she in her second marriage lived in great misery, he generously provided her and her husband with all the necessaries of life. One of his sons, R. Eleazar b. R. Jose the Galilean, became a distinguished teacher in the following generation and established the thirty-two hermeneutic rules of the Hagada.

6. *R. Simon b. Nanos*, also called simply Ben Nanos, was a great authority especially in the civil law, so that R. Ishmael recommended to all law students to attend the lectures of this profound teacher. His legal controversies were mostly with R. Ishmael and R. Akiba.

7. *R. Judah b. Baba,* who on account of his piety was called the Chasid, is noteworthy not only as a distinguished teacher, but also as

a martyr to Judaism. Contrary to the Hadrianic edict which, under extreme penalty, prohibited the ordination of teachers, he ordained seven[6] disciples of R. Akiba as Rabbis, and for this act was stabbed to death by the Roman soldiers.

8. *R. Jochanan b. Broka* was an authority especially in the civil law. Also his son R. Ishmael was a distinguished teacher who flourished in the following generation.

FOURTH GENERATION.

This generation extended from the death of R. Akiba to the death of the patriarch R. Simon b. Gamaliel IL, from the year 139 to about 165. Almost all leading teachers of this generation belong to the latter disciples of R. Akiba.

(1) R. Meir; (2) R. Jehuda (ben Ilai); (3) R. Jose (ben Chalafta); (4) R. Simon (b. Jochai); (5) R. Elazar (b. Shamua); (6) R. Jochanan the Sandelar; (7) R. Elazar b. Jacob; (8) R. Nehemia; (9) R. Joshua b. Korcha; (10) R. Simon b. Gamaliel. Strack counts all of them in the third generation, and adds, (11) Elazar b. Jose the Galilean; (12) Ishmael b. Jochanan b. Beroka; (13) Abba Schaul; (14) Chananiah b. Akiba; (15) Chananiah b. Akashya; (16) Jose b. Akabyah; (17) Issi b. Jehuda; (18) Nehuraye; (19) Abba Jos b. Dusthai.

Characteristics and Biographical Sketches.

1. *R. Meir*, the most prominent among the numerous disciples of R. Akiba, was a native of Asia Minor and gained a subsistence as a skilful copyist of sacred Scripture. At first, be entered the academy of R. Akiba, but finding himself not sufficiently prepared to grasp the lectures of this great teacher, he attended, for some time, the school of R. Ishmael, where he acquired an extensive knowledge of the law. Returning then to R. Akiba and becoming his constant and favored disciple, be developed great dialectical powers, R. Akiba soon recognized his worth and preferred him to other disciples by ordaining him at an early date. This ordination was later renewed by R. Judah b. Baba. On account of the Hadrianic persecutions, R. Meir had to flee from Judea, but after the repeal of those edicts, he returned and joined his colleagues in reëstablishing the Sanhedrin in the city of

206

Usha, in Galilee. His academy was in Emmaus, near Tiberias, and for a time also in Ardiscus, near Damascus, where a large circle of disciples gathered around him. Under the patriarch R. Simon b. Gamaliel II., he occupied the dignity of a *Chacham* (advising Sage), in which office he was charged with the duty of preparing the subjects to be discussed in the Sanhedrin. A conflict which arose between him and the patriarch seems to have induced him to leave Palestine and return to his native country, Asia Minor, where he died. R. Meir's legal opinions are mentioned almost in every Masechta of the Mishna and Boraitha. His greatest merit was that he continued the labors of R. Akiba in arranging the rich material of the oral law according to subjects, and in this way prepared the great Mishna compilation of R. Judah Hanasi. Besides being one of the most distinguished teachers of the law, he was also a very popular lecturer (Hagadist), who used to illustrate his lectures by interesting fables and parables. Of his domestic life it is known that he was married to Beruria, the learned daughter of the celebrated teacher and martyr R. Chananiah b. Teradyon. The pious resignation which he and his noble wife exhibited at the sudden death of their two promising sons has been immortalized by a popular legend in the Midrash.

2. *R. Jehuda b. Ilai* is generally called in the Mishna simply R. Jehuda. After having received instruction in the law from his father, who had been a disciple of R. Eliezer b. Hyrkanos, be attended the lectures of R. Tarphon, and became then one of the distinguished disciples of R. Akiba. On account of his great eloquence he is called, "The first among the speakers." Also his piety, modesty and prudence are highly praised. He gained a modest subsistence by a mechanical trade, in accordance with his favored maxims: "Labor honors man," and "He who does not teach his son a trade, teaches him, as it were, robbery." Having been one of the seven disciples who after the death of R. Akiba were ordained by R. Juda b. Baba contrary to the Hadrianic edict, he had to flee. After three years he returned with his colleagues to Usha and became one of the prominent members of the resuscitated Sanhedrin. The patriarch R. Simon ben Gamaliel honored him greatly, and appointed him as one of his advisers. As expounder of the law he was a great authority, and is very often

quoted in all parts of the Mishna and Boraitha. His legal opinions generally prevail, when differing from those of his colleagues R. Meir and R. Simon. To him is also ascribed the authorship of the essential part of the Siphra. The Hagada of the Talmud records many of his beautiful sayings, which characterize him not only as a noble-hearted teacher, but also as a sound and clearheaded interpreter of Scriptures. He, for instance, denied the literal meaning of the resurrection of the dead bones spoken of in Ezekiel, ch. XXXVII., but declared it to be merely a poetical figure for Israel's rejuvenation. (Sanhedrin, p. 278.)

R. Jehuda had two learned sons who flourished as teachers in the following generation.

3. *R. Jose b. Chalafta*, in the Mishna called simply R. Jose, was from *Sepphoris*, where already his learned father had established a school. Though by trade a tanner, be became one of the most distinguished teachers of his time. He was a disciple of R. Akiba and of R. Tarphon. Like his colleagues he was ordained by R. Juda b. Baba, and on this account had to flee to the south of Palestine, whence he later on returned with them to Usha. For having kept silent when in his presence R. Simon made a slighting remark against the Roman government, he was banished to Asia Minor. When permitted to return, he settled in his native city, Sepphoris, where he died at an advanced age. Besides being a great authority in the law, whose opinions prevail against those of his colleagues R. Meir, R. Jehuda and R. Simon, he was an historian to whom the authorship of the chronological book *Seder Olam* is ascribed.

4. *R. Simon b. Jochai* from Galilee, in the Mishna called simply R. Simon, was likewise one of the most distinguished disciples of R. Akiba, whose lectures he attended during thirteen years. "Be satisfied that I and thy creator know thy powers," were the words with which this teacher comforted him, when he felt somewhat slighted on account of a certain preference given to his younger colleague R. Meir. He shared the fate of his colleagues in being compelled to flee after ordination. Afterwards, he joined them at the new seat of the Sanhedrin in Usha. On a certain occasion he gave vent to his bitter feeling against the Romans, which was reported to the Roman gover-

nor, who condemned him to death. He, however, escaped this fate by concealing himself in a cave, where he is said to have remained for several years, together with his son, engaged in the study of the law, and subsisting on the fruit of the carob-trees which abounded there in the neighborhood. In the meantime political affairs had taken a favorable turn, so that he had no longer to fear any persecution; he left his hiding place and reopened his academy at *Tekoa*, in Galilee, where a circle of disciples gathered around him. He survived all his colleagues, and in his old age was delegated to Rome, where he succeeded in obtaining from the emperor (Marcus Aurelius) the repeal of some edicts against the Jewish religion.

In the interpretation of the law, R. Simon departed from the method of his teacher R. Akiba, as he inclined to the view of R. Ishmael that "the Torah speaks the common language of man," and consequently regarded logical reasoning as the proper starting point for legal deductions, instead of pleonastic words, syllables and letters. In accordance with this sound principle, he tried to investigate the evident motive of different biblical laws, and to make conclusions therefrom for their proper application. In regard to treating and arranging the oral law, however, he followed the method of R. Akiba in subsuming various provisions under guiding rules and principles. R. Simon is regarded as the author of the *Siphre*, though that work in its present shape shows many additions by the hands of later authorities.[7]

5. *R. Elazar b. Shamua*, in the Mishna simply R. Elazar, was among those of R. Akiba's disciples who in consequence of the Hadrian edicts went to the South, whence he went to Nisibis. He does not, however, appear to have joined his colleagues when they gathered again at Usha. He is regarded as a great authority in the law. The place of his academy is not known, but it is stated that his, school was always overcrowded by disciples eager to hear his learned lectures. Among his disciples was also the later patriarch R. Jehuda. On a journey, he visited his former colleague R. Meir at Ardiscos, in Asia Minor, and with him had discussions on important questions of the law, which are recorded in the Mishna and Boraitha.

6. *R. Jochanan the Sandelar* had this surname probably from his

trade in sandals. Born in Alexandria in Egypt, he came to Palestine to attend the lectures of R. Akiba, and was so faithful a disciple that he visited this teacher even in prison, in order to receive instruction from him. His legal opinions are occasionally recorded in the Mishna as well as in the Tosephta and Boraitha.

7. *R. Elazar* (or Eliezer) *b. Jacob* was a disciple of R. Akiba and later a member of the Sanhedrin in Usha. This teacher must not be confounded with a former teacher by that name who flourished in the second generation.

8. *R. Nechemia* belonged to the last disciples of R. Akiba and was an authority especially in the sacrificial law, and in laws concerning levitical purification. His controversies are mostly with R. Juda b. Ilai. He is said to have compiled a Mishna collection which was embodied in the Tosephta.

9. *R. Joshua b. Korcha* is supposed by some to have been a son of R. Akiba, who, on one occasion, is called by such a surname (meaning the bald head); but this supposition is very improbable, for it would be strange that the son of so illustrious a man should not rather have been called by his father's proper name, and that he should never have alluded to his celebrated parent or to any of his teachings.[8]

R. Joshua b. K. belonged to the authorities of this generation, though only a few of his opinions are recorded in the Mishna.

10. *R. Simon b. Gamaliel* was the son and successor of the patriarch Gamaliel II. of Jabne. In his youth, he witnessed the fall of Bethar, and escaped the threatened arrest by flight. After the death of the emperor Hadrian, he returned to Jabne where he, in connection with some teachers, reopened an academy, and assumed the hereditary dignity of a patriarch. As the returning disciples of R. Akiba, who were the leading teachers of that generation, preferred Usha as the seat of the new Sanhedrin, R. Simon was obliged to transfer his academy to that city, and appointed R. Nathan as Ab Beth-din (vice-president), and R. Meir as Chacham (advising sage, or speaker). Both of these officers had to retire however, when found planning his deposal on account of some marks of distinction introduced in order to raise the patriarchal dignity. He did not enjoy the privilege of his predecessors to be titled Rabban (our teacher), but like the other

teachers, he was simply called Rabbi (my teacher),[9] probably because many of his contemporaries were superior to him in learning. Still, his legal opinions, which are frequently quoted in the Mishna and Boraitha, give evidence that he was a man of considerable learning and of sound and clear judgment as well as of noble principles. He introduced several legal provisions for the protection of the rights of women and slaves, and for the general welfare of the community. All his opinions expressed in the Mishna, with the exception of only three cases, are regarded by later teachers as authoritative (Halakha). His discussions recorded in the Mishna and Boraitha are mostly held with his celebrated son, R. Jehuda Hanasi. R. Simon b. Gamaliel appears to have been acquainted also with the Greek language and sciences.

Apart from the great circle of teachers mentioned above, the disciples of R. Ishmael b. Elisha formed a school in the extreme South of Judea (Darom), where they continued the methods of their teacher. Of this separate school, called *Debe R. Ishmael*, only two members are mentioned by name: *R. Josiah* and *R. Jonathan*.

FIFTH GENERATION.

This generation extends from the death of R. Simon b. Gamaliel II., to the death of R. Jehuda Hanasi (from 165 to about 200).

The following are the most prominent teachers of this generation:

(1) R. Nathan (the Babylonian); (2) Symmachos; (3) R. Jehuda, Hanasi (the Patriarch), called simply Rabbi; (4) R. Jose b. Juda; (5) R. Elazar b. Simon; (6) R. Simon b. Elazar. Strack places these in the fourth generation and adds (7) Dustayi b. Janai; (8) Simeon b. Jehuda, of the village Akum; (9) Achia b. Joashai; (10) Jacob; (11) Itzchok; (12) Eliezer b. Simeon b. Johai; (13) Pinchas b. Jaier; (14) Ischmael b. Jos; (15) Menachem b. Jos (b. Chialaphta); (16) Jehudah b. Lakish; (17) Elazar Charkaper; (18) Abba Elazar b. Gamla; (19) Simon b. Jos b. Lecunia; (20) Simon b. Menascha; (21) Jehudah b. Tamah.

The junior sages of the fifth generation Strack quotes thus: (1) Hyye Rabbi (the Great); (2) Eliezer b. Kappara; (3) Simeon b. 'Halafta; (4) Lewi b. Sissi; (5) Simai.

Both Mielziner and Strack do not count Simon Shezurri, one of the great Tanaim. who belongs to the third generation, and who is mentioned in the Mishna several times, and of whom it is said (Menachoth, 30 b), "Everywhere the name of Simeon Shezurri is mentioned, the Halakha prevails in accordance with him." We would also count Wradimus b. R. Jose though according to some he was identical with Menachem, and who was one of the greatest Tanaim in the time of Rabbi. (See I. H. Weiss, p. 06.) [See Appendix No. I.] His father, R. Jose, quotes him as the author of a Halakha (Tosephtha, Baba Metzia).

Characteristics and Biographical Sketches.

1. *R. Nathan* was the son of one of the exilarchs in Babylon, and probably received his education in his native country. For some unknown reasons he emigrated to Judea, and on account of his great learning he was appointed by the patriarch, R. Simon b. Gamaliel, to the dignity of Ab-Beth-din (chief justice or vice-president), in the Sanhedrin of Usha. He had to retire from this office because of his and R. Meir's dissension with the patriarch, but was soon reinstated and became reconciled with the Synhedrial president, who held him in high esteem. Also the suceeding patriarch, R. Jehuda, with whom he had many discussions on questions of the law, speaks of him; with great respect. R. Nathan was not only an authority in the rabbinical law, especially in jurisprudence, but appears also to have been well versed in mathematics, astronomy and other sciences. To him is ascribed the authorship of Aboth, de R. Nathan, which is a kind of Tosephta to Pirke Aboth.

2. *Symmachos* was a prominent disciple of R. Meir and, distinguished for his great dialectical powers. After the death of his teacher, he as well as other disciples of R. Meir were excluded from the academy of R. Jehuda Hanasi, as they were charged with indulging in sophistical disputations in order to display their dialectical sagacity, instead of seeking after truth. Nevertheless the Mishna as well as the Tosephta makes mention of the opinions of Symmachos. His renown lay in the rabbinical jurisprudence, in which he laid down certain principles often referred to in the Talmud.

3. *R. Jehuda (Juda) Hanasi,* by way of eminence simply called

Rabbi, was a son of the patriarch R. Simon b. Gamaliel II., and is said to have been born on the same day when R. Akiba was executed. His principal teachers were R. Simon b. Jochai and R. Elazar b. Shamua, under whose guidance his intellectual capacity and splendid talents early developed. Besides his immense knowledge of the whole range of the traditional law, he had a liberal education in secular branches and was especially acquainted with the Greek language, which he preferred to the Syriac, the popular language of Palestine at that time. After the death of his father he succeeded him in the dignity of patriarch, and became the chief authority, eclipsing all other teachers of that generation. Though blessed with great riches, he preferred to live in a simple style and applied his wealth to the maintenance of his numerous pupils and to charitable works. The seat of his academy was first at Beth-Shearim, afterward at Sepphoris, and also at Tiberias. Among his most distinguished disciples were: R. Chiya; (Simon) bar Kappara; Levi bar Sissi; R. Abba Areca, later called Rab; Mar Samuel, and many others. He is said to have been in a friendly relation with one of the Roman emperors, either Marcus Aurelius, or more probably, Lucius Verus Antoninus. By virtue of his authority R. Jehuda abolished several customs and ceremonies which, though sanctified by age, had become impracticable through the change of times and circumstances. His most meritorious work, by which be erected for himself a monument of enduring fame, was the completion of the Mishna compilation which henceforth became the authoritative code of the traditional law and superseded all similar compilations made by former teachers.

4. R. *Jose ben Juda* (b. Ilai) belonged to the great teachers of that generation and was a friend of R. Jehuda Hanasi. His legal opinions are frequently recorded in the Mishna as well as in the Tosephta.

5. R. *Elazar b. Simon* (b. Jochai) was a disciple of R. Simon b. Gamaliel and of R. Joshua b. Korcha. Although an authority in the rabbinical law to whom even the patriarch sometimes yielded, he incurred the severest censure of his colleagues for having, on a certain occasion, lent his assistance to the Romans in prosecuting some Jewish freebooters.

6. R. *Simon b. Elazar* (probably E. b. Shamua), was a disciple of

R. Meir, whose opinions he often quotes. He established several important principles, especially in the civil law.

SIXTH GENERATION.

To this generation belong the younger contemporaries and disciples of R. Juda Hanasi. They are not mentioned in the Mishna, but in the Tosephta and Boraitha, and are therefore termed semi-Tanaim, who form a connecting link between the period of Tanaim and that of the Amoraim. Their names are:

(1) Plimo; (2) Ise b. Juda; (3) R. Elazar b. Jose; (4) R. Ishmael bar Jose; (5) R. Juda b. Lakish; (6) R. Chiya; (7) R. Acha; (8) R. Abba (Areca).

There is no sixth generation according to Strack, and all who are mentioned here he includes in the fifth generation. We have to remark that all the eight mentioned above by Mielziner, as they formed the last generation of the Tanaim, are also named Amoraim; and therefore we find stated in many places in the Talmud where one of the above-mentioned is in conflict with a Mishna or a Boraitha: "He is a Tana, and has the right to differ with the authorities of the Mishna or the Boraitha."

The most prominent among these semi-Tanaim were R. Chiya and R. Abba (Areca).

1. *R. Chiya* (bar Abba) the elder, which epithet is to distinguish him from a later Amora by the same name, was a Babylonian who came at an already advanced age to Palestine, where he became the most distinguished disciple and friend of R. Jehuda Hanasi. He and his disciple R. Oshaya (or Hoshaya) are regarded as the principal authors or compilers of the Tosephta.

2. *R. Abba* (Areca) a nephew of R. Chiya, was likewise a Babylonian, and a disciple of R. Jehuda Hanasi, after whose death he returned to his native country, where, under the historical name of Rab, he became the principal Amora. (See the following chapter.)

Of other distinguished teachers flourishing in this generation and in the beginning of the period of the Amoraim, we have to mention especially *R. Janai* (the elder), and *R. Jonathan* (the elder). The former lived in Sepphoris and was one of the teachers of R. Jochanan bar Naphacha, the greatest among the Palestinian Amoraim.

---

1. This comparatively great length of the first generation is easily explained by the circumstance that it refers to the duration of the prevailing Schools of Shamai and Hillel, and not, as in the subsequent generations, to that of the activity of a single leading teacher.
2. Shamai and Hillel themselves differ in three questions only. (See Eduyoth, p. 5.) Their schools, however, differ in 316 Halakhas.
3. Strack counts him and Zadok among the first generation.
4. We have added him as his omission by Mielziner can be attributed only to forgetfulness as his preceeding sages were also disciples of R. Johanan b. Zakkai, and for the same reason we have added Papus, who was a contemporary of R. Aqiba and of whom the Talmud speaks highly.
5. 22, 23 and 24 were out of Palestine.
6. We are aware only of six mentioned in vol. i.
7. The Cabbalists ascribe to him the compiling of the Zohar, which was revealed by Moses d' Leon. The Talmud also speaks of him as the one to whom miracles occurred frequently.
8. That R. Akiba had a son by the name of R. Joshua is stated in a Boraitha; but the identity of this son with R. Joshua b. Korcha is conclusively disproved by the Tosaphist Rabenu Tam in his remarks on Sabbath 150a, and B. Bathra 113a.
9. There are, however, some passages in the Mishna and Gemara in which he is called Rabban.

Chapter 3
The Amoraim or Expounders of the Mishna

As the Mishna compilation of R. Jehuda Hanasi became the authoritative code of the oral Law, the activity of the teachers was principally devoted to expounding this code. This was done as well in the academies of *Tiberias, Sepphoris, Cæsarea* in Palestine, as in those of *Nahardea, Sura,* and later of *Pumbaditha* and some other seats of learning in Babylonia. The main object of the lectures and discussions in those academies was to interpret the often very brief and concise expression of the Mishna, to investigate its reasons and sources, to reconcile seeming contradictions, to compare its canons with those of the Boraithoth, and to apply its decisions and established principles to new cases not yet provided for. The teachers who were engaged in this work, which finally became embodied in the Gemara, are called *Amoraim,* meaning speakers, interpreters, expounders.[1] They were not as independent in their legal opinions and decisions as their predecessors, the Tanaim and semi-Tanaim, as they had not the authority to contradict Halakhoth and principles accepted in the Mishna or Boraitha. The Palestinian Amoraim, having generally been ordained by the Nasi, had the title of *Rabbi,* while the Babylonian teachers of that period had only the title of *Rab* or of *Mar.*

The period of Amoraim extends from the death of R. Jehuda

Hanasi to the compilation of the Babylonian Talmud; that is, from the beginning of the third to the end of the fifth century. This period has been divided by some into six, by others into seven, minor periods or generations, which are determined by the beginning and the end of the activity of the most prominent teachers flourishing during that time.

The number of Amoraim who are mentioned in the Talmud amounts to several hundreds. The most distinguished among them, especially those who presided over the great academies, are contained in the following chronological tables, of the six generations of Amoraim.[2]

THE FIRST GENERATION OF AMORAIM.

A. Palestinian (219-279).
1. R. Chanina bar Chama.
2. R. Jochanan (bar Napacha).
3. R. Simon ben Lakish (Resh Lakish).
4. R. Joshua ben Levi.
B. Babylonian (219-257).
1. Abba Areca, called simply Rab.
2. (Mar) Samuel.

Strack adds to the first generation of the Palestinian, (5) Hama b. Biza; (6) Janai; (7) Jehuda; and (8) Hiskiah sons of Hyye; (9) Bnya or Bnaah; (10) Pdaya or Jehuda b. Pdaya; (11) Hoshia b. Hanninah b. Biza, named Rabbh the Great; (12) Jose b. Zimra; (13) Simon b. Yehozodak.

To the Babylonian Amoraim he adds, (3) Shila; (4) Abba b. Abba (father of Mar Samuel); (5) Kama[3]; (6) Mar Uqba (the Exilarch).

All the Palestinian Amoraim named here are very often mentioned in the Babylonian Talmud, and as their biographical sketches are interesting we could not omit them.

Biographical Sketches.

A. PALESTINIAN AMORAIM.

During this generation R. Gamaliel III. and R. Judah II. were successively the patriarchs.

1. R. *Chanina bar Chama* (born about 180, died 260), was a disciple of R. Jehuda Hanasi, whose son and successor, R. Gamaliel III., bestowed on him the title of Rabbi. He then presided over his own academy in Sepphoris and stood in high regard on account of his learning, modesty and piety. As teacher he was very conservative, transmitting that only which he had received by tradition, without ever allowing himself an independent decision. Of his prominent contemporaries are: R. *Ephes*, who reopened a school at Lydda, in South Judea; *Levi b. Sissi* (called simply Levi), who, though not presiding over an academy, was a distinguished teacher, and later emigrated to Babylonia; further *Chizkia*, who was a son of R. Chiya the Elder, and whose teachings are frequently quoted in the Talmud. This Chizkia, who had not the title of Rabbi, must not be mistaken for R. Chizkia, who belonged to the third generation.

2. R. *Jochanan bar Napacha*, in general called simply R. Jochanan (born about 199, died 279), was in his early youth a disciple of R. Jehuda Hanasi, later of R. Oshaya in Cæsarea, also of R. Janai, and especially of R. Chanina b. Chama. He then founded his own academy in Tiberias, which henceforth became the principal seat of learning in the Holy Land. By his great mental powers he excelled all his contemporaries, and is regarded the chief Amora of Palestine. In expounding the Mishna he introduced an analytical method, and laid down certain rules for the final decision in such cases in which the Tanaim expressed opposite opinions. His legal teachings, ethical aphorisms, and exegetical remarks, transmitted by his numerous disciples, form the principal elements of the Gemara. He is supposed to have laid the foundation of the Palestinian Talmud, though, in its present shape, this work can not have been compiled before at least one century after R. Jochanan's death.[4]

3. R. *Simon b. Lakish*, whose name is generally abbreviated to Resh Lakish, was a man who combined great physical strength with a noble heart and a powerful mind. It is said that in his youth he was

compelled by circumstances to gain his livelihood as a gladiator or soldier, until making the acquaintance of R. Jochanan, who gained him for the study of the law and gave him his sister in marriage. Having developed extraordinary mental and dialectical powers, he became R. Jochanan's most distinguished friend and colleague. In the interpretation of the Mishna and in legal questions they differed, however, very often, and their numerous controversies are reported in the Babylonian Talmud as well as in the Palestinian. Also is his Hagadic teachings, Resh Lakish was original and advanced some very rational views.

4. *R. Joshua b. Levi* (ben Sissi) presided over an academy in Lydda. He is regarded as a great authority in the law, and his decisions prevail even in cases where his celebrated contemporaries, R. Jochanan and Resh Lakish differ from him. Though himself a prolific Hagadist, he disapproved of the vagaries of the Hagada, and objected to their being written down in books. The circumstance that, on a certain occasion, his prayer for rain proved to be efficient, probably gave rise to the mystic legends with which the fancy of later generations tried to illustrate his great piety.

To other celebrities flourishing in this generation belongs R. *Simlai* of Lydda, who later settled in Nahardea. He was reputed less as teacher of the Halakha than for his ingenious and lucid method of treating the Hagada.

B. BABYLONIAN AMORAIM.

1. *Abba Areca* (or Aricha) was the real name of the chief Babylonian Amora, who, by way of eminence, is generally called *Rab* (the Teacher). He was born about 175 and died 247. As an orphaned youth he went to his uncle, the celebrated R. Chiya in Palestine, to finish his studies in the academy of R. Jehuda Hanasi. The mental abilities which he displayed soon attracted general attention. After the death of R. Jehuda, Abba returned to his native country, and in the year 219 founded the academy in Sura, where 1,200 pupils flocked around him from all parts of Babylonia. His authority was recognized even by the most celebrated teachers in Palestine. Being

regarded as one of the semi-Tanaim, he ventured in some instances even to dispute some opinions accepted in the Mishna, a privilege otherwise not accorded to any of the Amoraim. Most of his decisions, especially in ritual questions, obtained legal sanction, but in the civil law his friend Samuel in Nahardea was his superior. Over one hundred of his numerous disciples, who transmitted his teachings and decisions to later generations, are mentioned in the Talmud by their names.

2. *Samuel*, or Mar Samuel, was born about 180 in Nahardea, died there 257. His father, Abba bar Abba, and Levi b. Sissi were his first teachers. Like Rab he went to Palestine and became a disciple of Rabbi Jehuda Hanasi, from whom, however, he could not obtain the ordination. After his return to Nahardea, he succeeded R. Shela in the dignity of president of the academy (Resh-Sidra) in that city. Besides the law, he cultivated the sciences of medicine and astronomy. As Amora he developed especially the rabbinical jurisprudence, in which he was regarded as the greatest authority.[5] Among other important principles established by him is that of *"Dina d'malchutha Dina,"* that is, the civil law of the government is as valid for the Jews as their own law. The most friendly and brotherly relation prevailed between Samuel and Rab, although they often differed in questions of the law. After Rab's death (247), his disciples recognized Samuel as the highest religious authority of Babylonia. He died about ten years later, leaving behind numerous disciples, several of whom became the leading teachers in the following generation.

A distinguished contemporary of Samuel was *Mar Uqba*, at first head of the court in Kafri, and later Exilarch in Nahardea.

THE SECOND GENERATION OF AMORAIM.

A. Palestinian (279-320).
1. R. Elazar b. Pedath.
2. R. Arne.
3. R. Assi.
4. R. Chiya bar Abba.
5, Simon bar Abba.

6. R. Abbuhu.

7. R. Zera (Zeira).

B. Babylonian (257-320).

1. Rab Huna.

2. Rab Juda, bar Jecheskel.

3. Rab Chisda (or Chasda).

4. Rab Shesheth.

5. Rab Nachman b. Jacob.

To the second generation of the Palestinian, Strack adds, (8) Jehudah the Second (son of Gamalia III.), (Johanan and Simon b. Lakish Strack refers to the second generation); (9) Hilfa or Ilfa; (10) Alexanderi; (11) Khana; (12) Chia bar Joseph; (13) Jos b. Chaninah; (14) Abba b. Zabdah, and (15) Simlaie.

To the Babylonian Strack adds, (6) Ktinah; (7) Adda b. Ahba; (8) Rabba b. Abuhu, and (9) Mathna.

Remarks and Biographical Sketches.

A. PALESTINIAN AMORAIM.

The patriarchate during this generation was successively in the hands of R. Gamaliel IV., and R. Judah III.

1. R. *Elazar ben Pedath*, generally called simply R. Elazar, like the Tana R. Elazar (ben Shamua), for whom he must not be mistaken, was a native of Babylonia, and a disciple and later an associate of R. Jochanan, whom he survived. He, enjoyed great authority and is very often quoted in the Talmud.

2. and 3. R. *Ame* and R. *Assi* were likewise Babylonians, and distinguished disciples of R. Jochanan. After the death of R. Elazar they became the heads of the declining academy in Tiberias. They had the title only of "Judges, or the Aaronites of the Holy Land," and subordinated themselves to the growing authority of the teachers in Babylonia. Rabbi Assi is not to be confounded with his contemporary the Babylonian Amora Rab Assi, who was a colleague of Rab Saphra and a disciple of Rab in Sura.[6]

4. and 5. R. *Chiya bar Abba* and *Simon bar Abba* were probably brothers. They had emigrated from Babylonia and became disciples

of R. Jochanan. Both were distinguished teachers, but very poor. In questions of the law they were inclined to rigorous views.

6. *R. Abbahu* of Cæsarea, disciple of R. Jochanan, friend and colleague of R. Ame and R. Assi, was a man of great wealth and of a liberal education. He had a thorough knowledge of the Greek language, and favored Greek culture. Being held in high esteem by the Roman authorities, he had great political, influence. He seems to have had frequent controversies with the teachers of Christianity in Cæsarea. Besides being a prominent teacher whose legal opinions are quoted in all parts of the Palestinian and Babylonian Talmud, he was a very popular lecturer.

7. *R. Zeira* (or Zera), was a Babylonian and a disciple of Rab Juda bar Jecheskel, but dissatisfied with the hair-splitting method prevailing in the academies of his native country, he emigrated to Palestine where he attended the lectures of R. Elazar b. Pedath in Tiberias, and tried, in vain, to unlearn his former method of study. Having been ordained as Rabbi, he became one of the authorities in Palestine, together with R. Ame, R. Assi and R. Abbuhu.

B. BABYLONIAN AMORAIM.

1. *Rab Huna* (born 212, died 297) was a disciple of Rab, whom, after Mar Samuel's death, he succeeded as president of the academy in Sura. In this office he was active for forty years. He employed fifteen assistants to repeat and explain his lectures to his 800 disciples. Highly revered for his great learning and his noble character, he enjoyed an undisputed authority to which even the Palestinian teachers R. Ame and R. Assi voluntarily subordinated themselves.

2. *Rab Juda bar Jecheskel*, generally called simply R. Juda (or Jehuda), was a disciple of Rab, and also of Samuel. The latter teacher, whose peculiar method he adopted and developed, used to characterize him by the epithet, "the acute." He founded the academy in Pumbaditha, but after R. Huna's death he was chosen as his successor (Resh Methibta), at Sura, where after two years (299), he died at an advanced age.

3. *Rab Chisda* (or Chasda) belonged to the younger disciples of

Rab, after whose death he attended also the lectures of R. Huna. But from the latter teacher he soon separated on account of a misunderstanding between them, and established a school of his own. At the same time, he was one of the Judges in Sura. After Rab Juda's death, R. Chisda, though already above eighty years old, became head of the academy in Sura, and remained in this office for about ten years.

4. *Rab Shesheth*, a disciple of Rab and Samuel, was member of the court in Nahardea. After the destruction of that city he went to Mechuza; later he settled in Silhi, where he founded an academy. Being blind, he had to rely upon his powerful memory. He was R. Chisda's opponent in the Halakha, and disapproved of the hair-splitting dialectical method which had come in vogue among the followers of Rab Juda in Pumbaditha.

5. *Rab Nachman b. Jacob*, called simply Rab Nachman, was a prominent disciple of Mar Samuel. By his father-in-law, the exilarch Abba bar Abuha, he was appointed chief justice in Nahardea. After Mar Samuel's death, he succeeded him as rector of the academy in that city. When two years later (259), the city of Nahardea was destroyed, R. Nachman settled in Shechan-Zib. He is regarded as a great authority especially in the rabbinical jurisprudence, in which he established many important principles. Among others, he originated the rabbinical oath, that is, the purging oath imposed in a law suit on claims even in cases of general denial on the part of the defendant.

Of other teachers belonging to this generation, who, though not standing at the head of the leading academies, are often quoted in the Talmud, the following must be noted:

(*a*) *Rabba bar bar Chana*, who was a Babylonian and son of Abba bar Chana. After having attended the academy of R. Jochanan in Palestine, he returned to his native country, where he frequently reported the opinions of his great teacher. He is also noted for the many allegorical narratives ascribed to him in the Talmud.

(*b*) *Ulla* (b. Ishmael), was a Palestinian who frequently travelled to Babylonia, where he finally settled and died. Although without the title of Rabbi or Rab, he was regarded as a distinguished teacher whose opinions and reports are often mentioned.

THE THIRD GENERATION OF AMORAIM.

A. Palestinian (320-359).

1. R. Jeremiah.
2. R. Jonah.
3. R. Jose.

B. Babylonian (320-375).

1. Rabba bar Huna.
2. Rabba bar Nachmani.
3. Rab Joseph (bar Chiya).
4. Abaye.
5. Rabha.
6. Rab Nachman bar Isaac.
7. Rab Papa.

To the Palestinian, Strack adds, (4) Samuel b. Nachman (in the Babylonian he is mentioned as Nachmani); (5) Itzhak the second (his contemporary in Babylonia is Nachman b. Jacob); (6) Lewi; (7) Abuhu; (8) Ami; (9) Assi; (10) Hyya b. Abba II. (Elazar b. Pedath he quotes in the third generation); (11) Simeon b. Abba; (12) Simur (also Zera is mentioned among the second generation); (13) Samuel b. Itzhak; (14) Hilla or Illeh; (15) Zrika; (16) Hoshia the second; (17) Chananiah (the colleague of the Rabbinat)[7]; (18) Janai b. Ishmael; (19) Joshua; (20) Ban b. Mamal (in Babylonia named Abba b. Mamal); (21) Jacob b. Ide; (22) Itzhak b. Nachma; (23) Maysha; (24) Bibe; (Haggi and Jeremiah Strack quotes as belonging also to the fourth generation).

To the Babylonian, Strack adds, (8) Chisda; (9) Hamnuna; (10) Shesheth; (11) Nachma b. Jacob; (12) Rabba b. b. Hanna; (13) Ulla b. Ishmael; (14) Rabba b. Nachmene, and (1) Joseph b. Hiah.

Remarks and Biographical Sketches.

A. PALESTINIAN AMORAIM.

The patriarch of this period was Hillel II., who introduced the fixed Jewish calendar.

224

In consequence of the persecutions and the banishment of several religious teachers under the emperors Constantine and Constantius, the Palestinian academies entirely decayed. The only teachers of any prominence are the following:

1. *R. Jeremiah* was a Babylonian and disciple of R. Zeira, whom he followed to Palestine. In his younger days, when still in his native country, he indulged in propounding puzzling questions of trifling casuistry, by which he probably intended to ridicule the subtile method prevailing among some of the contemporary teachers, and on this account he was expelled from the academy. In the Holy Land he was more appreciated, and, after the death of R. Abbahu and R. Zeira, was acknowledged as the only authority in that country.

2. *R. Jonah* was a disciple of R. Ila (Hila) and of R. Jeremiah.

His opinions are frequently quoted, especially in the Palestinian Talmud.

3. *R. Jose* (bar Zabda), colleague of R. Jonah, was one of the last rabbinical authorities in Palestine.

It is probable that the compilation of the Palestinian Talmud was accomplished about that time, though it cannot be stated by whom.

B. BABYLONIAN AMORAIM.

1. *Rabba* (or Rab Abba) *bar Huna* was not, as erroneously supposed by some, the son of the exilarch Huna Mari, but of Rab Huna, the disciple and successor of Rab. After the death of R. Chisda (309), he succeeded him in the dignity of president of the academy in Sura. Under his presidency, lasting thirteen years, this academy was eclipsed by that of Pumbaditha, and after his death it remained deserted for about fifty years until Rab Ashe restored it to its former glory.

2. *Rabba bar Nachmani*, in the Talmud called simply Rabba was born 270, and died 330. He was a disciple of Rab Huna, Rab Juda and Rab Chisda, and displayed from his youth great dialectical powers on account of which he was characterized as "the uprooter of mountains." Selected as head of the academy of Pumbaditha, he attracted large crowds of hearers by his ingenious method of teaching.

In his lectures which commented on all parts of the Mishna, he investigated the reason of the laws and made therefrom logical deductions. Besides, he tried to reconcile seeming differences between the Mishna, the Baraithoth, and the traditional teachings of later authorities. He also liked to propound puzzling problems of the law, in order to test and sharpen the mental powers of his disciples. A charge having been made against him by the Persian government that many of his numerous hearers attended his lectures in order to evade the poll-tax, he fled from Pumbaditha and died in solitude.

3. *Rab Joseph* (bar Chiya) was a disciple of Rab Juda and Rab Shesheth, and succeeded his friend Rabba in the dignity of president of the academy in Pumbadita, after having once before been elected for this office, which he declined in favor of Rabba. On account of his thorough knowledge of the sources of the Law, to which be attached more importance than to ingenious deductions, he was called Sinai. Besides being a great authority in the rabbinical law, he devoted himself to the Targum of the Bible, especially of the prophetical books. In his old age he became blind. He died in the year 333, after having presided over the academy of Pumbaditha only for three years.

4. *Abaye*, surnamed Nachmani (b. 280, d. 338) was a son of Kaylil and a pupil of his uncle Rabba bar Nachmani, and of Rab Joseph. He was highly esteemed not only for his profound knowledge of the law and his mastership in Talmudical dialectics, but also for his integrity and gentleness. After Rab Joseph's death he was selected as head of the academy in Pumbaditha, but tinder his administration, which lasted about five years, the number of hearers in that academy decreased considerably, as his more talented colleague *Raba* had founded a new academy in Machuza which attracted greater crowds of pupils. Under these two Amoraim the dialectical method of the Babylonian teachers reached the highest development. Their discussions, which mostly concern some very nice distinctions in the interpretation of the Mishna, in order to reconcile conflicting passages, fill the pages of the Talmud.[8] In their differences concerning more practical questions, the opinion of Raba generally prevails, so that later authorities pointed out only six cases

in which the decision of Abaye was to be adopted against that of his rival.

5. *Raba* was the son of Joseph b. Chama in Machuza. He was born 299, and died 352. In his youth he attended the lectures of Rab Nachman and of R. Chisda. Later, he and Abaye were fellow-students in the academy of Rabba bar Nachmani. Here he developed his dialectical powers, by which he soon surpassed all his contemporaries. He opened an academy in Machuza which attracted a great number of students. After Abaye's death this academy supplanted that in Pumbaditha and during Raba's lifetime became almost the only seat of learning in Babylonia. His controversies with his contemporaries, especially with his rival colleague, Abaye, are very numerous. Wherever an opinion of Abaye is recorded in the Talmud, it is almost always followed by the contrary view and' argument of Raba.

6. *Rab Nachman b. Isaac* was a disciple of Rab Nachman (b. Jacob), and afterward an officer as Resh Calla in the academy of Raba. After the death of the latter he was made president of the academy in Pumbaditha, which now resumed its former rank. In this capacity he remained only four years (352-356), and left no remarkable traces of his activity. Still, less significant was the activity of his successor, *R. Chama* from Nahardea, who held the office for twenty-one years (356-377).

7. *Rab Papa* (bar Chanan), a disciple of Abaye and Raba, founded a new school in Nares, in the vicinity of Sura, over, which he presided for nineteen years (354-375). He adopted the dialectical method of his former teachers without possessing their ingenuity and their independence, and consequently did not give satisfaction to those of his hearers who had formerly attended the lectures of Raba. One of his peculiarities was that he frequently refers to popular proverbs people say.[9]

THE FOURTH GENERATION OF BABYLONIAN AMORAIM (375-427).

A. Sura.

1. Rab Ashe.

B. Pumbaditha.

1. Rab Zebid.

2. Rab Dime.

3. Rafram.

4. Rab Kahana.

5. Mar Zutra.

C. Nahardea.

Amemar.

To the fourth generation Strack adds, (1) Jeremiah (who though a Babylonian native, emigrated to Palestine, and was counted among the Palestinian); (2) Haggi; (3) Juda the third (Nassi), son of Gamaliel the fourth; (4) Jona; (5) Josa the second (colleague of Jona); (6) Pinchas (who also emigrated from Babylonia); (7) Judan; (8) Chelbo; (9) Hisda; (10) Chinna; (11) Tabbi; (12) Juda b. Pazi, from Lydda, and (13) Jehoshua of Siknin. Concerning the fourth generation of Babylonian, he counts also Abbaye and Rabba, and adds to the list of Mielziner, Rabba b. Mari, Rabbi b. Ulla, and Rabha b. Shilla. Strack does not distinguish between the colleges of Sura, Pumbaditha and Nahardea.

Remarks and Biographical Sketches.

A. *Rab Ashe* (son of Simai bar Ashe) was, at the age of twenty, made president of the reopened academy of Sura, after the death of Rab Papa, and held this office for fifty-two years. Under his presidency, this academy, which had been deserted since the time of Rabba bar Huna, regained its former glory with which Rab had invested it. Combining the profundity of knowledge which formerly prevailed in this academy with the dialectic methods developed in that of Pumbaditha, be was generally recognized as the ruling authority, so that his contemporaries called him by the distinguishing title of *Rabbana* (our teacher). Invested with this great authority, Rab Ashe was enabled to assume the task of sifting, arranging and compiling the immense material of traditions, commentaries and discussions on the Mishna, which, during the two preceding centuries, had accumulated in the Babylonian academies. In the compilation and revision of this gigantic work, which is embodied in the Gemara, he was occupied for over half a century, and still he did not complete it entirely, but this was done, after his death, by his disciples and successors.

B. During the long period of Rab Ashe's activity at the academy in Sura, the following teachers presided successively over the academy in Pumbaditha:

1 *Rab Zebid* (b. Oshaya), who succeeded Rab Chama and held the office for eight years (377-385).

2. *Rab Dime* (b. Chinena) from Nahardea, presiding only for three years (385-388).

3. *Rafram bar Papa* the elder, in his youth a disciple of Raba, succeeded R. Dime (388-394).

4. *Rab Kahana* (b. Tachlifa), likewise a disciple of Raba, was one of the former teachers of R. Ashe. In an already advanced age, he was made president of the academy of Pumbaditha, and died in the year 411. This Rab Cabana must not be mistaken for two other teachers of the same name, one of whom had been a distinguished disciple of Rab, and the other (Rab, Cahana b. Manyome), a disciple of Rab Juda b. Jecheskel.

5. *Mar Zutra*, who, according to some historians, succeeded Rab Cahana as rector of the school in Pumbaditha (411-414), is probably identical with Mar Zutra b. Mare, who shortly afterwards held the high office as Exilarch. In the rectorship of Pumbaditha he was succeeded by *Rab Acha bar Raba* (414-419), and the latter by *Rab Gebiha* (419-433).

C. *Amemar*, a friend of Rab Ashe, was a distinguished judge and teacher in Nahardea. When his former teacher Rab Dime became president of the academy in Pumbaditha, he succeeded him in the rectorship of that of Nahardea, from 390 to about 422. With him this once so celebrated seat of learning passed out of existence.

THE FIFTH GENERATION OF BABYLONIAN AMORAIM
(427-468).

A. Sura.

1. Mar Jemar (Maremar).

2. Rab Ide bar Abin.

3. Mar bar Rab Ashe.

4. Rab Acha of Difte.

B. Pumbaditha.

1. Rafram II.

2. Rechumai.

3. Rab Sama b. Rabba.

To the fifth generation of Palestinian Strack adds, (1) Abba b. Kohen; (2) Abba Mare; (3) Mattanjah; (4) Mana the second b. Jona; (5) Chananiah the second; (6) Jos b. Bune; (7) Jona of Bozrae; (8) Tanhum, and (9) Chiah b. Adda the second.

To the Babylonian fifth generation he counts, (1) Nachman b. Itzhak; (2) Papa; (3) Huna b. Johusua.

Remarks and Biographical Sketches.

A. 1. Mar Jemar (contracted to Maremar), who enjoyed high esteem with the leading teachers of his time, succeeded his colleague and friend, Rab Ashe, in the presidency of the academy in Sura, but held this office only for about five years, (427-432).

2. *Rab Ide* (or Ada) *bar Abin*, became, after Mar Jemar's death, president of the academy at Sura, and held this office for about twenty years (432-452). He as well as his predecessor continued the compilation of the Talmud which Rab Ashe had commenced.

3. *Mar bar Rab Ashe*, whose surname was Tabyome, and who, for some unknown reasons, had been passed over in the election of a successor to his father, was finally made president of the academy in Sura, and filled this office for thirteen years, (455-468.). In his frequent discussions with contemporary authorities, he exhibits independence of opinion and great faculties of mind.

4. *Rab Acha of Difte*, a prominent teacher, was on the point of being elected as head of the academy of Sura, but was finally defeated by Mar bar Rab Ashe, who aspired to that office which his father had so gloriously filled for more than half a century.

B. The academy of Pumbaditha, which had lost its earlier influence, had during this generation successively three presidents, of whose activity very little is known, namely:

1. *Rafram II.*, who succeeded Rab Gebihah, from 433 to 443.

2. *Rab Rechumai*, from 443-456.

3. *Rab Sama b. Rabba*, from 456-471.

Toward the end of this generation, the activity of both academies was almost paralyzed by the terrible persecutions which the Persian King Firuz instituted against the Jews and their religion.

THE SIXTH AND LAST GENERATION OF BABYLONIAN AMORAIM (468-500).

A. Sura.

1. Rabba Thospia (or Tosfaah).
2. Rabina.

B. Pumbaditha.

Rab Jose.

To the sixth generation of Palestinian Strack adds, (1) Samuel b. Jose b. Bune, and to the Babylonian, (1) Ashi; (2) Rabban bar Thachlifa; (3) Mar b. Rabbina; (4) Mar Zutra. Meremar and Tospha he counts to the seventh generation, whilst Mielziner counts them to the sixth.[10]

---

1. In a more restricted meaning the term *Amora* (from אמר, to say, to speak) signifies the same as *Methurgeman* (the interpreter), that is, the officer in the academies who, standing at the side of the lecturer or presiding teacher, had to announce loudly and explain to the large assembly what the teacher just expressed briefly and in a low voice.

   The term *Tana*, which generally applies only to the teachers mentioned in the Mishna and Boraitha, is in the period of Amoraim sometimes used also to signify one whose special business it was to recite the memorized Boraithoth to the expounding teachers. In this sense the term is to be understood in the phrase: A Tana (teacher) repeated a Boraitha (or taught same) before so and so, etc.

2. Some scholars count the semi-Tanaim as the first generation, and have consequently seven instead of six generations. The period of Palestinian Amoraim being much shorter than that of the Babylonian, ends with the third generation of the latter. Frankel in his introduction to the Palestinian Talmud, treating especially of the Palestinian Amoraim, divides them also into six generations.

3. Who was appointed by Mar Samuel to examine Rab. (Will be translated in Tract Kethubath.)

4. As to further characteristics of this and the other prominent Amoraim, the following works may be consulted: Graetz, "History of the Jews," Vol. IV.; Z. Frankel, "Mebo"; I. H. Weiss, "Dor Dor," Vol. III.; I. Hamburger, "Real Encyclopädie," Vol. II. Besides, J. Fürst, "Kultur und Literaturgeschichte der Juden in

Asien," which treats especially of the Babylonian academics and teachers during the period of the Amoraim.

5. Mar Samuel made also a compilation of Boraithoth, which is quoted in the Talmud by the phrase "the disciples of Samuel."

6. See Tosephoth Chullin, 19a.

7. There are eight Tanaim and twenty-three Amoraim named Chananiah. We do not remember who was called so as Strack did.

8. The often very subtle argumentations of these two teachers became so proverbial that the phrase "the critical questions of Abaye and Raba" is used in the Talmud as a signification of acute discussions and minute investigations.

9. This Rab Papa must not be mistaken for an elder teacher by the same name, who had ten sons, all well versed in the law, one of whom, Rafram, became head of the academy of Pumbaditha in the following generation. Neither is Rab Papa identified with Rab Papi, a distinguished lawyer who flourished in a former generation.

10. We refrain from giving our own opinion on the differences between the generations of Strack and those of Mielziner; for the reason, we confess, that we do not understand why only those named here should be mentioned among the different generations, whilst each of them has so many contemporaries named by Halpern in his special collection of Tanaim and Amoraim, which takes up a great part in Halakha p. 38 as well as in Hagada in both Talmuds and Medrashim. I. H. Weiss's method is to give the particulars of those who have much contributed to the development of the oral law; but nevertheless he mentioned many of the great men without particulars. Should we say that Mielziner has adopted his method while Strack did not, it would also not be correct. There are many whom Weiss speaks of lengthily whilst Mielziner does not mention them at all and *vice versa*. The modern scholars like Bacher, and others, took the trouble to write particulars of each one mentioned by Strack although even they omitted many who are mentioned by Halpern, and therefore we hesitate to give our own opinion on this matter.

Chapter 4
The Classification of Halakha and Hagada in the Contents of the Gemara

The collection of the commentaries and discussions of the Amoraim on the Mishna is termed *Gemara*. (See our Brief Introd., Vol. I., of our Edition.) Besides being a discursive commentary on the Mishna, the Gemara contains a vast amount of more or less valuable material which does not always have any close connection with the Mishna text, as legal reports, historical and biographical information, religious and ethical maxims and homiletical remarks.

The whole subject-matter embodied in the Gemara is generally classified into *Halakha* and *Hagada*.

To *Halakha*[1] belongs that which has bearing upon the law; hence all expositions, discussions and reports which have the object of explaining, establishing and determining legal principles and provisions. The principal branches of the Halakha are indicated by the names of the six sections of the Mishna, named in Chap. IV. of this work.

The *Hagada*[2] comprises everything not having the character of Halakha; hence all historical records, all legends and parables, all doctrinal and ethical teachings and all free and unrestrained interpretations of Scripture.

According to its different contents and character, the Hagada may be divided into:

1. *Exegetical* Hagada, giving plain or homiletical and allegorical explanations of biblical passages.

2 . *Dogmatical* Hagada, treating of God's attributes and providence, of creation, of revelation, of reward and punishment, of future life, of Messianic time, etc.

3. *Ethical* Hagada, containing aphorisms, maxims, proverbs, fables, sayings, intended to teach and illustrate certain moral duties.

4. *Historical* Hagada, reporting traditions and legends concerning the lives of biblical and post-biblical persons or concerning national and general history.

5. *Mystical* Hagada, referring to Cabala, angelology, demonology, astrology, magical cures, interpretation of dreams, etc.

6. *Miscellaneous* Hagada, containing ancedotes, observations, practical advice, and occasional references to various branches of ancient knowledge and sciences.

Hagadic passages are often, by the way, interspersed among matters of Halakha, as a kind of diversion and recreation after the mental exertion of a tiresome investigation or a minute discussion on a dry legal subject. Sometimes, however, the Hagada appears in larger groups, outweighing the Halakha matter with which it is loosely connected.

Concerning the Palestinian Talmud, its Halakhas and Hagadas, see Chap. V. of this volume. However, as an appendix we add that which was written by Mielziner about this matter.

There are two compilations of the Gemara, which differ from each other in language as well as in contents; the one made in Palestine is called *Jerushalmi*, the Jerusalem Gemara or Talmud; the other, originating in Babylonia, is called *Babli*, the Babylonian Gemara or Talmud.

COMPILATION OF JERUSHALMI, THE PALESTINIAN TALMUD.

As no academy existed in Jerusalem after the destruction of the second Temple, the customary appellation *Jerusalem* Talmud is rather a misnomer. More correct is the appellation the Palestinian Talmud, or the Gemara of the teachers of the West.

Maimonides in the introduction to his Mishna commentary ascribes the authorship of the Palestinian Talmud to the celebrated teacher R. Jochanan, who flourished in the third century. This statement, if literally taken, cannot be correct, since so many of the teachers quoted in that Talmud are known to have flourished more than a hundred years after R. Jochanan. This celebrated Amora may, at the utmost, have given the first impulse to such a collection of commentaries and discussions on the Mishna, which was continued and completed by his successors in the academy of Tiberias. In its present shape the work is supposed to belong to the fourth or fifth century. Some modern scholars assign its final compilation even to a still later period; namely, after the close of the Babylonian Talmud.[3]

The Palestinian Gemara, as before us, extends only over thirty-nine of the sixty-three Masechtoth contained in the Mishna, namely all Masechtoth of Seder Zeraim, Seder Moed, Nashim and Nezikin, with the exception of Eduyoth and Aboth. But it has none of the Masechtoth belonging to Seder Kodashim, and of those belonging to Seder Teharoth it treats only of Masecheth Nidda. (See Chap. V.)

Some of its Masechtoth are defective; thus the last four Perakim of Sabbath and the last Perek of Maccoth are wanting. Of the ten Perakim belonging to Masecheth Nidda it has only the first three Perakim and a few lines of the fourth.

There are some indications that elder commentators were acquainted with portions of the Palestinian Gemara which are now missing, and it is very probable that that Gemara originally extended to all or, at least, to most of the Masechtoth of the Mishna. The loss of the missing Masechtoth and portions thereof may be explained partly by the many persecutions which interrupted the activity of the Palestinian academies, partly by the circumstance that the Palestinian Gemara did not command that general attention and veneration which was bestowed on the Babylonian Gemara.

COMPILATION OF BABLI, THE BABYLONIAN TALMUD.

The compilation of the Babylonian Talmud is generally ascribed to Rab Ashe, who for more than fifty years (375-427), officiated as head of the academy in Sura. It is stated that it took him about thirty years to collect, sift and arrange the immense material of this gigantic work. During the remaining second half of his activity he revised once more the whole work and made in it many corrections.[4]

But Rab Ashe did not succeed in finishing the gigantic work. It was continued and completed by his disciples and successors, especially by the last Amoraim, Rabina II., who from 488 to 499 presided over the academy in Sura, and R. Jose, the school-head of Pumbaditha. Some additions were made by the Saboraim, and even by some still later hands.

The Gemara of the Babylonian Talmud covers only thirty-seven Masechtoth (tracts) of the Mishna, namely:

Of Zeraim only one, Berachoth, omitting the remaining ten Masechtoth;

Of Moed eleven, omitting only Shekalim, which in our Talmud editions is replaced by the Palestinian Gemara;[5]

Of Nashim all of the seven Masechtoth belonging to that division;

Of Nezikim eight, omitting Eduyoth and Aboth;[6]

Of Kodashim nine, omitting Middoth and Kinnim. In Thamid only chapters I., II. and IV. are provided with Gemara, but not chapters III., V., VI. and VII.

Of Teharoth only Nidda, omitting eleven Masechtoth.

There being no traces of the Gemara. missing to twenty-six Masechtoth, it is very probable that this part of the Gemara has never been compiled, though those; Masechtoth have undoubtedly also been discussed by the Babylonian Amoraim, as is evident from frequent references to them in the Gemara on the other Masechtoth. The neglect of compiling these discussions may be explained by the circumstance that those Masechtoth mostly treat of laws which had no practical application outside of Palestine. This is especially the case with the Masechtoth of Zeraim, except Berachoth, and those of

236

Teharoth, except Nidda. It was different with the Masechtoth belonging to Kodashim which, though treating of the sacrificial laws, are fully discussed in the Babylonian Talmud, as it was a prevailing opinion of the Rabbis that the merit of being engaged with the study of those laws was tantamount to the actual performance of the sacrificial rites. (See Talm. Menachoth, 110a.)[7]

The absence of Gemara on the Masechtoth Eduyoth and Aboth is easily accounted for by the very nature of their contents, which admitted of no discussions.

THE TWO GEMARAS COMPARED WITH EACH OTHER[8]

The Palestinian and the Babylonian Gemaras differ from each other in language and style as well as in material, and in the method of treating the same, also in arrangement.

As regards the language, the Palestinian Gemara is composed in the West Aramaic dialect which prevailed in Palestine at the time of the Amoraim.

The language of the Babylonian Gemara is a peculiar idiom, being a mixture of Hebrew and East Aramaic, with an occasional sprinkling of Persian words. Quotations from Mishna and Boraitha, and sayings of the elder Amoraim are given in the original, that is, the New Hebrew (Mishnic) language, while forms of judicial and notary documents and popular legends of later origin are often given in the Aramaic idiom.

Although the Palestinian Gemara extends to two more Masechtoth than the Babylonian, its total material amounts only to about one third of the latter. Its discussions are generally very brief and condensed, and do not exhibit that dialectic acumen for which the Babylonian Gemara is noted. The Hagada in the Palestinian Gemara includes more reliable and valuable historical records and references, and is, on the whole, more rational and sober, though less attractive than the Babylonian Hagada, which generally appeals more to the heart and imagination. But the latter, on many occasions, indulges too much in gross exaggerations, and its popular sayings, especially those evidently interpolated by later hands, have often an admixture of superstitious views borrowed from the Persian surroundings.

The arrangement of the material in the two Talmuds differs in this, that in the Babylonian, the Gemara is attached to the single paragraphs of the Mishna, while in the Palestinian all paragraphs (the retermed Halakhoth), belonging to one Perek of the Mishna, are generally placed together at the head of each chapter. The comments and discussions of the Gemara referring to the successive paragraphs are then marked by the headings, Halakha 1, Halakha 2, and so on.

The two Gemara collections make no direct mention of each other as literary works. But the names and opinions of the Palestinian authorities are very often quoted in the Babylonian Gemara; and in a similar way, though not to the same extent, the Palestinian Gemara mentions the views of the Babylonian authorities. This exchange of opinions was effected by the numerous teachers who are known to have emigrated or frequently travelled from the one country to the other,

The study of the Babylonian Talmud, having been transplanted from its native soil to North Africa, and the European countries (especially Spain, France, Germany and Poland), was there most sedulously and religiously cultivated in the Jewish communities, and gave rise to an immense Rabbinical literature. The Palestinian Talmud never enjoyed such general veneration and attention. Eminent Rabbis alone were thoroughly conversant with its contents, and referred to it in their writings. It is only in modern times that Jewish scholars have come to devote more attention to this Talmud, for the purpose of historical and literary investigations.

---

1. *Halakha* means custom, usage, practice; then, an *adopted rule*, a *traditional law*. In a more extended meaning, the term applies to matters bearing upon that law.

2. *Hagada* or *Haggada* means that which is related, a tale, a saying, an individual utterance which claims no binding authority. Regarding this term, see W. Bacher's learned and exhaustive article, "The Origin of the Word Hagada (Agada)," in the *Jewish Quarterly Review* (London), Vol. IV., pp. 406-429. As to fuller particulars concerning Halakha and Hagada, see Zunz's "G. Vortraege," pp. 57-61 and 83 sq.; also Hamburger's "Real Encyclopädie," H., the articles Halacha and Agada, also above, Vol. I., Chap. V.

3. Critical researches on this subject are found in Geiger's "Jued. Zeitschrift I. Wissenschaft," 1870; Z. Frankel's "Mebo," p. 46 sq., and in Wiesner's "Gibeath Jeruschalaim" (Vienna, 1872).

I. H. Weiss ("Dor Dor," III., p. 114 sq.) regards R. Jose (bar Zabda), who was a colleague of R. Jonah and one of the last authorities in Palestine, as the very compiler of the Pal. Talmud which in the following generation was completed by R. Jose bar Bun (Abun).

4. Those scholars who maintain that the Mishna was not written down by R. Jehuda Hanasi, but that he merely arranged it orally (see Chap. IV.), maintain the same in regard to Rab Ashe's compilation of the Gemara, without being able to state when and by whom it was actually committed to writing. Against this opinion it has been properly argued that it must be regarded as absolutely impossible for a work so voluminous, so variegated in contents and so full of minute and intricate discussions, as the Talmud, to have been orally arranged and fixed, and accurately transmitted from generation to generation. On the strength of this argument and of some indications found in the Talmud, Z. Frankel (in his "Mebo," p. 47) even regards it as very probable that Rab Ashe in compiling the Gemara made use of some minor compilations which existed before him, and of some written records and memoranda containing short abstracts of the academical discussions in the preceding generations. Collecting and arranging these records, he partly enlarged them by fuller explanations, partly left them just as he found them. Some traces of such memoranda, made probably by R. Ashe's predecessors, are still found in numerous passages of the Talmud.

5. In our new edition in Vol. VIII., we supplied a new brief commentary by Rodkinson.

6. We have placed Aboth de Rabbi Nathan under the Mishna instead of the missing Gemara Jurisprudence, Vol. I. (IX.).

7. This reason appears doubtful to us as, according to the sages, the study of the Torah, no matter of which of its branches, is esteemed higher than sacrifices and they also were not very much in favor of sacrifices at large, just as little as the old prophets. Apart from this we find there lengthy discussions about things which have never and could never have existed. We therefore think that the Gemara was composed of all the Mishnayoths, and those which are missing were simply lost in the course of time. Secondly, discussions to subjects of every Mishna are scattered in the Talmud, but were not collected, and, indeed, a Rabbi of Ishbitza in Poland, Gershon Henich Lener, took the trouble to gather the Gemara belonging to the section *Purification* and publish them in a very voluminous book, in 1836, with the approbation of most of the Russian and Polish rabbis. (See particulars of this in our Phylacterian Retus, p. 122.)

8. About this subject we have spoken in the first volume of this work. However, we will not omit what was said by Mielziner concerning this matter, as it is very reasonable.

Chapter 5
Apocryphal Appendices to the Talmud and Commentaries

Besides the Masechtoth contained in the Mishna and the two Gemaras, there are several Masechtoth composed in the form of the Mishna and Tosephta, that treat of ethical, ritual, and liturgical precepts. They stand in the same relation to the Talmud as the Apocrypha to the canonical books of the Bible. When and by whom they were composed cannot be ascertained. Of these apocryphal treatises, the following are appended to our editions of the Talmud:

1. *Aboth d'Rabbi Nathan,*[1] divided into forty-one chapters and a kind of Tosephta to the Mishnic treatise "Pirke Aboth," the ethical sentences of which are here considerably enlarged and illustrated by numerous narratives. In its present shape, it belongs to the post-Talmudic period, though some elements of a Boraitha of R. Nathan (who was a Tana belonging to the fourth generation) may have been embodied therein.[2]

2. *Sopherim* (the Scribes), containing, in twenty-one chapters, rules for the writing of the scrolls of the Pentateuch, and, of the book of Esther; also Masoretic rules, and liturgical rules for the service on Sabbath, Feast and Fast days. R. Asher already expressed (in his Hilchoth Sepher Thora) the opinion that this Masecheth Sopherim belongs to the period of the Gaonim.[3]

3. *Ebel Rabbathi* (the large treatise on Mourning),[4] euphemisti-

cally called *Semachoth* (Joys), is divided into fourteen chapters, and treats, as indicated by the title, of rules and customs concerning burial and mourning. It is not identical with a treatise under the same title, quoted already in the Talmud (Moed Katon, 24a, 26a; Kethuboth, 28a), but seems to be rather a reproduction of the same with later additions.[5]

4. *Callah* (the bride, the woman recently married). This minor Masechta, being likewise a reproduction of a Masechta by that name, mentioned already in the Talmud (Sabbath, 114a; Taanith, 10b; Kiddushin, 49b; Jer. Berachoth, II., 5), treats in one chapter of the duties of chastity in marriage, and in general.

5. *Derech Eretz*[6] (the conduct of life), divided into eleven chapters, the first of which treats of prohibited marriages, and the remaining chapters, of ethical, social and religious teachings. References to a treatise by that name are made already in the Talmud (B. Berachoth, 22a, and Jer. Sabbath, VI., 2).

6. *Derech Eretz Zuta* (the conduct of life, minor treatise), containing ten chapters, replete with rules and maxims of wisdom.[7]

7. *Perek Ha-shalom* (chapter on Peace) consists, as already indicated by the title, only of one chapter, treating of the importance of peacefulness.

Remark: Besides these apocryphal treatises appended to our editions of the Talmud under the general title of "Minor Treatises," there are seven lesser Masechtoth which were published by Raphael Kirchheim from an ancient manuscript. (Frankfort on the Main, 1851.)

COMMENTARIES.

The Necessity for such Commentaries.

The Talmud offers to its students great difficulties, partly on account of the peculiar idiom in which it is written, and which is intermixed with so numerous, often very mutilated, foreign words; partly on account of the extreme brevity and succinctness of its style, the frequent use of technical terms and phrases, and mere allusions to matters discussed elsewhere; partly also on account of the circumstance that, in consequence of elliptical expressions, and in the absence of all punctuation marks, question and answer, in the most intricate discussions, are sometimes so closely interwoven that it is not easy to discern at once where the one ends and the other begins. To meet all these difficulties, which are often very perplexing, numerous commentaries have been written by distinguished Rabbis. Some of the commentaries extend to the whole Talmud, or a great portion thereof; others exclusively to the Mishna, or some of its sections.

Up to date new commentaries upon commentaries appear, so that in the last edition printed in Vilna, more than a hundred additional commentaries are given (an illustration of which we give at the end of this chapter). We therefore do not care to point them out. Moreover they all are commentaries to the text which do not belong to our new edition. However, the commentaries exclusively on the Mishna we deem to be interesting for some readers and therefore do not omit them.

Commentaries Exclusively on the Mishna.

1. The first to write a commentary on the whole Mishna was *Moses Maimonides* (XII. century). He commenced it in the twenty-third year of his age, in Spain, and finished it in his thirtieth year, in Egypt. This commentary was written in Arabic, manuscripts of which are to be found in the Bodleian Library at Oxford, and in some other libraries. From the Arabic it was translated into Hebrew by several scholars, flourishing in the XIII. century; namely, Seder Zeraim, by Jehuda Charizi; Seder Moed, by Joseph Ibn Alfual; Seder Nashim, by Jacob Achsai (or Abbasi[8]); Seder Nezikin, by Solomon b. Joseph, with the exception of Perek Chelek in Sanhedrin and Masecheth Aboth, including the ethical treatise Sh'mone Perakim, introducing the latter, which were translated by Samuel Ibn Tibbon; Seder Kodashim, by Nathanel Ibn Almuli; the translator of Seder Teharoth is not known. These translations are appended to all Talmud editions, after each Masechta, under the heading of Commentary of Maimonides.

The characteristic feature of this commentary of Maimonides consists in this, that it follows the analytical method, laying down at the beginning of each section the principles and general views of the subject, and thereby throwing light upon the particulars to be explained, while Rashi in his Talmud commentary adopted the synthetical method, commencing with the explanation of the particulars, and thereby leading to a clear understanding of the whole of the subject-matter.

2. Several distinguished Rabbis wrote commentaries on single sections of the Mishna, especially on those Masechtoth to which no Babylonian Gemara (and hence no Rashi) exists. Of these commentaries the following are found in our Talmud editions:

(a) *Rashi's Commentary* on all Masechtoth of Seder Zeraim, except Berachoth, and all Masechtoth of Seder Teharoth, except Nidda, by *R. Simson* of *Sens* (XII. century), the celebrated Tosaphist.

(b) *Asheri's Commentary* on the same Masechtoth, by *R. Asher b. Yechiel* (XIII. century), the author of the epitome of the Talmud which is appended to all Masechtoth.

(c) *Rashi's Commentary* on Masecheth Middoth, by *R. Shemaya*, who is supposed to have been a disciple of Rashi.

(d) *Rabad's Commentary* on Masecheth Eduyoth, by R. Abraham b. David (XII. century), the celebrated author of critical annotations on Maimonides' Talmudical code.

(e) Commentary on the Masechtoth Kinnim and Tamid by an anonymous author.

3. *R. Obadya of Bertinoro* in Italy, and Rabbi in Jerusalem (d. in the year 1510), wrote a very lucid commentary on the whole Mishna, which accompanies the text in most of our separate Mishna editions. He follows the analytic method of Rashi, and adds to each paragraph of the Mishna the result of the discussion of the Gemara.

4. *Additions of Yom Tob.* Additional comments by *Yom Tob Lipman Heller*, Rabbi of Prague and Cracow (XVII. century). These comments, likewise extending to all parts of the Mishna, and accompanying its text on the opposite side of Bartinoro's commentary in most of our Mishna editions, contain every valuable explanations and critical remarks.

5. Of shorter commentaries to be found only in some special editions of the Mishna text the following may be mentioned:

(a) *Tree of Life*, by *Jacob Chagiz*, Rabbi in Jerusalem (XVII. century), the author of a Talmudical terminology, *Techilath Chochma*.

6. *Full Spoon of Delight*, by Senior Phoebus (XVIII. century). This commentary is an abstract of Bertinoro's and Yom Tob Lipman Heller's commentaries.

(b) *Spoon of Delight*, by *Isaac Ibn Gabbai* in Leghorn (XVII. century), is generally based on the commentaries of Rashi and Maimonides.[9]

"*Tefereth Israel*" to all Mishnayoth, by Israel Liphschitz, a very reasonable commentary.

---

1. In our new edition it is translated in Vol. I. (IX.) and divided into paragraphs to each Mishna of Aboth.
2. Compare Zunz, "Gottesd. Vortraege," p. 108, sq.--Solomon Taussig published in his "Neve Sholom" (Munich, 1872), from a manuscript of the Library in Munich, a recension of the Aboth d'Rabbi Nathan which differs considerably from that printed in our Talmud editions. The latest edition of Aboth d. R. N. in two recensions from MSS. with critical annotations was published by S. Schechter (Vienna, 1887).
3. See Zunz, GD. V., p. 95, sq. The latest separate edition of Masecheth Sopherim from a MS. and with a German commentary was published by Joel Mueller (Leipsic, 1878).
4. Translated by us in Vol. VIII. with a brief commentary by Rodkinson.
5. See Zunz, G. V., p. 90, and N. Brüll "Die Talm. Tractate Uber Trauer um Verstorbene" (Jahrbücher für Jüd. Geschichte und Literatur, L, Frankfurt a. M.), p. 1-57. M. Klotz published "Der Talm. Tractat Ebel Rabbathi nach Handschriften bearbeitet, überzetzt und mit Anmerkungen versehen," Frankf. on the Main, 1892.
6. Also these three are translated in Vol. I. (IX.) of our new edition.
7. On both of these Masechtoth Derech Eretz, see Zunz, GD. V., pp. 110-112. See also Abr. Tawrogi, "Der Talm. Tractat Derech Erez Sutta Kritisch bearbeitet, übersetzt und erläutert" (Berlin, 1835).
8. See Graetz, "Geschichte d. J.", Vol. VII. p. 302.
9. The commentaries of the Palestinian Talmud we omit, but not the Epitomes, etc., which seem to us of interest for the reader.

Chapter 6
Epitomes, Codifications, Manuscripts and Printed Editions of the Talmud

INTRODUCTORY.

Since the Babylonian Talmud was considered by most of the Jewish communities in all countries as the source of the rabbinical law by which to regulate the religious life, it is but natural that already at a comparatively early period attempts were made to furnish abstracts of the same for practical purposes. This was done partly by epitomes or compendiums which, retaining the general arrangement and divisions of the Talmud, bring its matter into a narrower compass by omitting its Hagadic and unnecessary passages, and abridging the legal discussions; and partly by codes in which the results of the discussed legal matter is presented in a more systematic order. The first attempts in this direction were made by R. Jehudai Gaon of Sura (VIII. century), in his book *Halachoth Ketuoth* (Abridged Halakhoth), and by R. Simon of Kahira (--IX. century) in his *Halachoth Gedoloth*. 'Both of these two works, which afterwards coalesced into one work, still extant under the latter title, were, however, eclipsed by later master works of other celebrated Rabbinical authorities.

245

A. EPITOMES.

The principal epitomes or compendiums of the Talmud are by the following authors:

1. R. *Isaac Alfasi* (after the initials, called "Rif," born in 1013 near the city of Fez in Africa, died in 1103 as Rabbi at Lucena in Spain) wrote an excellent compendium, which he called "Halakhoth," but which is usually called by the name of its author, Alpassy. In this compendium he retains the general arrangement, the language and style of the Talmud, but omits, besides the Hagada, all parts and passages which concern laws that had become obsolete since the destruction of the Temple. Besides, he condensed the lengthy discussions, and added his own decision in cases not clearly decided in the Talmud.

REMARK.--Alfasi's compendium comprises in print three large folio volumes in which the text is accompanied by Rashi's Talmud commentary, and besides by numerous commentaries, annotations and glosses, especially those by R. Nissim b. Reuben (ר״ן); by R. Zerachia Halevi (Maor); by R. Mordecai b. Hillel; by R. Joseph Chabiba (Nimuke Joseph), and by some other distinguished Rabbis.

2. R. *Asher b. Jechiel*, a German Rabbi, later in Toledo, Spain, where he died in 1327, wrote a compendium after the pattern of that of Alfasi and embodied in the same also the opinions of later authorities. This compendium is appended in our Talmud editions to each Masechta, under the title of the author, Rabbennu Asher.

R. Jacob, the celebrated son of this author, added to that compendium an abstract of the decisions contained in the same, The Extract of Asher's Decisions.

B. CODES.

1. *Mishne Torah*, "Repetition of the Law," by R. Moses Maimonides, flourishing in the XII. century. This is the most comprehensive and systematically arranged Code of all the Laws scattered through the two Talmuds, or resulting from the discussions in the

same. Occasionally also the opinions of the post-Talmudic authorities, the Gaonim, are added.

This gigantic work, written throughout in Mishnic Hebrew in a very lucid and attractive style, is divided into *fourteen* books; hence its additional name, Sepher Ha-yad (having the numerical value of 14), and by way of distinction, it was later called "Yad Hachazaka," The Strong Hand. Every book is, according to the various subjects treated therein, divided into Halakhoth, the special names of which are given at the head of each of those fourteen books. The Halakhoth are again subdivided into chapters (Perakim), and these into paragraphs.

2. *Sephar Mitzvath Godol* (abbreviated S. M. G.), the great Law book, by the Tosaphist R. Moses of Coucy, in France (XIII. century). This work arranges the Talmudical law according to the 613 precepts which the Rabbis found to be contained in the Pentateuch, and is divided into 248 positive and 365 negative commandments.

REMARK--A similar work, but on a smaller scale, is "Sephar Mitzvath Gaton," also called "Amude Golah," by R. Isaac b. Joseph, of Corbeil (d. 1280).

3. *Turim* (the Rows of Laws), by R. Jacob, son of that celebrated R. Asher b. Jechiel who was mentioned above. The work is divided into four parts, called: *Tur Orach Chayim*, treating of Liturgical Laws; *Tur Yore Dea*, treating of the Ritual Laws; *Tur Eben Ha-ezer*, on the Marriage Laws, and *Tur Choshen Mishpat*, on the Civil Laws. Each of these four books is subdivided according to subjects under appropriate headings, and into chapters, called Simanim. This code differs from that of Maimonides in so far as it is restricted to such laws only which were still in use outside of Palestine, and as it embodies also rules and customs which were established after the close of the Talmud. Besides, it is not written in that uniform and pure language, and in that lucid style, by which the work of Maimonides is characterized.

4. *Shulchan Aruch* (The Prepared Table), by *R. Joseph Karo* (XVI. century), the same author who wrote the commentaries on the codes of Maimonides and of R. Jacob b. Asher. Taking the last-mentioned code (Turim) and his own commentary on the same as

basis, and retaining its division into four parts as well as that into subjects and chapters, he subdivided each chapter (Siman), into paragraphs, and so remodelled its contents as to give it the proper shape and style of a law book. This Shulchan Aruch, together with the numerous annotations added to it by the contemporary R. Moses Isserles, was up to our time regarded by all rabbinical Jews as the authoritative code by which all questions of the religious life were decided.

Constant reference to the four Codes mentioned above are made in the marginal glosses which are found on every page of the Talmud, under the heading of "*En Mishpat, Ner Mitzwuah.*" It is the object of these glosses to show, at every instance when a law is quoted or discussed in the Talmud, where the final decision of that law is to be found in the various codes. The authorship of these marginal glosses is ascribed to R. Joshua Boas Baruch (XVI. century). The same scholar wrote also the glosses headed *Torah Or* which are found in the space between the Talmud text and Rashi's commentary, and which indicate the books and chapters of the biblical passages quoted in the Talmud, besides the very important glosses in the margins of the pages, beaded *Massoreth Ha-shas*, which give references to parallel passages in the Talmud. The last mentioned glosses were later increased with critical notes by Isaiah Berlin (Pik), Rabbi in Breslau (d. 1799).

C. COLLECTIONS OF THE HAGADIC PORTIONS OF THE TALMUD.

While the above-mentioned Compendiums and Codes are restricted to abstracting only the legal matter (Halakha) of the Talmud, R. *Jacob ibn Chabib*, flourishing at the beginning of the sixteenth century, collected all the Hagadic passages, especially of the Babylonian Talmud. This very popular collection, which is usually printed with various commentaries, has the title of *En Jacob*; in some editions it is also called *En Israel*.

R. *Samuel Jafe*, flourishing in the latter part of that century, made a similar collection of the Hagadic passages Palestinian Talmud, with

248

an extensive commentary under the title of *Y'phe Mareh* (Vienna, 1590, and Berlin, 1725-26). An abridged edition with a short commentary was published under the title of *Benyan Jerusalem* (Lemberg, 1860).

D. MANUSCRIPTS.

In consequence of the terrible persecutions of the Jews during the middle ages, and the destruction of their libraries, so often connected therewith, and especially in consequence of the vandalism repeatedly perpetrated by the Church against the Talmud,[1] only a very limited number of manuscripts of the same have come down to our time. Codices of single *Sedarim* (sections) and *Masechloth* (tracts or treatises) are to be found in various libraries of Europe, especially in the Vatican Library of Rome, and in the libraries of Parma, Leyden, Paris, Oxford, Cambridge, Munich, Berlin and Hamburg. The only known complete manuscript of the Babylonian Talmud, written in the year 1369, is in possession of the Royal Library of Munich A fragment of Talmud Pesachim, of the ninth or tenth century, is preserved in the University Library of Cambridge, and was edited with an autotype facsimile, by W. H. Lowe, Cambridge, 1879.

The Columbia College in the city of New York lately acquired a collection of manuscripts containing the treatises *Pesachim, Moed Katon, Megilla*, and *Zebachim* of the Babylonian Talmud. These manuscripts came from Southern Arabia, and date from the year 1548.[2]

Manuscripts of the *Mishna* or of single Sedarim thereof, some of which dating from the thirteenth century are preserved in the libraries of Parma, of Berlin, of Hamburg, of Oxford, and of Cambridge. That of the last-mentioned library was edited by W. H. Lowe: "The Mishna on which the Palestinian Talmud Rests," etc., Cambridge, 1883.

Of the *Palestinian Talmud* the only manuscript, of considerable extent, is preserved in the Library of Leyden. See S. M. Schiller-Szinessy, "Description of the Leyden MS. of the Palestinian Talmud,"

Cambridge, 1878. Fragments of the Palestinian Talmud are also to be found in some other libraries, especially in those of Oxford and Parma.

Fuller information concerning MSS. of the Talmud is given in F. Lebrecht's "Handschriften und erste Ausgaben des Babyl. Talmud," Berlin, 1862. See also M. Steinschneider's "Hebraische Bibliographic," Berlin, 1862 and 1863.

E. THE TALMUD IN PRINT.

a. The Mishna Editions.

Already as early as the year 1492, the first edition of the Mishna, together with the commentary of Maimonides, appeared in Naples. It was followed by several editions of Venice (1546-50, and 1606), of Riva di Trento (1559), and of Mantua (1559-63). In the last-mentioned editions the commentary of Obadia di Bertinoro is added. The editions which have since appeared are very numerous. Those which appeared since the seventeenth century are generally accompanied, besides Bertinoro's commentary, by Lipman Heller's or some other shorter commentaries.

b. The Babylonian Talmud.

The first complete edition of the Babylonian Talmud was published by Daniel Bomberg in twelve folio volumes, Venice, 1520-23. Besides the text, it contains the commentary of Rashi, the Tosephoth, the Piske-Tosephoth, the compendium of Asheri, and the Mishna commentary of Maimonides. This original edition served as model for all editions which subsequently appeared at Venice, Basel, Cracow, Lublin, Amsterdam, Frankfort-on-the-Oder, Berlin, Frankfort-on-the-Main, Sulzbach, Dyhernfurt, Prague, Warsaw, Lemberg, and recently at Vienna and Wilna. The later editions were greatly, improved by the addition of valuable literary and critical marginal notes and appendices by learned rabbis. But the Basel and most of the subsequent editions, down almost to the present time, have been much mutilated by the official censors of the press, who expunged from the Talmud all those passages which, in their opinion, seemed to reflect upon Christianity, and, besides, changed expressions, especially names of nations and of sects, which they suspected as having reference to Christians.

The Amsterdam editions, especially the first (1644-48), escaped those mutilations at the hand of the censors, and are on this account considered very valuable. Most of the passages which have elsewhere been eliminated or altered by the censors have been extracted from the Amsterdam edition, and published in separate small books. Of these the following two may be mentioned: "Collected Omissions" and "The Omissions," Koenigsberg, 1860.[3]

A critical review of the complete editions of the Babylonian Talmud and of the very numerous editions of single Masechtoth since the year 1484, was published by Raphael Rabbinovicz, in his Hebrew pamphlet, Munich, 1877.[4]

The same author also collected and published very rich and important material for a critical edition of the Babylonian Talmud from the above-mentioned manuscript in the Royal Library of Munich and other manuscripts, as well as from early prints of single Masechtoth in various libraries. The title of this very extensive work, written in Hebrew, is *Dikduke Sopherim*, with the Latin title: *Variae lectiones in Mishnam et in Talmud Babylonicum*, etc., Munich 1868-86. The fifteen volumes in octavo which have appeared of this valuable work comprise only three and a half Sedarim of the six Sedarim of the Talmud. It is to be regretted that in consequence of the death of the learned author the completion of this important work has been suspended.

c. The Palestinian Talmud.

Of the Palestinian Talmud (Jerushalmi) only four complete editions appeared:

1. The first edition, published by Daniel Bomberg, Venice, 1523-24, in one folio volume, without any commentary.

2. The *Cracow* edition, 1609, with a short commentary on the margin.

3. The *Krotoshin* edition, 1866, with a commentary like that in the Cracow edition, but added to it are marginal notes, containing references to parallel passages in the Babylonian Talmud, and corrections of text readings.

4. The *Shitomir* edition, 1860-67, in several folio volumes, with various commentaries.

Besides these four complete editions, several parts have been published with commentaries.

------

1. It is stated that at the notorious *auto-da-fe* of the Talmud, held in the year 1249, at Paris, twenty-four cart-loads of Talmud tomes were consigned to the flames. Similar destructions of the Talmud were executed by the order of Pope Julius III., in first at Rome, then at Bologna and Venice, and in the following year the year 1553, in Ancona and other cities. Among the 12,000 tomes of the Talmud that were burned at Cremona, in the year 1559 (see Graetz's "Geschichte d. Juden," X., p. 382), were undoubtedly also numerous manuscripts, though most of them may have been printed copies.
2. See Max L. Margolis's "The Columbia College MS. of Meghilla Examined," New York, 1892.
3. In our "Schulchan Aruch und Seine Beziehungen, etc.," mentioned in our appendix about the Münster process, we give a clear explanation about all the corrections by the censor which does not fully agree with this remark. Concerning these omissions, see our "Concluding Words" to Vols. XVII. and XVIII.
4. This instructive pamphlet is also reprinted as an appendix to Vol. VIII. Of Dikduke Sopherim.

Chapter 7
Translations of the Talmud

A. THE MISHNA.

English Translations.

W. *Walton.* Translation of the treatises Sabbath and Erubin, London, 1718.

D. A. *de Sola* and M. I. *Raphall.* Eighteen treatises from the Mishna translated. London, 1843.

Joseph Barclay published under the title "The Talmud" a translation of eighteen treatises of the Mishna with annotations. London, 1878.

C. *Taylor.* Sayings of the Jewish Fathers (the treatise Aboth). Cambridge, 1877.

REMARK.--The treatise "Aboth" has been translated into almost all of the European languages.

B. THE BABYLONIAN TALMUD.

To translate the Mishna is a comparatively easy task. Its generally plain and uniform language and style of expression, and its compendious character could easily enough be rendered into another language, especially when accompanied by some explanatory notes. But it is quite different with the Gemara, especially the Babylonian. There are, of course, also passages in the Gemara which offer no great difficulties to a translator who is sufficiently familiar with the idiom in which the original is composed. We refer to the historical, legendary and homiletical portions (Hagadas), which the compilers have interspersed in every treatise. The main part of the Gemara, however, which is essentially of an argumentative character, giving minute reports of discussions and debates on the law, this part, so rich in dialectical subtilities, and so full of technicalities and elliptical expressions, offers to the translator almost insurmountable difficulties.

English Translations.

A. W. Streane. Translation of the treatise *Chagiga.* Cambridge, 1891.

Michael L. Rodkinson: Babylonian Talmud--Section Moed (Festivals). Complete, consisting of the following volumes: Vol. I.,[1] Tract Sabbath (first ten chapters); Vol. H., Tract Sabbath (continued), fourteen chapters; Vol. III., Tract Erubin (Mingling); Vol. IV., Tracts Skekalim (Duties), and Rosh Hashana (Hebrew Calendar); Vol. V., Tract Pesachim (Passover); Vol. VI., Tracts Yomah (Day of Atonement), and Hagiga (Holocaust); Vol. VII., Tracts Betzah (Feast), Succah (Tabernacles), and Moed Katan (Minor Festivals); Vol. VIII., Tracts Taanith (Fasts), Megilla (Book of Esther), and Ebel Rabbathi (Great Mourning).

Section Jurisprudence: Vol. I., Ethics of Judaism, (Tracts Aboth, Aboth of R. Nathan, Derech Eretz, Rabba and Zutta); Vol. H., Bab Kama (First Gate, eight chapters); Vol. III., Baba Metziah (Middle Gate), five chapters, and the last two of Baba Kama; Vol. IV., the last five chapters of Baba Metziah; Vol. V.-VI., Baba Bathra (Last Gate, five chapters in each); Vol. VII.-VIII., Sanhedrin; Vol. IX., Maccath, Shebuoth, and Eduyoth; Vol. X., Abuda Zara and Horioth, New York, 1896-1903.[2]

C. THE PALESTINIAN TALMUD.

a. Latin Translation.

Blasius Ugolinus, published in volumes XVII.-XXX. of his Thesaurus antiquitatum sacrarum. (Venice, 1755-65), the following treatises in Latin: Pesachim (vol. XVII.); Shekalim, Yoma, Succah, Rosh Hashanah, Taanith, Megilla, Chagiga, Betza, Moed Katan (vol. XVIII.); Maaseroth, Maaser Sheni, Challah, Orlah, Biccurim (vol. XX.); Sanhedrin, Maccoth (Vol. XXV.); Kiddushin, Sota, Kethuboth (vol. XXX.).

b. German Translations.

Joh. Jacob Rabe, besides translating Berachoth in connection with that treatise in the Babylonian Gemara, as mentioned above, published: Der Talmudische Tractat *Peah,* übersetzt und erläutert. Anspach, 1781.

August Wünsche. Der Jerusalemische Talmud in seinen haggadischen Bestandtheilen zum ersten Male in's Deutsche übertragen. Zurich, 1880.

c. French Translation.

Moise Schwab. Le Talmud de Jerusalem traduit pour la première fois. X. volumes. Paris, 1871-90.

D. GEMARA.

M. Schwab, the author of the French translation published in English: The Talmud of Jerusalem. Vol. I. Berachoth. London, 1886.

---

1. Of Vol. I. and IV. a second revised and enlarged edition was published.
2. See "Kritische Geschichte der Talmud Übersetzung" by Bischof, p. 62. In this book all the translations from both Talmuds in *all languages* and all tracts or parts of them, with criticisms, are mentioned. The English translations are given here for the English reader.

Chapter 8
Bibliography of Modern Works and Monographs on Talmudic Subjects

BIBLIOGRAPHY OF MODERN WORKS AND
MONOGRAPHS ON TALMUDIC SUBJECTS.
(Arranged with reference to subjects and in alphabetical order of
authors).

HAGADA.

W. *Bacher*. Die Agada der Tannaiten. Strasburg, Als. 1884;
Die Agada der Babylonischen Amoräer. Strasburg, Als.,
1878; Die Agada der Palästinischen Amoräer. Strasburg, Als., 1891;
Agada der Palästinischen Amoräer, published 1896, Vol. II., Die
Schueler Jochanan's, and 1899 Vol. III., Die letzten Amoräer des
heiligen Landes.

S. *Back*. Die Fabel im Talmud u. Midrasch (in Monatsschrift f.
Geschichte u. Wissenschaft d. Judenthums, XXIV., 1875; XXV.,
1876; XXIX., 1880; XXX., 1881; XXXII., 1883; XXXIII., 1884).

M. *Grünbaum*. Beiträge zur vergleichenden Mythologie aus der
Haggada (in Zeitschrift d. D. Morgenl. Gesellschaft, vol. XXXI.,
1877).

M. *Güdemann*. Mythenmischung in der Haggada (in Monatsschrift f. Geschichte u. Wissenschaft d. Judenthums, vol. XXV., 1876).

D. Hoffmann. Die Antonius Agadoth im. Talmud (in Magazin für Wissenschaft des Judenthums, vol. XIX., 1892).

ARCHÆOLOGICAL.

Ad. Brüll. Trachten der Juden im nachbiblischen Alterthum. Frankf. on the M., 1873.

Franz Delitzsch. Jüdisches Handwerkerleben zur Zeit Jesu, Elangen, 1879. Translated by B. Pick, "Jewish Artisan Life." New York, 1883.

M. H. Friedländer. Die Arbeit nach Bibel u. Talmud. Brünn, 1891.

L. Herzfeld. Metrologische Voruntersuchungen, Geld und Gewicht der Juden bis zum. Schluss des Talmuds (in Jahrbuch für Geschichte der Juden u. des Judenthums, vol. III., pp. 95-191, Leipsic, 1863).

Alex. Kohut. Ist das Schachspiel im Talmud genannt? (Z. d. D. M. G., XLVI., 130-39).

Leopold Löw. Graphische Requisiten und Erzeugnisse bei den Juden, Leipsic, 1870-71; Die Lebensalter in der jüd. Literatur. Szegedin, 1875.

H. Vogelstein. Die Landwirthschaft in Palestina zur Zeit der Mischna. Berlin, 1894.

B. Zuckerman. Ueber Talmudische Münzen u. Gewichte. Breslau, 1862; Das jüdische Maassystem. Breslau, 1867; Technologic u. Terminologie der Handverke in der P. Rieger Mischnah. Berlin, 1895.

BIOGRAPHICAL.

Sam. Back. Elischa ben Abuja, quellenmässig dargestellt. Frankf. on the M., 1891.

A. Blumenthal. Rabbi Meir, sein Leben u. Wirken. Frankf., 889.

M. Braunschweiger. Die Lehrer der Mischna, ihr Leben u. Wirken. Frankf. on the M., 1890.

S. Fessler. Mar Samuel, der bedeutendste Amora. Breslau, 1879.

M. Friedländer. Geschichtsbilder aus der Zeit der Tanaiten u. Amoräer. Brünn, 1879.

S. Gelbhaus. R. Jehuda Hanasi und die Redaction der Mischna. Vienna, 1876.

D. Hoffmann. Mar Samuel, Rector der Academie zu Nahardea. Leipsic, 1873.

M. D. Hoffmann. Biographie des Elischa ben Abuya. Vienna, 1870.

Armand Kaminka. Simon b. Jochai (chapter in the author's Studien zur Geschichte Galilaeas. Berlin, 1890).

Raphael Lévy. Un Tanah (Rabbi Mar), Étude sur la vie et l'enseignement d'un docteur Juif du II. siècle. Paris, 1883.

L. Lewin. R. Simon b. Jochai. Frankf. on M., 1893.

M. I. Mühlfelder. Rabh. Ein Lebensbild zur Geschichte des Talmud. Leipsic, 1873.

J. Spitz. Rabban Jochanan b. Sakkai, Rector der Hochschule zu Jabneh. Berlin, 1883.

I. Trenel. Vie de Hillel l'Ancient. Paris, 1867.

H. Zirndorf. Some Women in Israel (pp. 119-270, portraying distinguished women of the Talmudic age). Philadelphia, 1892.

F. Kauter. Beitraege zur Kenntniss des Rechtsystems und der Ethik Mar Samuels. Bern, 1895.

A. Kisch. Hillel der Alte, Lebensbild eines jued. Weisen. Prag., 1889.

CHRONOLOGY AND CALENDAR.

L. M. Lewisohn. Geschichte u. System des jüdischen Kalenderwesens. Leipsic, 1856.

B. Zuckermann. Materialien zur Entwickelung der altjüdischen Zeitrechnung. Breslau 1882.

CUSTOMS.

I. M. Cassanowicz. Non-Jewish religious ceremonies in the

Talmud (in Proceedings of the American Oriental Society). New York, 1894.

Joseph Perles. Die jüdische Hochzeit in nachbiblischer Zeit. Leipsic, 1860. Die Leichenfeierlichkeiten im. nachbiblischen Judenthum. Breslau, 1861.

REMARK.--An English translation of both of these two monographs is embodied in "Hebrew Characteristics," published by the American Jewish Publication Society. New York, 1875.

M. Fluegel. Gedanken uber religiöse Bräuche und Anschauungen. Cincinnati, 1888.

DIALECTICS.

Aaron Hahn. The Rabbinical Dialectics. A History of Dialecticians and Dialectics of the Mishna and Talmud. Cincinnati, 1879.

EDUCATION.

Blach-Gudensberg. Das Paedagogische im Talmud. Halberstadt, 1880.

M. Duschak. Schulgesetzgebung u. Methodik der alten Israeliten. Vienna, 1872.

Sam. Marcus. Zur Schul-Paedagogik des Talmud. Berlin, 1866.

Joseph Simon. L'éducation et l'instruction d'après la Bible et le Talmud. Leipsic, 1879.

E. Van Gelden. Die Volkeschule des juedischen Alterthums nach Talmudischen Quellen. Berlin, 1872.

J. Wiesen. Geschichte und Methodik der Schulwesens im talmudischen Alterthum. Strasburg, 1892.

J. Lewit. Darstellung der theoretischen und practischen Paedagogik im juedischen Alterthum. Berlin, 1896.

ETHICS.

M. Bloch. Die Ethik der Halacha. Budapest, 1886.

Herman Cohen. Die Nächstenliebe im Talmud. Ein Gutachten. Marburg, 1886.

M. Duschak. Die Moral der Evangelien u. des Talmuds. Bronn, 1877.

H. B. Fassel. Tugend- und Rechtslehre des Talmud. Vienna, 1848.

M. Lazarus. Die Ethik des Judenthums. Frankfort a. M., 1898. Translated into English. (The Ethics of Judaism), by Henriette Szold, Vol. 1. Philadelphia, 1900-01.

E. Grünebaum. Die Sittenlehre des Judenthums andern Bekentnissen gegenüber. Strasburg, 1878.

M. Güdemann. Nächstenliebe. Vienna, 1890.

Alex. Kohut. The Ethics of the Fathers. A series of lectures. New York, 1885.

L. Lazarus. Zur Charakteristik der talmudischen Ethik. Breslau, 1877.

Marc. Lévy. Essai sur la morale de Talmud. Paris, 1891.

Luzzatto. Israelitische Moraltheologie, dcutsch von Al. Joel. Breslau, 1870.

S. Schaffer. Das Recht und seine Stellung zur Moral nach talmudischer Sitten- und Rechtslehre. Frankf. on the M., 1889.

N. J. Weinstein, Geschichtliche Entwickelung des Gebotes der Nächstenliebe innerhalb des Judenthums, kritisch beleuchtet. Berlin, 1891.

M. L. Rodkinson. Ahbath Adam ah pe Torah She Balpeh. In Hebrew--a booklet in the periodical Hakol, Vol. VT. Vienna, 1885. Translated into German as "Nächstenliebe nach den Talmud" in manuscript.

EXEGESIS.

W. Bacher. Exegesis and Bible Criticism. Ein Woerterbuch der bibelexegetischen Kunstsprache der Tannaiten. Leipsic, 1899.

M. Eisenstadt. Ueber Bibelkritik in der talmud. Literatur. Berlin, 1894.

H. S. Hirschfeld. Halachische Exegese. Berlin, 1840; Die Hagadische Exegese. Berlin, 1847.

S. Waldberg. Darke Hashinnuyim, on the methods of artificial interpretation of Scriptures in the Talmud and Midrash (in Hebrew). Lemberg, 1870.

GEOGRAPHY AND HISTORY.

A. Berliner. Beiträge zur Geographie u. Ethnographie Babyloniens im. Talmud u. Midrasch. Berlin, 1883.

J. Derenbourg. Essai Sur l'histoire et la géographie de la Palestine d'après les Talmuds et les autres sources rabbiniques. Paris, 1867.

H. Hildesheimer. Beiträge zur Geographie Palästinas. Berlin, 1886.

Armand Kaminka. Studien zur Geschichte Galilaeas. Berlin, 1890.

Ad. Neubauer. La géographie du Talmud. Mémoire couronné par l'académie des inscriptions et belles-lettres. Paris, 1868.

LAW.

a. In General.

Jacques Levy. La jurisprudence du Pentateuque et du Talmud. Constantine, 1879.

S. Mayer. Die Rechte der Israeliten, Athener und Römer. Leipsic, 1862-66.

M. Mielziner. Legal Maxims and Fundamental Laws of the Civil and Criminal Code of the Talmud. Cincinnati, 1898.

M. W. Rapaport. Der Talmud und sein Recht (in Zeitschrift fuer Vergleichende Rechtswissenschaft, XIV. Band. Stuttgart, 1900).

I. L. Saalschütz. Das Mosaische Recht, nebst den vervollständigenden thalmudisch-rabbinischen Bestimmungen. 2d Edition, Berlin, 1853.

S. Schaffer. Das Recht u. seine Stellung zur Moral nach talmudischer Sitten- und Rechtslehre. Frankf. on the M., 1889.

I. M. Wise. The Law (in the Hebrew Review, Vol. I., pp. 12-32. Cincinnati, 1880).

b. Judicial Courts.

Adolph Buechler. Das Synhedrion in Jerusalem. Vienna, 1902.

E. Hoffmann. Der oberste Gerichtshof in der Stadt des Heiligthums. Berlin, 1878.

J. Klein. Das Gesetz ueber das gerichtlische Beweisverfabren nach mosaisch-talmudischen Rechte. Halle, 1885.

J. Selden. De Synedriis et praefecturis juridicis veterum Ebraeorum. London, 1650; Amsterd., 1679; Frankf., 1696.

c. Evidence in Law.

I. Blumenstein. Die verschiedenen Eidesarten nach mosaisch-talmudischem Rechte. Frankf. on the M., 1883.

Z. Frankel. Der Gerichtliche Beweis nach mosaisch-talmudischem Rechte. Berlin, 1846.

D. Fink. "Miggo" als Rechtsbeweis im. bab. Talm. Leipsic, 1891.

d. Criminal Law.

O. Bähr. Das Gesetz über falsehe Zeugen, nach Bibel u. Talmud. Berlin, 1862.

P. B. Benny. The Criminal Code of the Jews. London, 1880.

M, Duschak. Das mosaisch-talmudische Strafrecht. Vienna, 1869.

J. Fürst. Das peinliche Rechtsverfahren im jüd. Alterthum. Heidelberg, 1870.

E. Goitein. Das Vergeltungsprinzip im bibl. u. talmudischen Strafrecht (in Zeitschrift für Wissenschaft d. J. Vol. XIX.

S. Mendelsohn. The Criminal Jurisprudence of the ancient Hebrews compiled from the Talmud and other rabbinical writings. Baltimore, 1891.

Thonisson. La peine de mort dans le Talmud. Brussels, 1886.

Julius Vargha. Defence in criminal cases with the ancient Hebrews, translated from the first chapter of the author's large work "Vertheidigung in Criminalfällen," and published in the Hebrew Review, Vol. I., pp. 254-268. Cincinnati, 1880.

I. Wiesner. Der Bann in seiner geschichtlichen Entwickelung auf dem Boden des Judenthums. Leipsic, 1864.

e. Civil Law.

L. Auerbach: Das jüdische Obligationsrecht. Berlin, 1871.

M. Bloch. Die Civilprocess-Ordnung nach mosaisch-rabbinischem Rechte. Budapest, 1882.

H. B. Fassel. Das mosaisch-rabbinische Civilrecht. Gr. Kanischa, 1852-54; Das mosaisch-rabbinische Gerichtsverfahren in civilrechtlischen Sachen. Gr. Kanischa, 1859.

S. Keyzer. Dissertatio de tutela secundum jus Talmudicum. Leyden, 1847.

f. Inheritance and Testament.

M. Bloch. Der Vertrag nach mosaisch-talmud. Rechte. Budapest, 1892; Das mosaisch-talmud. Erebrecht. Budapest, 1890;

L. Bodenheimer. Das Testament. Crefeld, 1847.

Eduard Gans. Grundzüge des mosaisch-talmudischen Erbrechts (in Zunz's Zeitschrift für die Wissenschaft des Judenthums, p. 419 sq.).

M. Mielziner. The Rabbinical Law of Hereditary Succession. Cincinnati, 1900.

Moses Mendelssohn. Ritualgesetze der Juden, betreffend Erbschaften Vormundschaft, Testamente, etc. Berlin, 1778, and several later editions.

M. W. Rapaport. Grundsaetze des (talmudischen) Intestaterbrechts und Schenkungen (in Zeitschrift fuer Vergleichende Rechts Wissenschaft, XIV. Band. Stuttgart, 1900.

Joh. Selden. De Successionibus in bona defuncti ad leges Hebraeorum. London, 1646; Frankf., 1696.

A. Wolff. Das Juedische Erbrecht. Berlin, 1888.

g. Police Law.

M. Bloch. Das mosaisch-talmudische Polizeirecht. Budapest, 878. Translated into English by I. W. Lilienthal in the Hebrew Review, Vol. I. Cincinnati, 1891.

h. Law of Marriage and Divorce.

P. Buchholz. Die Familie nach mos.-talmud. Lehre. Breslau, 1867.

M. Duschak. Das mosaisch-talmudische Eherecht. Vienna, 1864.

Z. Frankel. Grundlinien des mosaisch-talmud. Eherechts. Breslau, 1860.

S. Holdheim. Die Autonomie der Rabbinen und das Princip der jüdischen Ehe. Schwerin, 1847.

L. Lichtschein. Die Ehe nach mosaisch-talm. Auffassung. Leipsic, 1879.

M. Mielziner. The Jewish Law of Marriage and Divorce in ancient and modem times, and its relation to the law of the State. Cincinnati, 1884.

Joh. Selden. Uxor Ebraica sive de nuptiis et divortiis, etc. London, 1646.

I. Stern. Die Frau im Talmud. Zurich, 1879.

D. W. Amram. The Jewish Law of Divorce. Philadelphia, 1896.

i. Laws Concerning Slavery.

D. Farbstein. Das Recht der freien und der unfreien Arbeiter nach juedish-talmudischen Recht. Frankfort o. M., 1896.

M. Mielziner. Verhältnisse der Sklaven bei den alten Hebräern nach biblischen und talmudischen Quellen. Copenhagen (Leipsic), 1859.

REMARK.--An English translation of this treatise was published by Prof. H. I. Schmidt in the *Gettysburg Evang. Review*, Vol. XIII., No. 51, and reprinted in the *Am. Jew's Annual*. Cincinnati, 1886.

I. Winter. Stellung der Sklaven bei den Juden. Breslau, 1886.

Zadok-Kahn. L'esclavage selon la Bible et le Talmud (Paris, 1867); Sklaverei nach Bibel u. Talmud. Deutsch von Singer. Berlin, 1888.

LINGUISTICS.

A. Berliner. Beiträge zur hebräischen Grammatik im Talmud u. Midrasch. Berlin, 1879.

Ad. Brüll. Fremdsprachliche Redensarten u. Wörter in den Talmuden u. Midraschim. Leipsic, 1869.

N. Brüll. Fremdsprachliche Wörter in den Talmuden u. Midraschim (in Jahrbücher für jüd. Geschichte u. Literatur, I., 123-220). Frankf. o. M., 1874.

Sam. Kramer. Griechische und Lateinische Lehnwoerter in Talmud, Midrasch u. Targum. 2 vols. Berlin, 1898-99.

Jos. Perles. Etymologische Studien zur Kunde der rabbinischen Sprache und Alterthümer. Breslau, 1871.

G. Rülf. Zur Lautleüre der aramäisch-talmudischen Dialecte. Breslau, 1879.

Mich. Sachs. Beiträge zur Sprach- und Alterthumsforschung. 2 volumes. Berlin, 1852-54-

A. Lieberman. Das Pronomen und das Adverbium des babyl.-talmudischen Dialecte. Berlin, 1895.

MATHEMATICS.

B. Zuckermann. Das Mathematische im Talmud. Beleuchtung und Eläuterung der Talmudstellen mathematischen Inhalts. Breslau, 1878.

MEDICINE, SURGERY, ETC.

Jos. Bergel. Die Medizin der Talmudisten. Leipsic, 1885.

Joach. Halpern. Beiträge zur Geschichte der talm. Chirurgie. Breslau, 1869.

A. H. Israels. Collectanea Gynaecologica ex Talmude Babylonico. Gröningen, 1845.

L. Katzenelsson. Die Osteologie der Talmudisten. Eine talmudisch-anatonische Studie (in Hebrew). St. Petersburg, 1888.

R. I. Wunderbar. Biblisch-talmudische Medicin. 2 Volumes. Riga (Leipsic), 1850-60.

NATURAL HISTORY AND SCIENCES.

Jos. Bergel. Studien über die naturwissenschaftlichen Kenntnisse der Talmudisten. Leipsic, 1880.

M. Duschak. Zur Botanik des Talmud. Budapest, 1870.

L. Lewysohn. Die Zoologie des Talmuds. Frankf. on the M., 1858.

Imm. Löw. Aramaische Pflanzennamen. Leipsic, 1881.

PARSEEISM IN THE TALMUD.

Alexander Kohut. Was hat die talm. Eschatologie aus dem Parsismus aufgenommen? (in Z. d. D. M. G., Vol. XXI., pp. 552-91); Die jüdische Angelologie und Daemonologie in ihrer Abhängigkeit vom Parsismus (Leipsic, 1866); Die talmudisch-midraschische Adamssage in ihrer Rückbeziehung auf die pers. Yima und Meshiasage (in Z. d. D. M. G., XXV., pp. 59-94); Die Namen der pers. u. babylonischen Feste im Talmud (in Kobak's Jeschurun, Vol. VIII., 49-64). The same subject in Revue des Études Juives, Vol. XXIV.

POETRY.

S. *Sekles.* The Poetry of the Talmud. New York, 1880.

PROVERBS, MAXIMS, PARABLES.

L. *Dukes.* Rabbinische Blumenlese (Leipsic, 1844); Rabbinische Sprachkunde (Vienna, 1851).

J. R. *Fürstenthal.* Rabbinische Anthologie. Breslau, 1834.

Giuseppe Levi. Parabeln, Legenden u. Gedanken aus Talmud u. Midrasch, aus dem Italienischen ins Deutsche übetragen von L. Seligmann. Leipsic, 1863

Löwenstein. Sentenzen, Sprüche u. Lebensregeln aus dem, Talmud. Berlin, 1887.

Henry Cohen. Talmudic Savings. Cincinnati, 1895.

G. *Tabenhaus.* Echoes of Wisdom, or Talmudic Sayings, Part I. Brooklyn, 1900.

PSYCHOLOGY.

M. *Jacobson.* Versuch einer Psychologie des Talmud Hamburg, 1878.

I. *Wiesner.* Zur talmudischen Psychologie (in Magazin für jüdische Geschichte und Literatur, Vol. I., 1874, and II. 1875).

RELIGIOUS PHILOSOPHY AND HISTORY.

M. Friedländer. Den Dosa und seine Zeit, oder Einfluss der heidnischen Philosophie auf das Judenthum u. Christenthum. Prague, 1872.

M. Güdemann. Religionsgeschichtliche Studien. Leipsic, 1876.

M. Joel. Blicke in die Religionsgeschichte zu Anfang des II. Jahrhunderts. Breslau, 1880.

A. Nager. Die Religionsphilosophic des Talmud. Leipsic, 1864.

SUPERNATURALISM AND SUPERSTITION.

Gideon Brecher. Das Transcendentale, Magik und magische Heilarten im Talmud. Vienna, 1850.

David Joel. Der Aberglaube und die Stellung des Judenthums zu demselben. 2 parts. Breslau, 1881-3.

Alex. Kohut. Jüdische Angelologie u. Daemonologic in ihrer Abhängigkeit vom Parsismus. Leipsic, 1866.

Sal. Thein. Das Princip des planetarischen Einflusses nach der Anschauung des Talmud. Vienna, 1876.

S. Wolffsohn. Oneirologie im Talmud, oder der Traum nach Auffassung des Talmuds. Breslau, 1874.

POPULAR TREATISES AND LECTURES ON THE TALMUD.

Tobias Cohn. Der Talmud. Ein Vortrag. Vienna, 1866.

Arsem Darmstetter. The Talmud (translated from the French by Henriette Szold). Philadelphia, 1897.

Emanuel Deutsch. What is the Talmud? (in the Quarterly Review for October, 1867, reprinted in the Literary Remains, New York, 1874).

M. Ehrentheil. Der Geist des Talmud. Breslau, 1887-

J. Eschelbacher. Zwei Reden ueber den Talmud. Frankfort o. M., 1897.

Karl Fischer. Gutmeinung über den Talmud. Vienna, 1883.

H. Goitein. Anklaeger und Vertheidiger des Talmud. Frankf. o. M., 1897.

Sams. Raph. Hirsch. Beziehung des Talmuds zum Judenthum und zur sozialen Stellung seiner Bekenner. Frankf. o. M., 1884.

P. I. Hershon. Talmudic Miscellany. London, 1880.

P. L. Hershon. Treasures of the Talmud. London, 1882.

Abram S. Isaacs. Stories from the Rabbis. New York, 1893.

A. Jellinek. Der Talmud. Zwei Reden (Vienna, 1865); Der Talmudjude. 4 Reden (Vienna, 1882-83).

M. Joel. Gutachten über den Talmud. Breslau, 1877.

Albert Katz. Der wahre Talmudjude. Die wichtigsten Grundsätze des talmudischen Schriftthums über das sittliche Leben des Menschen. Berlin, 1893.

S. Klein. Die Wahrheit über den Talmud (aus dem Französischen "La verité sur le Talmud," übersetzt von S. Mannheimer. Basel, 1860.

Isidore Loeb. La Controverse sur le Talmud sous Saint Louis. Paris, 1881.

H. Polano. The Talmud, Selections from the contents of that ancient book. London, 1876.

Ludwig Philippson. Zur Characteristik des Talmuds (in "Weltbewegende Fragen." Vol. II., pp. 349-40. Leipsic, 1869).

Em. Schreiber. The Talmud. A series of (4) Lectures. Denver, 1884.

L. Stern. Ueber den Talmud. Vortrag. Wurzburg, 1875.

J. Stern. Lichtstrahlen aus dem Talmud. Zurich, 1883.

A. A. Wolff. Talmudfjender (the Enemies of the Talmud), in Danish. Copenhagen, 1878.

August Wünsche. Der Talmud. Eine Skizze. Zurich, 1879.

M. L. Rodkinson. What is the Talmud? (A book in Hebrew, the first chapter of which is translated into English as an appendix to the Pentateuch. Its language and characters). Chicago, 1894. In the first prospectus issued by the New Amsterdam Book Co., it is republished with additional remarks.

Chapter 9
Why Should Christians Feel Interested in the Talmud?

Many learned men, as is well known to any student, have in each century since the close of the Talmud written about the necessity of Talmudic studies, even for non-Jews. We have, nevertheless selected for quotation some statements of modern scholars of this century, to the effect that the study of the Talmud is highly useful to Christian theologians.

Christian theology and Jewish theology having really followed two parallel paths, the history of either cannot be understood without the history of the other. Numberless material details of the gospels find, moreover, their commentary in the Talmud. . . The distinction of epochs is here very important, the compilation of the Talmud extending from the year 200 to the year 500 nearly.--*Renan's "Life of Jesus," Introduction.*

Is the literature that Jesus was familiar with in his early years yet in existence in the world? Is it possible for us to get at it? Can we ourselves review the ideas, the statements, the modes of reasoning and thinking, on moral and religious subjects, which were current in his time, and must have been revolved by him during those silent thirty years when he was pondering his future mission? To such inquiries the learned class of Jewish rabbis answer by holding up the

Talmud. Here, say they, is the source from whence Jesus of Nazareth drew the teachings which enabled him to revolutionize the world; and the question becomes, therefore, an interesting one to every Christian, What is the Talmud? . . .

The Talmud, then, is the written form of that which, in the time of Jesus, was called the Traditions of the Elders, and to which he makes frequent allusions. What sort of book is it?

The answer is at first sight discouraging to flesh and spirit. The Talmud appears to view in form of fourteen heavy folio volumes, of thick, solid Hebrew and Aramaic consonants, without a vowel to be seen from the first word of the first volume to the last word of the last. Such is the Jewish Talmud, including both the Jerusalem and the Babylonian. Who can read it? It can be read, for it has been read . . .

The Talmud is the great repository of the mental products of a most vigorous and vivid race of thinkers, through long ages of degradation, persecution, oppression, and sorrow; and, as such, few human works are more worthy of, or will better repay, the student of human nature . . .

What light it may shed on the words of Jesus and Paul to know the modes of thought which were such a perfect world in their time! When Paul speaks of his studies at the feet of Gamaliel, one of the principal authors of the Talmud, of his profiting in the matters of law above many of his equals, we see him, an ardent young enthusiast, on the way to become an accomplished rabbi, perhaps even a Nasi, in some future day, and we understand what he means when he says, "But what things were gain tome, these I counted loss to Christ." It was a whole education and a whole life's work that he threw at the feet of his new Master.

Looking at the Talmud in contrast with any other ancient sacred writings extant in the world, except the Bible, we must be struck with its immense superiority . . .

I desire, in conclusion, to express my obligations to the ponderous erudition of the two older standard authors on this subject . . .

The writings of Dukes, an author of our own day, are especially rich in regard to Rabbinic proverbs and apologues; and in one of his prefaces he expresses the hope that they may be of some use even to that rather numerous body of Christians who give little other evidence of being Christians at all, except that of hating the Jews.-- *Atlantic Monthly*, Vol. 21, p. 673, sq.

The science of our day owes to itself the duty of studying the Talmud impartially. It will judge worthy of its attention this monument of a religion and a civilization whose influence has not been void in the world, and whatever its absolute value may be adjudged to be, science will understand it, and study its formation and development. It will demand of the, Talmud instruction, or, at least, information, almost as varied as the subjects coming within the compass of science. The historian will address himself to it for light upon the history of the earliest centuries of the Christian era, and of the centuries immediately preceding it, and though not seeking in it precise data, which it cannot furnish, he will be sure to find a faithful picture of the beliefs and ideas of the Jewish nation on its moral and spiritual life. The naturalist will ask of it numerous questions concerning the sciences, physical, natural, or medical. Has it ever occurred to any one to compile, if not the fauna, at least the flora of the Talmud; that is, of the Palestine and Babylonia contemporary with the Empire? It were easy with it as a basis to furnish a second edition of Pliny's *Natural History*, certainly as valuable as the first. The lawyer will question it on the history of its jurisprudence, will investigate whether, how, and by what intermediaries Roman law and Persian customs influenced it, and it will be a curious study to compare the results that two different civilizations, directed by opposite principles, have reached in the *jus civile* and the *jus Talmudicum*, The mythologist will dive into its legends, and, by a nice application of the comparative method, determine the history of Midrashic mythology. The philologist will devote himself to the language--that abrupt, rough language by means of which the Talmud seems to please itself in heaping up obscurities of form over those of the thought, and he will be sure to make more than one happy find. For, says the author of the *History of the Semitic Languages*, "the lexical spoliation and grammatic analysis of the

Talmudic language, according to the methods of modem philology, remain to be made . . . That language fills a hiatus in the history of Semitic idioms.

Finally, the philosopher will demand of the Talmud the explanation of Judaism and the history of Jewish institutions, and as the Talmudic books offer the completest expression thereof, and as he has at hand all the component elements, a scrupulous analysis will give him the law of the development of the Jewish religion.--*Darmesteter*, "The Talmud," p. 96.

Here we have an attempt-and the attempt is praiseworthy--to put the Talmud, or the substance of it, into *plain English*, and for this the Christian reader, if not the learned rabbi, must be grateful to the translator.--Independent, April 7, 1899.

Published in the second prospectus issued by the New Talmud Publishing Co., adding to them some remarks of Mielziner's address to the senior class of the Union Hebrew College at Cincinnati, some years ago:

"To impress you the more with the necessity of the Talmudic studies for a clear conception of Judaism and its history, I could also quote the opinions of many of our greatest scholars, but shall confine myself only to a quotation from the writings of two of our most renowned scholars whom none will suspect of having been biased by a too great predilection for the Talmud; one is the late Dr. Geiger, and the other our great historian, the late Dr. Jost.

"*Geiger (Das Judenthum und seine Geschichte*, I., p. 15 5) in speaking of the Talmud and the rabbinical literature, says:

"'Gigantic works, productions of gloomy and brighter periods are here before us, monuments of thought and intellectual labor; they excite our admiration. I do not indorse every word of the Talmud, nor every idea expressed by the teachers in the time of the Middle Ages, but I would not miss a tittle thereof. They contain an acumen and power of thought which fill us with reverence for the spirit that animated our ancestors, a fulness of sound sense, salutary maxim-s-a freshness of opinion often bursts upon us that even to this day exercises its enlivening and inspiring effect.'

272

"*Jost* in his *Geschichte des Judenthum's und seiner Secten*, II., 202, characterizes the Talmud by the following masterly words:

'"The Talmud is a great mine, in which are imbedded all varieties of metals and ores. Here may be found all kinds of valuables, the finest gold and rarest gems, as also the merest dross. Much has been unearthed that has realized countless profit to the world. The great spiritual work whose outcome has been apparent in the advancement of religion has shown that the Talmud is not only of incalculable value in the pursuit of wisdom, but that it has a self-evident significance for all times, which can not be shown by any mere extracts from its pages, and that it can not be disregarded on the plea of its antiquity as valueless in the knowledge of the Jewish religion. Indeed it is and must remain the chief source of this knowledge, and particularly of the historical development of the Jewish religion. More than this, it is the abode of that spirit which has inspired that religion, these many centuries, that spirit from which even those who sought to counteract it could not escape. It is and will remain a labyrinth with deep shafts and openings, in which isolated spirits toil with tireless activity, a labyrinth which offers rich rewards to those who enter impelled by the desire to gain, not without hidden dangers to those who venture wantonly into its mazes and absorb its deadly vapors. Religion has created this work, not indeed to give utterance in an unsatisfactory way to the great questions of Deity and Nature, Mortality and Eternity, and not to carry on controversies upon the proper formulation of articles of faith, but to give expression to a religion of deed, a religion designed to accompany man from the first steps in his education until he reaches the grave, and beyond it; a guide by which his desires and actions are to be regulated at every moment, by which all his movements are to be guarded, that takes care even of his food and drink, of his pleasures and pains, of his mirth and sorrow, and seeks to elevate him, at all times, to an enunciation of the purest faith.

'"It is thus that this spirit, which breathes from the Talmud, enters into the nation's inmost life. It offers repeated recitals of the various modes of thinking, practising, believing, of the true and false representations, of hopes and longings, of knowledge and error, of the great lessons of fate, of undertakings and their consequences, of utterances and their effects, of persons and their talents and inaptitudes, of words and examples, of customs, both in matters of public worship and private life; in short, of all the happenings, past or contemporary, in the time which the Talmud comprises, *i.e.*, a period of nearly one thousand years, excluding the Bible times.

"'Hence, also, its great value to antiquarians in the frequent allusions to facts, opinions and statements, to modes of expression and grammatical construction, to peculiarities of every kind, which at the same time afford a view of the development of mankind, such as no other work of the past gives.

"'To treat the Talmud with scorn because of its oddness, on account of much that it contains that does not conform to our maturer modes of thinking, because of its evident errors and misconceptions--errors from ignorance or errors in copying--to throw it overboard, as it were, as useless ballast, would be to insult all history, to deprive it of one of its strongest limbs, to dismember it.

"'To dam up its channels by taking away the Talmud, would be to close the access to the head waters and living sources of the Jewish religion, and thus leave her again in a desert land, after the tables of the law have already called forth a world of life and activity. It would be turning one's back, as it were, denying and disregarding one's own. There is a historical justification for the sharply defined modes of worship and religious forms that have their embodiment in set words and in fixed deeds. For this we must look to the Talmud. Judaism is rooted in the Talmud and would be tossed about in mid-air if torn from its soil, or require a new planting and a new growth.'

"In conclusion, my young friends, let me say this:

"If our College had no other purpose than to graduate common Sabbath school teachers who should be able to occasionally deliver popular though superficial lectures, the study of the Talmud, as well as that of our rabbinical and philosophical literature, might have been stricken from the course of your studies. But our College has a higher aim and object. Its object is to educate future guides and leaders of our congregations, to educate banner-bearers of Judaism, representatives and cultivators of Jewish knowledge and literature.

"You can never expect to answer this purpose without a thorough knowledge of, and familiarity with, that vast literature that offers us the means to follow and understand the religious formation, the growth and the entire course of development of Judaism from its beginning to the present time."

Chapter 10
Opinions on the Value of the Talmud by Gentiles and Modern Jewish Scholars

No literary monument of antiquity has ever been subject to so different and opposite views and opinions, as the Talmud. Its strict followers generally looked upon it as the very embodiment of wisdom and sagacity, and as a work whose authority was second only to that of the Bible. In the non-Jewish literature it was often decried as "one of the most repulsive books that exist," as "a confused medley of perverted logic, absurd subtilities, foolish tales and fables, and full of profanity, superstition, and even obscenity," or at the most, as "an immense heap of rubbish at the bottom of which some stray pearls of Eastern wisdom are hidden."

It is certain that any of those who thus assumed to pass a condemning judgment upon the gigantic work of the Talmud never read nor were able to read a single page of the same in the original, but were prompted by religious prejudice and antagonism, or they based their verdict merely on those disconnected and often distorted passages which Eisenmenger and his consorts and followers picked out from the Talmud for hostile purposes.

Christian scholars who had a deeper insight into the Talmudical literature, without being blinded by religious prejudices, expressed themselves quite differently on the character and the merits of that work, as may be seen from the following few quotations.

Johann Buxtorf, in the preface to his Lexicon Chald. et Talmudicum, says: "The Talmud contains many legal, medical, physical, ethical, political, astronomical, and other excellent documents of sciences, which admirably commend the history I of that nation and time; it contains also luminous decisions of antiquity; excellent sayings; deep thoughts, full of grace and sense; and numerous expressions which make the reader not only better, but also more wise and learned, and which, like unto flashing jewels, grace the Hebrew speech not less than all those Greek and Roman phrases adorn their languages."

Other favorable opinions expressed by Christian scholars of the sixteenth to eighteenth centuries are collected in Karl Fischer's "Gutmeinung über den Talmud der Hebräer." Vienna, 1883.

Of such scholars as belong to our time, the following may be quoted here:

The late Professor Delitzsch in his *"Jüdisches Handwerkerleben zur Zeit Jesu,"* says:

"Those who have not in some degree accomplished the extremely difficult task of reading this work for themselves, will hardly be able to form a clear idea of this polynomical colossus. It is an immense speaking-hall, in which thousands and tens of thousand of voices, of at least five centuries, are heard to commingle. A law, as we all know from experience, can never be so precisely formulated that there does not remain room for various interpretations; and question upon question constantly arises as to the application of it to the endless multiplicity of the existing relations of life. just imagine about ten thousand decrees concerning Jewish life classified according to the spheres of life, and in addition to these, about five hundred scribes and lawyers, mostly from Palestine and Babylon, taking up one after another of these decrees as the topic of examination and debate, and, discussing with hair-splitting acuteness every shade of meaning and practical application; and imagine, further, that the fine-spun thread of this interpretation of decrees is frequently lost in digressions, and that, after having traversed long distances of such desert-sand, you find, here and there, an oasis, consisting of sayings and accounts of more general

277

interest. Then you may have some slight idea of this vast, and of its kind, unique, juridic codex, compared with whose compass all the law-books of other nations are but Lilliputians, and beside whose variegated, buzzing market din, they represent but quiet study-chambers."

7. Alexander, in his book on *The Jews; their Past, Present and Future* (London, 1870), says:

"The Talmud, as it now stands, is almost the whole literature of the Jews during a thousand years. Commentator followed upon commentator, till at last the whole became an immense bulk; the original Babylonian Talmud alone consists of 2,947 folio pages. Out of such literature it is easy to make quotations which may throw an odium over the whole. But fancy if the production of a thousand years of English literature, say, from the "History" of the Venerable Bede to Milton's "Paradise Lost," were thrown together into a number of uniform folios, and judged in like manner; if because some superstitious monks wrote silly "Lives of Saints," therefore the works of John Bunyan should also be considered worthless. The absurdity is too obvious to require another word from me, Such, however, is the continual treatment the Talmud receives both at the hand. of its friends and of its enemies. Both will find it easy to quote in behalf of their preconceived notions, but the earnest student will rather try to weigh the matter impartially, retain the good he can find even in the Talmud, and reject what will not stand the test of God's word."

The impartial view of the Talmud taken by modern Jewish scholars may be seen from the following opinion expressed by the late *Professor Graetz* in his "History of the Jews" (vol. IV., 309 sq.).

The Talmud must not be considered as an ordinary literary work consisting of twelve folios; it bears not the least internal resemblance to a single literary production; but forms a world of its own which must be judged according to its own laws. It is, therefore, extremely difficult to furnish a specific sketch of the Talmud, seeing that a familiar standard or analogy is wanting. And however thoroughly a man of consummate talent may have penetrated its spirit and become conversant with its peculiarities, he would scarcely succeed in such a task, It may, in some respects, be compared with the Patristic literature, which sprang up simultaneously. But on closer inspection, this comparison will also fail. . . .

"The Talmud has at different times been variously judged on the most heterogeneous assumptions, it has been condemned and consigned to the flames; simply because it was presented in its unfavorable aspect without taking into consideration its actual merits. It cannot be denied that the Babylonian Talmud labors under some defects, like any other mental product, which pursues a single course with inexorable consistency and undeviating dogmatism. These defects may be classified under four heads: the Talmud contains some unessential and trival subjects, which it treats with much importance and a serious air; it has adopted from its Persian surroundings superstitious practices and views, which presuppose the agency of intermediate spiritual beings, witchcraft, exorcising formulas, magical cures and interpretations of dreams and, hence, are in conflict with the spirit of Judaism; it further contains several uncharitable utterances and provisions against members of other nations and creeds; lastly it favors a bad interpretation of Scripture, absurd, forced and frequently false commentations. For these faults the whole Talmud has been held responsible and been denounced as a work devoted to trifles, as a source of immorality and trickery, without taking into consideration that it is not a work of a single author who must be responsible for every word, and if it be so, then the whole Jewish people was its author. Over six centuries are crystallized in the Talmud with animated distinctness, in their peculiar costumes, modes of speech and of thought, so to say a literary Herculaneum and Pompeii, not weakened by artistic imitation, which transfers a colossal picture to the narrow limits of a miniature.

It is, therefore, no wonder, if in this world sublime and mean, great and small, serious and ridiculous, Jewish and heathen elements, the altar and the ashes, are found in motley mixture. Those odious dicta of which Jew-haters have taken hold were in most cases nothing else but the utterances of a momentary indignation, to which an individual had given vent and which were preserved and embodied in the Talmud by over-zealous disciples, who were unwilling to omit a single expression of the revered ancients. But these utterances are richly counterbalanced by the maxims of benevolence and philanthropy towards every man, regardless of creed and nationality, which are also preserved in the Talmud. As counterpoise to the rank superstition, there are found therein sharp warnings against superstitious, heathen practices (Darke Emori), to which subject a whole section, under the name of *Perek Emorai*, is devoted.[1]

"The Babylonian Talmud is especially characterized and distinguished from the Palestinian, by high-soaring contemplations, a keen understanding, and flashes of thought which fitfully dart through the mental horizon. An incalculable store of ideas and incentives to thinking is treasured in the Talmud, but not in the form of finished themes that may be appropriated in a semi-somnolent state, but with the fresh coloring of their inception. The Babylonian Talmud leads into the laboratory of thought, and its ideas may be traced from their embryonic motion up to a giddy height, whither they at times soar into the region of the incomprehensible. For this reason it became, more than the Jerusalemean, the national property, the vital breath, the soul of the Jewish people."

---

1. Sabbath, 66a; Toseptha, Ch. VII., VIII.

Chapter 11
Talmudical Ethics

"Ethics is the flower and fruit on the tree of religion. The ultimate aim of religion is to ennoble man's inner and outer life, so that he may love and do that only which is right and good. This is a biblical teaching which is emphatically repeated in almost every book of Sacred Scriptures. Let me only refer to the sublime word of the prophet Micah: 'He hath showed thee, O man, what is good, and what doth the Lord require of thee, but to do justice and to love kindness and to walk humbly with thy God?' (Micah vi., 8.)

"As far as concerns the Bible, its ethical teachings are generally known. Translated into all languages of the world, that holy book is accessible to every one and whoever reads it with open eyes and with an unbiased mind will admit that it teaches the highest principles of morality, principles which have not been surpassed and superseded by any ethical system of ancient or modern philosophy.

"But how about the Talmud, that immense literary work whose authority was long esteemed second to that of the Bible? What are the ethical teachings of the Talmud?

"Although mainly engaged with discussions of the Law, as developed on the basis of the Bible during Israel's second commonwealth down to the sixth century of the Christian era, the Talmud devotes also much attention to ethical subjects. Not only are one treatise of the Mishna (*Pirke Aboth*) and some Boraithoth (as *Aboth d'R. Nathan* and *Derech Eretz*) almost exclusively occupied with ethical teachings, but such teachings are also very abundantly contained in the Hagadic (homiletical) passages which are so frequently interspersed in the legal discussions throughout all parts of the Talmud.[1]

"It must be borne in mind that the Talmudical literature embraces a period of about eight centuries, and that the numerous teachers whose ethical views and utterances are recorded in that vast literature, rank differently in regard to mind and authority. At the side of the great luminaries, we find also lesser ones. At the side of utterances of great, clear-sighted and broad-minded masters with lofty ideas, we meet also with utterances of peculiar views which never obtained authority. Not every ethical remark or opinion quoted in that literature can, therefore, be regarded as an index of the standard of Talmudical ethics, but such opinions only can be so regarded which are expressed with authority and which are in harmony with the general spirit that pervades the Talmudic literature.

"Another point to be observed is the circumstance that the Talmud does not treat of ethics in a coherent, philosophical system. The Talmudic sages made no claim of being philosophers; they were public teachers, expounders of the Law, popular lecturers. As such, they did not care for a methodically arranged system. All they wanted was to spread among the people ethical teachings in single, concise, pithy, pointed sentences, well adapted to impress the minds and hearts, or in parables or legends illustrating certain moral duties and virtues. And this, their method, fully answered its purpose. Their ethical teachings did actually reach the Jewish masses, and influenced their conduct of life, while among the Greeks, the ethical theories and systems remained a matter that concerned the philosophers only, without exercising any educating influence upon the masses at large.

"Furthermore, it must be remembered that the Talmudical ethics is largely based on the ethics of the Bible. The sacred treasure of biblical truth and wisdom was in the minds and hearts of the Rabbis. This treasury they tried to enrich by their own wisdom and observation. Here they develop a principle contained in a scriptural passage, and give it a wider scope and a larger application to life's various conditions. There they crystallize great moral ideas into a pithy, impressive maxim as a guide for human conduct. Here they give to a jewel of biblical ethics a new lustre by setting it in the gold of their own wisdom. There again they combine single pearls of biblical wisdom to a graceful ornament for human life."--*M. Mielziner.*

There are many books written upon the ethics of the Talmud which are enumerated in the bibliography. The most excellent of these is the philosophical book of Professor Lazarus, "Ethik des Judenthums," in German, Frankfort o. M., 1898, the first volume of which is translated into English by the Jewish Publication Society. The second volume of this work, we have heard, is ready for or already in print.[2]

However, to enable the reader, to get an idea of the Talmud Ethics, without troubling him with the various books in different languages, an extract which was made by Mielziner shall be given in this book, whose selections are so excellent that practically we have nothing to add. We, however, would call the attention of the reader to a book written by us in our periodical *Hacol*, Vol. VI., Vienna, 1885 (translated into German but not yet published), in which the subject of love of mankind is explained in two parallels, that of the Talmud and that in which we have drawn a parallel between the conceptions of both Talmud and Evangelium as to the moral content of the principle of Love. An extract of this explanation we should like to give here:

The commandment in the Old Testament (Leviticus xix., 17): "Love thy neighbor as thyself," the Talmud interprets in a negative sense by the words of Hillel, the elder, thus: "That which thou likest not being done unto thyself do not unto thy neighbor," and this rule the Talmud adopts in all the ways of charity, and in all affairs in which man comes in contact with his fellow-man; *e.g.*, based upon this biblical commandment it is forbidden to betroth a woman before seeing her, for he may dislike her thereafter, and as one does not wish to be disliked himself, he must not cause another to be disliked. And so in all connections with one's neighbor, it is forbidden to do him any harm whatsoever, because one dislikes that he himself should be harmed. Also concerning the duties of charity, numerous special commandments are to be found in the Old Testament. The Talmud explains most of them negatively, viz.: "Thou shalt not leave thy neighbor to suffer any pain whatsoever, but thou shalt prevent it by supplying him with whatsoever thou canst afford." However, the rich man is not obliged to divide his money or property with the poor, nor to supply him with luxuries if the poor man had not been used to them before he became poor. (More details will be found in each subject mentioned further on.) Hence this obligation which is proper and in accordance with common sense, can be fulfilled by every one without any difficulty. The Evangelist, however, interprets the passage (Levit. xix., 17) in a positive sense (Matt. vii., 12): "Therefore all things *whatsoever* ye would that men should do to you, do ye even so to them, for this is the Law and the prophets." After a deep consideration, it is almost impossible for one to entirely fulfil this commandment. According to this, one must divide his money and property with those not possessing such. "Whatsoever ye would that men should do to you!" Who then would not want to be rich and to live luxuriously; to ride instead of going on foot, to be dressed in the best garments according to the latest style, etc.? Hence if one would like to live up to the words of the Evangelist, he must see that the life of his poor neighbor should be made exactly equal to his own life, which certainly can never and was never accomplished. The same is with the command in Luke vi., 2 9: "And unto him that smiteth thee on the one cheek offer also the other," which was never and will never be fulfilled, as this is against the nature of mankind, especially when one is in wrath whilst being beaten. Therefore nothing of this kind is to be found in the Talmud. On the contrary the Talmud says: "He who raises his hand to strike his neighbor is already considered wicked even before he has smitten him." The above-mentioned book quotes this parallel in every affair in which human beings come in contact with each other. It is remarkable that in the explanation of Deut. vi., 4, "Thou shalt love the Lord, thy God, etc.," the Talmud also does not interpret this literally, thinking that it is impossible to impose upon the heart to love, especially Him whom one has never seen, and of whom one has not even a correct idea. Therefore they interpreted this passage thus, "The name of the Lord shall be loved through thy treatment of thy fellow-men, viz. "thy commerce with men should be just and peaceful; thy 'yes' should be firm and thy 'no' unvariable; so that it should be proclaimed: 'Hail the man who follows the Law of the Lord, which is Love thy fellow-men! Therefore let us and our children also study this magnificent Law.' The result evidently is that the name of the Lord is glorified through thee ------"

All the ethics of the Talmud are thus set up with a view to make their observance possible in all their particulars, which is not the case with the teaching of the Evangelist.

Finally, we beg to quote the beginning of the first chapter of the above-mentioned book.--Abyye used to say: "One should be always keen in the fear of God; use meek talk, prevent wrath, bestow thy greeting upon every one in the market, even if he be a stranger. This will cause you to be loved by Heaven and liked by thy fellow-men." It was said about R. Yohanan b. Zakkai, that it never happened that he should have been greeted first (for he was it who greeted every one first, as soon as he perceived him).[3]

---

1. Also the Midrash, a post-Talmudic collection of extracts from popular lectures of the ancient teachers on biblical texts, contains an abundance of ethical teachings and maxims advanced by the sages of the Talmud, which must likewise be taken into consideration when speaking of Talmudical Ethics.
2. We cannot restrain ourselves from expressing our great sorrow over the death of this great man which occurred this year. He was our friend and patron, and many days and weeks we had been fortunate to spend in his company, when, in 1883, we had the pleasure to read before him the several thousand quotations from the Talmud, which we had prepared for his work, "Ethik des Judenthums," at his request. We certainly do not know how many of them he has made use of. However, he wrote us a few years ago that our name and service would be mentioned in the second volume of his book. To our great sorrow he departed before the second volume was published.
3. This paragraph is said by Abyye in pure Bible-Hebrew, which was not the language used by him in every-day talk. We infer from this and also from the expression *"he used to say,"* that he only quoted a traditional proverb which was established ever since the oral law had been started.

Chapter 12

Ethical Teachings of the Talmud

L et us now try to give a few outlines of the ethical teachings of the Talmud. In the first place, concerning

MAN AS A MORAL BEING.

In accordance with the teaching of the Bible, the rabbis duly emphasize man's dignity as a being created in the likeness of God. By this likeness of God they understand the spiritual being within us, that is endowed with intellectual and moral capacities. The higher desires and inspirations which spring from this spiritual being in man, are called *Yetzer tob*, the good inclination; but the lower appetites and desires which rise from our physical nature and which we share with the animal creation, are termed *Yetzer ha-ra*, the inclination to evil. Not that these sensuous desires are absolutely evil; for they, too, have been implanted in man for good purposes. Without them man could not exist, he would not cultivate and populate this earth, or, as a Talmudical. legend runs: Once, some over-pious people wanted to pray to God that they might be able to destroy the *Yetzer ha-ra*, but a warning voice was heard, saying. "Beware, lest you destroy this world!" Evil are those lower desires only in that they, if unrestrained, easily mislead man to live contrary to the demands and aspirations of his divine nature. Hence the constant struggle in man between the two inclinations. He who submits his evil inclination to the control of his higher aims and desires is virtuous and righteous. "The righteous are governed by the *Yetzer tob*, but the wicked by the *Yetzer ha-ra*. The righteous have their desires in their power, but the wicked are in the power of their desires."

FREE-WILL.

Man's free-will is emphasized in the following sentences: "Everything is ordained by God's providence, but freedom of choice is given to man." "Everything is foreordained by heaven, except the fear of heaven," or, as another sage puts it: Whether man be strong or weak, richer poor, wise or foolish depends mostly on circumstances that surround him from the time of his birth, but whether man be good or bad, righteous or wicked, depends upon his own free-will.

GOD'S WILL, THE GROUND OF MAN'S DUTIES.

The ground of our duties, as presented to us by the Talmudical as well as the biblical teachings, is that it is the will of God. His will is the supreme rule of our being. "Do His will as thy own will, submit thy will to His will." "Be bold as a leopard, light as an eagle, swift as a roe, and strong as a lion, to do the will of thy Father, who is in heaven."

MAN ACCOUNTABLE TO GOD FOR HIS CONDUCT.

Of man's responsibility for the conduct of his life, we are forcibly reminded by numerous sentences, as: "Consider three things, and thou wilt never fall into sin; remember that there is above thee an all-seeing eye, an all-hearing ear, and a record of all thy actions." And again, "Consider three things, and thou wilt never sin; remember whence thou comest, whither thou goest, and before whom thou wilt have to render account for thy doings."

HIGHER MOTIVES IN PERFORMING OUR DUTIES.

Although happiness here and hereafter is promised as reward for fulfilment, and punishment threatened for neglect of duty, still we are reminded not to be guided by the consideration of reward and punishment, but rather by love and obedience to God, and by love to that which is good and noble. "Be not like servants, who serve their master for the sake of reward." "Whatever thou doest, let it be done in the name of heaven" (that is, for its own sake).

DUTY OF SELF-PRESERVATION AND SELF-CULTIVATION.

As a leading rule of the duties of *self-preservation* and *self-cultivation*, and, at the same time, as a warning against selfishness, we have Hillel's sentence: "If I do not care for myself, who will do it for me? and if I care only for myself, what am I?"

The duty of *acquiring knowledge*, especially knowledge of the Divine Law (Torah), which gives us a clearer insight in God's will to man, is most emphatically enjoined in numerous sentences: "Without knowledge there is no true morality and piety." "Be eager to acquire knowledge, it does not come to thee by inheritance." "The more knowledge, the wore spiritual life." "If thou hast acquired knowledge, what dost thou lack? but if thou lackest knowledge, what hast thou acquired?" But we are also reminded that even the highest knowledge is of no value, as long as it does not influence our moral life. "The ultimate end of all knowledge and wisdom is man's inner purification and the performance of good and noble deeds." "He whose knowledge is great without influencing his moral life is compared to a tree that has many branches, but few and weak roots; a storm cometh and overturneth it."

LABOR.

Next to the duty of acquiring knowledge, that of *industrious labor* and *useful activity* is strongly enjoined. It is well known that among the ancient nations in general manual labor was regarded as degrading the free citizen. Even the greatest philosophers of antiquity, Plato and Aristotle, could not free, themselves of this deprecating view of labor. How different was the view of the Talmudic sages in this respect! They say: "Love labor, and hate to be a lord." "Great is the dignity of labor; it honors man." "Beautiful is the intellectual occupation, if combined with some practical work." "He who doles not teach his son a handicraft trade, neglects his parental duty." "He who lives on the toil of his hands is greater than he who indulges in idle piety."

In accordance with these teachings, some of the most prominent sages of the Talmud are known to have made their living by various kinds of handicraft and trade.

CARDINAL DUTIES IN RELATION TO FELLOW-MEN.

Regarding man's relation to fellow-men, the rabbis consider *justice*, *truthfulness*, *peaceableness* and *charity* as cardinal duties. They say, "The world (human society) rests on three things-- on justice, on truth and on peace."

JUSTICE.

The principle of *justice* in the moral sense is expressed in the following rules: "Thy neighbor's property must be as sacred to thee as thine own." "Thy neighbor's honor must be as dear to thee as thine own." Hereto belongs also the golden rule of Hillel: "Whatever would be hateful to thee, do not to thy neighbor."

TRUTH AND TRUTHFULNESS.

The sacredness of *truth* and *truthfulness* is expressed in the sentence: "Truth is the signet of God, the Most Holy." "Let thy yea be in truth, and thy nay be in truth." "Truth lasts forever, but falsehood must vanish."

Admonitions concerning *faithfulness* and *fidelity* to given promises are: "Promise little and do much." "To be faithless to a given promise is as sinful as idolatry." "To break a verbal engagement, though legally not binding, is a moral wrong." Of the numerous warnings against any kind of deceit, the following may be mentioned: "It is sinful to deceive any man, be he even a heathen." "Deception in words is as great a sin as deception in money matters." When, says the Talmud, the immortal soul will be called to account before the divine tribunal, the first question will be, "Hast thou been honest and faithful in all thy dealings with thy fellow-men?"

PEACEFULNESS.

Peace and harmony in domestic life and social intercourse as well as in public affairs are considered by the Talmudic sages as the first condition of human welfare and happiness, or as they express it: "Peace is the vessel in which all God's blessings are presented to us and preserved by us." "Be a disciple of Aaron, loving peace, and pursuing peace." To make peace between those in disharmony is regarded as one of the most meritorious works that secure happiness and bliss here and hereafter.

As virtues leading to peace, those of *mildness* and *meekness*, of *gentleness* and *placidity* are highly praised and recommended. "Be not easily moved to anger." "Be humble to thy superior, affable to thy inferior, and meet every man with friendliness." "He who is slow to anger, and easily pacified, is truly pious and virtuous." "Man, be ever soft and pliant like a reed, and not hard and unbending like the cedar." "Those who, when offended, do not give offence, when hearing slighting remarks, do not retaliate--they are the friends of God, they shall shine forth like the sun in its glory."

CHARITY.

The last of the principal duties to fellow-men is *charity*, which begins where justice leaves off. Professor Steinthal, in his work on General Ethics, remarks that among the cardinal virtues of the ancient philosophers we look in vain for the idea of *love* and *charity*, whereas in the teachings of the Bible, we generally find the idea of love, mercy and charity closely connected with that of justice. And we may add, as in the Bible so also in the Talmud, where charity is considered as the highest degree in the scale of duties and virtues. It is one of the main pillars on which the welfare of the human world rests.

The duty of *charity* (Gemilath Chesed) extends farther than to mere *almsgiving* (Tzedaka). "Almsgiving is practised by means of money, but charity also by personal services and by words of advice, sympathy and encouragement. Almsgiving is a duty towards the poor only, but charity towards the rich as well as the poor, nay, even towards the dead (by taking care of their decent burial)."

By works of charity man proves to be a true image of God, whose attributes are love, kindness and mercy. "He who turns away from works of love and charity turns away from God." "The works of charity have more value than sacrifices; they are equal to the performance of all religious duties."

Concerning the proper way of practising this virtue, the Talmud has many beautiful sentences, as: "The merit of charitable works is in proportion to the love with which they are practised." "Blessed is he who gives from his substance to the poor, twice blessed he who accompanies his gift with kind, comforting words." "The noblest of all charities is enabling the poor to earn a livelihood." He who is unable to give much shall not withold his little mite, for "as a garment is made up of single threads, so every single gift contributes to accomplish a great work of charity."

DUTIES CONCERNING SPECIAL RELATIONS.

Besides these principal duties in relation to fellow-men in general, the Talmud treats also very elaborately of duties concerning the various relations of life. Not intending to enter here into all details, we shall restrict ourselves to some of its ethical teachings in reference to the domestic relations, and regarding the relation to the country and the community.

THE CONJUGAL RELATION.

"First build a house and plant a vineyard (*i.e.*, provide for the means of the household), and then take a wife." "Let youth and old age not be joined in marriage, lest the purity and peace of domestic life be disturbed." "A man's home means his wife." "Let a man be careful to honor his wife, for he owes to her alone all the blessings of his house." "If thy wife is small, bend down to her, to take counsel from her." "Who is rich? He who has a noble wife." "A man should be careful lest he afflict his wife, for God counts her tears." "If in anger the one hand removed thy wife or thy child, let the other hand again bring them back to thy heart." "He who loves his wife as his own self, and honors her more than himself, and he who educates his children in the right way, to him applies the divine promise: Thou shalt know that there is peace in thy tent." "Tears are shed on God's altar for the one who forsakes the wife of his youth." "He who divorces his wife, is hated before God."

PARENTS AND CHILDREN.

"Parental love should be impartial, one child must not be preferred to the other." "It is a father's duty not only to provide for his minor children, but also to take care of their instruction, and to teach his son a trade and whatever is necessary for his future welfare." "The honor and reverence due to parents are equal to the honor and reverence due to God." "Where children honor their parents, there God dwells, there He is honored."

COUNTRY AND COMMUNITY.

Regarding duties to the country and the community, the Rabbis teach: "The law of the country is as sacred and binding as God's law." "Pray for the welfare of the government; without respect for the government, men would swallow each other." "Do not isolate thyself from the community and its interests." "It is sinful to deceive the government regarding taxes and duties." "Do not aspire for public offices; but where there are no men, try thou to be the man." "Those who work for the community shall do it without selfishness, but with the pure intention to promote its welfare."

GENERAL CHARACTERISTICS.

To these short outlines of Talmudical ethics let us add only a few general remarks. Being essentially a development of the sublime ethical principles and teachings of the Bible, the Talmudical ethics retains the general characteristics of that origin.

It teaches nothing that is against human nature, nothing that is incompatible with the existence and welfare of human society. It is free from the extreme excess and austerity to which the lofty ideas of religion and morality were carried by the theories and practices of some sects inside and outside of Judaism.

Nay, many Talmudical maxims and sayings are evidently directed against such austerities and extravagances. Thus they warn against the monastic idea of obtaining closer communion with God by fleeing from human society and by seclusion from temporal concerns of life: "Do not separate thyself from society." "Man's thoughts and ways shall always be in contact and sympathy with fellow-men." "No one shall depart from the general customs and manners." "Better is he who lives on the toil of his hand, than he who indulges in idle piety."

They strongly discountenance the idea of *celibacy*, which the Essenes, and later, some orders of the Church regarded as a superior state of perfection. The rabbis say: "He who lives without a wife is no perfect man." "To be unmarried is to live without joy, without blessing, without kindness, without religion and without peace." "As soon as man marries, his sins decrease."

While, on the one hand, they warn against too much indulgence in pleasures and in the gratification of bodily appetites and against the insatiable pursuit of earthly goods and riches, as well as against the inordinate desire of honor and power en the other hand, they strongly disapprove of the ascetic mortification of the body and abstinence from enjoyment, and the cynic contempt of all luxuries that beautify life. They say: "God's commandments are intended to enhance the value and enjoyment of life, but not to mar it and make it gloomy." "If thou hast the means, enjoy life's innocent pleasures." "He who denies himself the use of wine is a sinner." "No one is permitted to afflict himself by unnecessary fasting." "The pious fool, the hypocrite, and the pharisaic flagellant are destroyers of human society." "That which beautifies life and gives it vigor and strength, just as riches and honor, is suitable to the pious, and agreeable to the world at large."

Finally, one more remark: The Talmud has often been accused of being illiberal, as if teaching its duties only for Jews towards fellow-believers, but not also towards fellow-men in general. This charge is entirely unfounded. It is true, and quite natural, that in regard to the *ritual* and *ceremonial* law and practice, a distinction between Jew and Gentile was made. It is also true that we occasionally meet in the Talmud with an uncharitable utterance against the heathen world. But it must be remembered in what state of moral corruption and degradation their heathen surroundings were, at that time. And this, too, must be remembered, that such utterances are only made by individuals who gave vent to their indignation in view of the cruel persecutions whose victims they were. As regards *moral* teachings, the Talmud is as broad as humanity. It teaches duties of man to man without distinction of creed and race. In most of the ethical maxims, the terms *Adam* and *Beriyot*, "man," "fellow-men," are emphatically used; as: "Do not despise any man." "Judge every man from his favorable side." "Seek peace, and love fellow-men." "He who is pleasing to fellow-men is also pleasing to God." "The right way for man to choose is to do that which is honorable in his own eyes (*i.e.*, approved by his conscience) and at the same time honorable in the eyes of his fellow-men." In some instances, the Talmud expressly reminds that the duties of justice, veracity, peacefulness and charity are to be fulfilled towards the heathen as well as to the Israelites; as, "It is sinful to deceive any man, be he even a heathen." It is our duty to relieve the poor and needy, to visit the sick and bury the dead without distinction of creed and race."

294

"Thou shalt love thy neighbor as thyself" (Lev. xix., 18), this is, said R. Akiba, the all-embracing principle of the divine law. But *Ben Azai* said, there is another passage in Scriptures still more embracing; it is the passage (Gen. v., 2): "This is the book of the generations of man; in the day that God created man, he made him in the likeness of God." That sage meant to say, this passage is more embracing, since it clearly tells us who is our neighbor; not, as it might be misunderstood, our friend only, not our fellow-citizen only, not our co-religionist only, but since we all descend from a common ancestor, since all are created in the image and likeness of God, every man, every human being is our brother, our neighbor whom we shall love as ourselves.

The liberal spirit of Talmudic ethics is most strikingly evidenced in the sentence: "The pious and virtuous of all nations participate in the eternal bliss," which teaches that man's salvation depends not on the acceptance of certain articles of belief, nor on certain ceremonial observances, but on that which is the ultimate aim of religion name-ly, *Morality*, purity of heart and holiness of life.

Chapter 13
Method of Translation

The Method of our Translation into English of our Revised Text in
the "New Edition."

After having submitted the text of the Talmud to a thorough review, and carried out the corrections thus found necessary, we have come down to the conclusion that the translation of the Talmud into English in this corrected form would be although not one of the easiest, but a possible task.[1] Thus we made up our mind to start this task, having considered as our leading principle to carry it out in a manner that should facilitate the understanding of the Talmud to such English readers as are not conversant with the Hebrew text. Therefore we did not care to give the discussions of the Mishnas, Tosephtas and Boraithas which the Gemara quotes for the purpose of a contradiction, objection, or comparison with a distinguishing expression, as we thought it is immaterial for the English reader. The method of the Gemara, however, is to distinguish the expressions for the purpose of letting the reader know whether the quotation is from a Mishna, Tosephta, or Boraitha, or was only said by the Amoraim, the expounders of the Mishna, viz.: (1) *Tenan*, for the quotation of a Mishna; (2) *Tania*, for the quotation of a Tosephta or a Boraitha; (3) *Itemar*, for the quotation of that which was said by the Amoraim. Therefore in the first volume of our editions, for all the quotations we have used only one expression, "we have learned," or "it was taught." However, after we were criticised for this, we also adopted a method of distinguishing the quotations, which is printed in the Explanatory Remarks to each volume; namely: Remark 1. For a quotation from the Mishna, "we have learned in a Mishna," for a Tosephta or a Boraitha, "we have learned in a Tosephta or a Boraitha," and for the sayings of the Amoraim, "it was taught." Thus have we also corrected in the second edition of the first and the fourth volumes: Remark 2. To save space we did not adopt the method of the German translators who usually write question and answer to each paragraph where such is to be found; we have indicated the question by an interrogation point, and immediately follows the answer without being so marked. Coming to the third explanatory remark, in which we say that we translate only the second, we have to give here this explanation at length, as this treats about omissions from the text in the translation.

In our *Hakol*, vol. VI., No. 298, 1885, in which we announced that we desire to revise and correct the Talmud so as to make its translation possible into a living language, we gave some examples of the omissions necessary in Halakha and Hagada for this purpose. And we dare say that the examples were favorably received by eminent students of the Talmud. As an answer to another criticism in a Hebrew monthly in New York, *Ner Hamarobe*, we wrote a long article in the same about our method of the omissions in Halakha, claiming that in reality we *omit nothing* of importance of the whole text, in the shape given out by its compilers, and only that which we were certain to have been added by the dislikers of the Talmud for the purpose of degrading it we do omit. We cannot very well translate the whole article here for lack of space and time. We will therefore limit ourselves to pointing out the omissions of Halakha and Hagada with one or two examples: (1) Omitting repetitions, *e.g.*, in Tract Kethuboth 72b, there is a Mishna, "if one betroths a woman with the stipulation that she is not subject to any vows," and the whole Mishna with its Gemara is repeated in Tract Kedushin 58, without any change, and the Gemara to this Mishnayoth questions why the repetition? To which the same answer, "it was learned by the way," is repeated in both tracts. In our edition the Mishna will appear only once, in Tract Kedushin, and it is self-evident that the question and the answer of the Gemara falls off. However, the continuation which is if importance comes in the proper place. This is concerning the Mishnayoth. The discussions in the Gemara are repeated sometimes from one to fifteen times, some of them without any change at all, and some with change of little or no importance. In our edition we give the discussion only once, in its proper place. True, it is a great difficulty to go over all the repetitions, to mark the changes wherever they are, and to consider the matter thoroughly as to which is the most proper place for them. However, we did not spare time and careful study. And according to our ability we left it at the place which seemed to us to be proper and cancelling all other repetitions.[2] (2) There is a custom in the text when it brings a statement from an Amora (very seldom also from a Tana) which is in conflict with a Mishna or a Boraitha, and trying to reconcile them by a long discussion, and after it comes to the conclusion that such a reconciliation is impossible, it concludes that "if such was taught it must be so and so," contrary to the first statement. We in our edition translate only the conclusion, omitting the whole discussion, which partly or wholly is to be found elsewhere. (Examples of this are given in our above-mentioned article, and as they are very numerous, we cannot give them here). (3) Where there are two versions in the text under the term *Lishma achrena* (another version), or *Ika d'amri* (some say), or *Waibayith Aema* (if you wish, we may say), and the second is contrary or entirely different from the first, we mostly give the second only. However, we are very careful in omitting such. (See our concluding words in Vol. XVII., page 8), and as to the last phrase, *Waibayith Aema*, which in many places is said twice or thrice, the reader will find all of them translated in our translation, under the term, "if you wish it may be said so, and if you wish, it may be said so." (4) The reader will find in our edition foot-notes stating, "transferred from tract so and so," in Halakha as well as in Hagada. We do so when the subject treated is inserted in a place where it is disconnected with the preceding and following statement; however, there is a special discussion about the same subject in another tract. (Concerning Hagada we did so in Tract Sanhedrin, transferring Hagadas which have no connection in the preceding chapters, to the last (eleventh) chapter which is all Hagada. This is done for the purpose of preventing confusion in the reader's mind, which, while engaged in one subject, is abruptly confronted with a strange subject. (5) In a very few places we combine two Mishnayoths which are united in the editions of the separate Mishnayoths, but are divided in the Gemara into two or three (see Nedarim 32b and 33a), to which the Gemara questions "in accordance with what Tana the statement of this Mishna is given," and answers "in accordance with so and so," and the same it does with the divided Mishna with the same question and answer. (6) In places where the Gemara discusses in a long paragraph, "how was the case? Shall we assume so, then such a statement would be in the way, and if we assume so, another statement of so and so would be in the way," etc. The conclusion, however, is explained clearly and nicely. In such cases we often translate the conclusion only, omitting the discussion, which seems to us to be inserted only for the purpose of sharpening the mind. (However, we are very careful with such omissions, and if we see in them something of importance, we do not omit them.) To this point, may be added then that all the discussions usual in the Gemara why the Tana or the Amora A does not say like B, and why B does not say like C, and C like D, and then why D does not say like C, B, and A, etc. After then when the reason is given why A does not say like B, and B like C, it is again asked why should A not adopt the reason of B, etc., etc. We then give only the questions and answers of the first category, viz., why does not A agree with B and C, and B and C with A. We omit, however, the second category of the questions and answers for not adopting the reasons, which in many places occupy a whole column and after reading it, we do not find anything new or important, but simply repetitions after repetitions which confuse the mind of the reader without doing any good. (7) Questions which remain undecided and many of them are not at all practical but only imaginary, and very peculiar too,[3] we omit. Many of such questions were ascribed to the Amora Jeremiah, of whom

Rabha said that, "When he was in Babylonia he never understood what the Rabbis said." When he (Jeremiah) came to Palestine he expressed himself concerning the Babylonian scholars thus: "The Babylonians who are dwelling in a dark land are proclaiming dark Halakhath." It is the same to us if Jeremiah questioned the above-mentioned questions at the time he did not understand the Rabbis, or, as I. H. Weiss said, that he intended with such questions to ridicule the Rabbis, for at any rate such questions must not be placed in our edition. We have good reason to say that all such questions were inserted in the name of Jeremiah or other Amoraim, by the dislikers of the Talmud, who were to be found. from its very beginning, for the purpose of ridiculing it. We cannot agree with Weiss that Jeremiah himself put such questions, as for a similar question: "If it happened that one has put one foot into the Sabbath limit, and the other foot was still out of it, may he enter or not?" he was immediately driven out from the college. Hence, since the other questions ascribed to him are much worse in every respect than the one just mentioned, is it possible that he would be listened to and such inserted as undecided questions? We would also state that the above statement of the dark Halakhath by the Babylonian sages was also put in his mouth by the same people, as we cannot believe that such a great Amora like Jeremiah should throw stones in the valley from which he drank his water.

Finally, we will give one example concerning Hagadas, in Tract Zebachin, pp. 113a, in the discussion whether the flood was in Palestine or not, basing their statements upon Ecclesiastes, "there is no new thing under the sun," *i.e.*, no new creatures were created after the seven days of creation, and as there are to be found some creatures which, according to their size, could not enter into the ark of Noah, and we see their existence, it must be concluded that the flood which had destroyed all the creatures did not take place in Palestine, in which such creatures are to be found. The opponents of this say that the flood was in Palestine also, and of all kinds of the existing creatures, there were some in the ark. And when the last were objected to by the existence of *r'em* (wild-ox), which, according to Rabba b. b. Hannah, the size of its offspring of one day was equal to forty miles, hence it could not in any way be entered in the ark, the answer comes that its snout only was in the ark, and the rest of the body was swimming in the water.

Now we would ask any reader if it is possible that such a thing should be said by any sage of the Talmud, and especially by *Resh Lakish*, who was one of the greatest Amoraim of Palestine. As this Hagada was discussed in connection with a Halakha it must not by any means be taken as allegorical. It is therefore more than certain that one who desired to make the Talmud ridiculous put in the mouths of Jochanan and Resh Lakish the discussion about the r'em with such a ridiculous answer. Hence in our translation it must be omitted. There is another one which was put as a question: "May the high priest marry a pregnant virgin?" and to the question "how can a virgin be pregnant?" the answer comes that "perhaps she became pregnant in a bath where preceding her was a man who had left there his seed."[4] We do not believe that any one with common sense, and without partiality, can be found who would deny that such things were inserted by the Talmud haters only for the purpose of ridiculing the Talmud. It is self-evident then that in our edition such and numerous similar legends do not find place.

Concerning the translation itself, we translate almost literally but not slavishly. In those places where the text of the Gemara can be understood only with the aid of Rashi's commentary, we reproduce the sense without marking "Rashi." However, in those places where Rashi adds something to make the text better understood, we put Rashi's commentary in parentheses. See fifth remark on the copy-righting; but passages inserted from the Gemara itself we put in brackets. Those passages, however, which are not explained by Rashi or which we found the explanation more detailed in other commentaries, we translate according to the latter's, stating in the respective foot-note that it is according to so and so. Our only desire was to enable the English student, even laymen, to understand the sense without difficulty, in which, according to I. M. Wise in his review of Volume VIII., we have succeeded. We may state also that, though we have strictly followed our method, yet we were compelled in some places to deviate from the same. It was also impossible for us to arrange our new edition in accordance with the old edition; based upon the decision of Sherira Gaon that it is immaterial in what order the tracts should be brought, as the Gemara itself states that the consecutive order of the Mishna is not always to be taken seriously. However, each tract is numbered from page 1, so that if the reader prefers binding the tracts according to the former order he may do so. There are, however, many more points concerning our method which we omit for lack of space and time, especially since the method is fully traced in its main features.

---

1. See letter of Dr. M. Jastrow in the prospectus of our work.
2. In our edition, if such an omission comes from that which was already printed, we mark it in parentheses or in a foot-note: "repeated from tract or from volume so and so, page so and so," which could not do with the text which was not as yet translated.
3. E.g., נפלמןוהגג ותקעלביבמתו, the translation of which we do not care to give.
4. It seems to us that such were inserted by one against the belief that the Virgin Mary had borne Jesus.

Chapter 14
Criticism

In our table of contents to this history announced in the prospectus issued in 1897, we have inserted "A Reply to some Criticism." This would be in place if this history had been published at the time when the criticism was still new. Now, however, after the lapse of six years, during which new proper criticism has not appeared, a reply to what is almost forgotten would be out of place. We, however, cannot restrain ourselves to say a few words about criticism in general, and about our edition in special. In our opinion, true criticism must drive only to the point, *i.e.*, the critic has to show the author his mistakes and errors in such and such point, page or paragraph, based upon undoubted or uncontradictory evidence, or common sense, taking care, however, to avoid partiality and personality. Otherwise it is not criticism but attack. In our introduction to Vol. VII., we expressed our anxiety to face a *true* criticism, which has not appeared thus far as aught we know. As what concerns the criticism which appeared after the issue of the first volume, the same may be classified in three categories:

(*a*) Personality against the reviser of the first volume or against ourself. (*b*) Opposition on the part of those who disliked for some reason the idea of the Talmud being translated in any living language, no matter which; and (*c*) the views expressed by ignoramuses in all that concerns the Talmud and its study. It seems to us that a discussion would not persuade either of the three categories, as they indulged only in attacks lacking real evidence, nay, even a basis of probability on which they might have rested; *e.g.*, there were some who claimed that our edition is not scientifically arranged, our omissions mutilating the whole text at large; but these did not care to give any example, which might have served them as evidence.

Now, concerning the scientific point of view, we hold that no translation of the Talmud could answer the requirements of a scientific work, as the Talmud itself is nothing but a chaotic mass lacking any scientific order, and should a translator follow scientific tracks, the result of his work would be a treatise on, but not a translation of, the Talmud. And, as what regards the so-called mutilations, since no example was given, we cannot enter any discussion as to them. Our method was already clearly explained in a lengthy article in Hebrew, out of which it might have appeared that our method consists in these very mutilations, and if after that anybody accuses us of mutilating the text we have nothing to say but let him try to invent a better method.

However, regarding the criticism of the spelling of some ancient names, which we were not very careful about, and also as to the distinguishing of the quotations from divers Mishnas, Boraithas, etc., we have gratefully admitted its truth and accordingly corrected in the succeeding volumes as well as in the second edition of the first volume, as it can be seen in our answer to these criticisms in the American Hebrew, July 29, 1896, which the critic himself admitted thereafter that it was a gentlemanly answer, though it could not induce him to deny his policy. And what concerns other criticisms of the above categories we may conscientiously say that they were not worthy of any consideration whatsoever, as their basis was the very criticism of this prominent scholar, who encouraged them to attack, to scold, and to make use of any expression which is fit to disqualify the work at large in the eyes of its supporters.[1] As an evidence to this latter statement we beg to quote the editorial of *The American Israelite*, September 19, 1901.

"The complaint voiced through the Jewish press that Rodkinson's translation of the Talmud is not receiving the support which its merits deserve is very much in the nature of self-accusation. The truth is that the great undertaking has never been able to overcome the onslaught originally made upon it. Recognizing its great value, the late editor of this paper gave to the work from its initial conception his earnest encouragement and support, which, instead of being seconded by the Jewish press and rabbinate, was met by a torrent of abuse and misrepresentation. Now that his foresight has been justified, and the former detractors of the work complain that Jewish support is lacking, they have a chance to contemplate their own doings. If the example set by the late editor of this paper had been emulated instead of neglected and derided, there would not now be occasion to charge the Jewish public with want of appreciation.

"It was not among Jews alone that the insensate opposition to Dr. Rodkinson's difficult project was met with. As is perfectly natural, the non-Jewish press depended largely upon Jewish sources for their information in regard to the work, and therefore reflected the unfavorable opinions expressed by supposed Jewish authorities. As soon as unbiased reviewers were made aware of its merits, they changed their unfavorable attitude, but it was too late to overcome the prejudice created by the first impression. *To-day the non-Jewish press recognizes that it was misled into antagonizing the work, and speaks of it as a most important contribution to the world's stock of knowledge,* but it certainly must be disheartening to its editor and his publishers to convince possible purchasers that the authorities upon which they depend for information have experienced a change of heart. It is an old story, that with one moment's start a lie will not be overtaken by its refutation in a thousand years. It is impossible to wholly right the wrong, but at least amends can be made by those who through ignorance or malice misrepresented Dr. Rodkinson's great undertaking, and it is not by taking a fling at the Jews that this is to be accomplished. It is safe to classify the Jews as average human beings, who are neither better nor worse than the rest of mankind, and taking them as such, the proportion among them who encourage Jewish letters will not be found to fall below what can rightly be expected. This statement, however, does not include the Jews who have been blessed with superabundant riches, for the members of that class have not in this country given to Jewish literature the same support so common among the men of wealth who enable the literature of Christianity to be spread broadcast over the world."

---

1. To our great sorrow we must confess that they have succeeded in harming us both materially and morally. The material harm was that, as an immediate result of their attacks, an enormous amount of financial support had been refused to us. The moral harm they caused us was that, being at loss of the necessary funds, we could not submit our work to competent men for revising, and so the whole gigantic labor of issuing all which has been printed so far was carried out only through our own endeavors, to which no assistance, moral or material, was given us an the part of anybody. And with all our modesty we may say that, had we not been so energetic and strong-minded, our attackers would have succeeded in destroying the whole plan and annihilating the publication of our work. A great authority and most influential man in this city, seeing our struggles and troubles after we had already issued several volumes, offered us 6,000 as financial aid for the duration of three years, so as to complete the translation in this period and to submit to him afterwards the whole manuscript, for which he was willing to take the trouble upon himself to find a publisher who would undertake to publish it upon the plan of royalty. The above amount he calculated to obtain of three philanthropists, two Gentiles and one Hebrew. We, however, having conjectured who the Hebrew philanthropist might be, told him that if he meant Mr. ------, he was mistaken, for he is already influenced by the critics and therefore would not support this work. In fact, it was so, and the professor was reduced to drop the whole plan.

   This case was not the only one, There was another professor who promised to subscribe for twenty sets of our work for the purpose of distributing them among his friends. It was again the critic that prevented him from doing so.

   The Jewish Publication Society of America, whose aim it is to help authors in issuing their works, and who are constantly doing so, have not assisted us with a single cent, in spite of the fact that all the above-mentioned critics but one had not only retracted from and moderated their first statements, but afterwards wrote favorably about our translation in different periodicals and private letters, as can be seen from the Press comments, which will be placed on the last pages of this work.

   One cannot imagine our struggles and troubles at each issue of the volumes, and it is only our ideal that the edition of the Talmud should be completed which spurs us to continue, We rely upon the divine help, that it will not cease to grant us further on the assistance which it has lent us to the completion of the two large sections issued by us.

Chapter 15
The Arrangement of the Six Sections in Their Sixty Tracts

Section Zeraim (Plants) contains eleven tractates, viz.: Berachoth (Benediction), supplied with Gemara, both Palestinian and Babylonian, Peah (Corner tithe), Dmai (Uncertain), Khilayim (Mixtures), Shebüt (Sabbatical year), Therumoth (Heave offering), Maasheroth (Tithes), Maaser Sheni (Second tithes), Chala (Dough), Orla (Fruit trees during the first three years), and Biccurim (First fruit), all of which are not supplied with Babylonian Gemara. The laws of all of them concern Palestine at that time the Temple was in existence.

Section Nashim (Women) contains seven tracts, viz.: Yebamoth (Levirate marriage), Khethuboth (Marriage contracts), Nedarim. (Vows), Nazir (Nazarite), Sota (Suspicious women), Gittin (Divorces), Kiddushin (Betrothals).

Section Kodashim (Holiness), eleven tracts: Zebachim (Sacrifices), Menachoth (Meal-offering), Chulin (Profane things), Bechoroth (First born), Arachin (Estimations), Themura (Exchange), Kherithoth (Excisions), Me-ila (Trespass), Thamid (Daily offerings), Middoth (Measurements) and Kinnim (Birds' nests). All the above tracts, besides Chulin, treat about sacrifices, offerings used at the time of the Temple. Chulin, however, speaks of the laws of slaughtering and of the meats that may be used.

Section Tcharoth (Purification), twelve tracts, viz.: Khelim (Vessels), Ohaloth (Tents), Nego-im (Leprosy), Parah (Heifer), Teharoth (Purification), Mikvaoth (Wells), Nidda (Menstruous), Mach-shirim (Preparations), Zabim (Running issues), Tebul-Yom (Legal-day bath), Yadayim (Hands), and Uktzin (Stalks of fruit); to all of them, except Nidda, there is no Gemara, for the reason stated above (Vol. II., p. 42). The tract Nidda, however, treats about women menstruous and all the laws of sexual intercourse.

Section Moed (Festivals), twelve tracts (in our Edition 13), and Section Nezikin (Jurisprudence), ten tracts (in our Edition 13), which are already published in the English language.

THE END

www.ingramcontent.com/pod-product-compliance
Lightning Source LLC
Chambersburg PA
CBHW010754150726
48196CB00007B/560